CodeIgniter 1.7

Improve your PHP coding productivity with the free
compact open source MVC CodeIgniter framework!

Jose Argudo Blanco

David Upton

BIRMINGHAM - MUMBAI

CodeIgniter 1.7

First published: November 2009

Production Reference: 1031109

Published by Packt Publishing Ltd.
32 Lincoln Road
Olton
Birmingham, B27 6PA, UK.

ISBN: 978-1-847199-48-5

www.packtpub.com

Cover Image by Vinayak Chittar (vinayak.chittar@gmail.com)

Credits

Authors

Jose Argudo Blanco

David Upton

Reviewer

Pascal Kriete

Acquisition Editor

Douglas Paterson

Development Editor

Swapna Verlekar

Technical Editor

Dhwani Devater

Indexer

Hemangini Bari

Editorial Team Leader

Abhijeet Deobhakta

Project Team Leader

Lata Basantani

Project Coordinator

Poorvi Nair

Proofreader

Chris Smith

Graphics

Nilesh R Mohite

Production Coordinator

Dolly Dasilva

Cover Work

Dolly Dasilva

About the Authors

Jose Argudo Blanco is a web developer from Valencia, Spain. After finishing his studies he started working for a web design company. After working for six years for that company and some others, he decided to work as a freelance.

Now, after some years have passed, he thinks it's the best decision he has ever taken—a decision that let him work with the tools he likes, such as CodeIgniter, Joomla!, CakePHP, JQuery, and other well-known open source technologies.

For the past few months he has also reviewed some books for Packt Publishing, such as *Magento 1.3 Theme Design, Magento: Beginner's Guide, Joomla! 1.5 SEO, Symfony 1.3 Web Application Development*, and *Joomla! with Flash*. The one yet to be published is *Magento Development with PHP*.

He has put a lot of effort into this book and hopes it's very useful for the readers.

To my girlfriend Silvia whose support helps me every day, to my brother, maybe some day we will work together, to my parents for being always there, and, of course, to Swapna, Poorvi, and all the Packt team, without their help, and Pascal's advices this book couldn't have been possible.

David Upton is a director of a specialized management consultancy company, based in London but working around the world. His clients include some of the world's largest companies. He is increasingly interested in web-enabling his work, and seeking to turn ideas into robust professional applications by the simplest and easiest route. So far he has written applications for two major companies in the UK. His other interests include simulation, on which he writes a weblog that takes up far too much of his time, and thinking.

About the Reviewer

Pascal Kriete is a developer from Germany. Although his background lies in engineering, after a short, unsuccessful stint in traditional server/client administration he found his way into freelance web development. Looking to streamline his development workflow—as freelancers want to do—he discovered CodeIgniter and began actively participating in the community. This involvement quickly spread to the ExpressionEngine forums and by the end of 2008 Pascal joined the EllisLab team as a Technical Support Specialist. He has since moved on to become a member of the development team, where he continues to polish code and gets to interact with an ever growing number of third-party developers.

Table of Contents

Preface	1
Chapter 1: Introduction to CodeIgniter	**7**
What can CodeIgniter do for you?	**7**
Save time	8
Make your site more robust	9
Keep your links up-to-date automatically	10
Preventing database SQL injection attacks and form prepping	10
Protect your site from XSS attacks	12
Make your code bolder	13
Send email attachments without hassles	13
Save bandwidth by zipping files that users need to download	14
What CI doesn't do	**14**
Yes, but…what is CodeIgniter? What are frameworks?	**15**
Comparing CI to other open source solutions (CakePHP and Joomla!)	**16**
What to choose	17
License	**19**
Summary	**20**
Chapter 2: Setting up a CodeIgniter Site	**21**
Prerequisites	**21**
Installing CodeIgniter	**22**
Exploring the file structure	23
Does it work?—checking our CI installation	26
The configuration file	26
Autoloading libraries, helpers, and so on	28
Mod rewrite and apache .htaccess to achieve nice URL rewrites	29
Moving the application directory and the system directory—benefits	31
Summary	**32**

Chapter 3: Navigating Your Site   33

MVC: Model-View-Controller   34

But how does all this work?   36
- The welcome controller   38
- Working with views   39
- The default controller   40

CodeIgniter syntax rules   42
- Controller   43
- View   43

Types of files or classes on a CI site   43

Designing a better view   46

Designing a better controller   48
- Getting parameters to a function   49
- Passing data to a view   50

How CI classes pass information and control to each other   52
- Calling views   52
- Calling functions directly   52
- Interacting with controllers   52
- An example of a CI helper—the URL helper   53
- A simple library example—creating a menu   55

Summary   57

Chapter 4: Using CI to Simplify Databases   59

Configuration settings   60

Designing the database for our site   61

Active Record   62

Advantages of using the Active Record class   63
- Saving time   63
- Automatic functionality   64
- Read queries   66
- Displaying query results   69
- Create and update queries   69
- Delete queries   72

Mixing Active Record and "classic" styles   72

Dealing with complex queries   73

Summary   76

Chapter appendix: MySQL query to set up the website's database   76

Chapter 5: Simplifying HTML Pages and Forms   81

Writing a view   81

Long and short PHP syntax and other CodeIgniter style guidelines   83
- File format   84
- PHP closing tag   86

Nesting views   86

Practical issues of site architecture   89

CI's form helper—entering data   **91**

Form helper advantage one: Clarity   92

Form helper advantage two: Automation   95

My display model   **96**

CI's form validation class: Checking data easily   **98**

Setting up validation   98

Setting up the controller   99

Setting up forms   100

Let's pack it all together   100

Summary   **103**

Chapter 6: Simplifying Sessions and Security   **105**

Continuing with our practical site using CI   **105**

Moving around the site   106

Security/Sessions: Using another CI library class   **111**

Turning sessions into security   115

But what about logout?   117

Isn't there anything already built?   **118**

Security   **122**

Summary   **124**

Chapter 7: CodeIgniter and Objects   **125**

Object-oriented programming   **125**

The CI super-object   126

Copying by reference   129

Adding your own code to the CI super-object   130

Problems with the CI super-object   132

Summary   **135**

Chapter 8: Improving Our Application with Third-Party Code   **137**

Creating a helper   **137**

Creating a library   **139**

Sitemap   141

Explanation for My_Parser.php   144

Google charts plugin   145

Summary   **151**

Chapter 9: Using CI to Communicate   **153**

Using the FTP class to test remote files   **153**

Machines talking to machines again: XML-RPC   **157**

Getting the XML-RPC server and client in touch with each other   158

Formatting XML-RPC exchanges   160

Debugging   162

Issues with XML-RPC   163

Talking to humans for a change—the email class	163
Twitter	168
Summary	169
Chapter 10: How CI Helps to Provide Dynamic Information	**171**
The date helper—converting and localizing dates	172
The Calendar class	175
Working with text—the text helper	177
Going international—the Language class	179
Making HTML tables the easy way—the Table class	181
Caching pages	183
Summary	185
Chapter 11: Using CI to Handle Files and Images	**187**
The file helper	188
The download helper	192
The file upload class and CI's image class	193
CI's image class	196
Easy file compression with CI's zip class	199
Summary	200
Chapter 12: Moving Your Site to the WWW	**201**
Errors and error pages	208
So, should we update if a new version of CI comes out?	210
Steps/advice to follow when updating our CI version	211
Summary	212
Chapter 13: CRUD—or Putting It All Together	**213**
Building our CRUD controller, model, and views	214
Upgrading our CRUD	231
Pagination class	232
Putting some order into our records	235
Summary	239
Chapter 14: The Verdict on CI	**241**
Organizing the files of our site	242
Organizing the logic of our site	242
A model	243
A controller	243
A view	244
Centralized configuration	244
Code conventions	245
Database tools	245
Simpler and more powerful code	246

Adding security to our site	**246**
Making our site more scalable and our code more reusable	**247**
Documentation and community	**247**
Summarizing all that CI offers	**248**
Summary	**248**
Chapter 15: Resources and Extensions	**249**
CI's user forums	**250**
Video tutorials	252
Available plugins and libraries	252
AJAX or JavaScript	253
Authentication	253
PDF generation	254
Comparisons: Which charting library to use?	254
HTML purifier	256
CRUD—the final frontier	256
Invoicing	**257**
Additional resources	**258**
Some books that could help	258
Resources for other programs: XAMPP Lite, MySQL, and PHP	259
Summary	**260**
Appendix	**261**
What we need to use the library	**261**
Adding products to the cart	**263**
Showing the cart to our clients	**268**
Summary	**275**
Index	**277**

Preface

CodeIgniter (CI) is a powerful open source PHP framework with a very small footprint, built for PHP programmers who need a simple and elegant toolkit to create full-featured web applications. CodeIgniter is an MVC framework, similar in some ways to the Rails framework for Ruby, and is designed to enable, not overwhelm. This book explains how to work with CodeIgniter in a clear logical way.

What this book covers

Chapter 1: Introduction to CodeIgniter, will introduce you to what frameworks are, and specifically we will talk about CI and how it can help in our day to day work. We will see what CI offers and what it doesn't.

Chapter 2: Setting up a CodeIgniter Site, will help you to prepare the basic configuration of your site, studying CI's structure and config files. At the end you will have a working CI installation.

Chapter 3: Navigating Your Site, will cover some important topics, like the MVC pattern and how CI handles this pattern, and we will make an example controller just to see how all this works.

Chapter 4: Using CI to Simplify Databases, helps you to start working with databases. This is a very important topic. CI will really help us at this point, so we are going to see in detail all the tools at our disposal, including Active Record.

Chapter 5: Simplifying HTML Pages and Forms, will help you with HTML and form helpers, which are some important tools you will find in CodeIgniter; we will see some examples about their usage and introduce form validation.

Chapter 6: Simplifying Sessions and Security, will cover some important security features of CI, which will help make your site more secure. As we will also talk about sessions we will build a simple login feature.

Chapter 7: CodeIgniter and Objects, introduces a bit on object-oriented programming and how CI makes use of it, including the use of the CI super object, and how we can modify and use it.

Chapter 8: Improving Our Application with Third-Party Code, will help you take some rest from the hard work you have done in the previous chapters. We will see some third-party code that we can easily add to our site, improving it, and adding interesting functionalities.

Chapter 9: Using CI to Communicate, explains how CI helps us in communication. Communication is an important part of every site. We will see the ftp class, email class, and XML-RPC class and, of course, the possibility to add more as we need!

Chapter 10: How CI Helps to Provide Dynamic Information, will show some more useful helpers and classes, this will include the date helper, text helper, and table and language classes. All of this will help in the development of our site, not only in reducing code, but in adding powerful features to our working toolbox.

Chapter 11: Using CI to Handle Files and Images, will be about files, uploading, downloading, and compressing them, of course, all with CI classes! As always those classes will make our life easier. Image treatment also has some space in the chapter as CI has some nice features to crop, reduce, watermark, and so on.

Chapter 12: Moving Your Site to the WWW, will finally show you how to upload your site to a shared host or similar. Here we will see in detail how to do that, and also what kind of error we can expect to encounter.

Chapter 13: CRUD – or Putting It All Together, will be a chapter of "putting it all together", where we'll take time to recap and emphasize the most important topics covered to the moment. Insert, edit, and remove records from the database are some topics we will see here, but also ordering and pagination of results.

Chapter 14: The Verdict on CI, will summarize the key points of CI, not to forget anything, as every little thing CI offers will be of great help.

Chapter 15: Resources and Extensions, will give a list of resources and third-party code — we don't want to reinvent the wheel! We will take a look at some useful extensions such as authentication, PDF generation, invoicing, and much more.

The *Appendix* will introduce a new and interesting CI feature, the cart class; building a store has never been easier!

What you need for this book

Only basic PHP and HTML knowledge is needed to understand this book.
All the rest is explained here from top to bottom. You won't get lost!

Who this book is for

This book is not only for PHP developers who want to be more productive at work,
but also for those who are new to web programming and are searching for a useful
tool that helps in their work. If you are tired of writing the same code again and
again, this book is for you. If you want to create more robust and easier-to-maintain
PHP sites, again this book is for you. But this book is really for you if you want to
enjoy PHP programming with a framework that really helps you.

Conventions

In this book, you will find a number of styles of text that distinguish between
different kinds of information. Here are some examples of these styles, and an
explanation of their meaning.

Code words in text are shown as follows: "Our `password` variable contains a
password that looks quite secure, but will produce a problem in our query."

A block of code will be set as follows:

```
$this->load->database('websites');
$query = $this->db->get('sites');
foreach ($query->result() as $row)
{
  print $row->url;
}
```

When we wish to draw your attention to a particular part of a code block, the
relevant lines or items will be shown in bold:

```
<head>
  <!DOCTYPE html PUBLIC '-//W3C//DTD XHTML 1.0
  Strict//EN'http:\/\/www.w3.org/TR/xhtml1/DTD/xhtml1-strict.dtd'>
  <html xmlns='http:\/\/www.w3.org/1999/xhtml'>
  <title>Web test Site</title>
    <link rel="stylesheet" type="text/css" href="<?php echo
    $base."/".$css;?>">
</head>
```

New terms and **important words** are shown in bold. Words that you see on the screen, in menus or dialog boxes for example, appear in our text like this: "When you click on the **Buy** button, you will be returned to this page again".

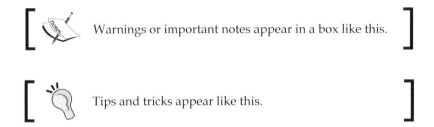

Warnings or important notes appear in a box like this.

Tips and tricks appear like this.

Reader feedback

Feedback from our readers is always welcome. Let us know what you think about this book—what you liked or may have disliked. Reader feedback is important for us to develop titles that you really get the most out of.

To send us general feedback, simply drop an email to feedback@packtpub.com, and mention the book title in the subject of your message.

If there is a book that you need and would like to see us publish, please send us a note in the **SUGGEST A TITLE** form on www.packtpub.com or email suggest@packtpub.com.

If there is a topic that you have expertise in and you are interested in either writing or contributing to a book, see our author guide on www.packtpub.com/authors.

Customer support

Now that you are the proud owner of a Packt book, we have a number of things to help you to get the most from your purchase.

Downloading the example code for the book

Visit http://www.packtpub.com/files/code/9485_Code.zip to directly download the example code.

[The downloadable files contain instructions on how to use them.]

Errata

Although we have taken every care to ensure the accuracy of our contents, mistakes do happen. If you find a mistake in one of our books—maybe a mistake in text or code—we would be grateful if you would report this to us. By doing so, you can save other readers from frustration, and help us to improve subsequent versions of this book. If you find any errata, please report them by visiting http://www.packtpub.com/support, selecting your book, clicking on the **let us know** link, and entering the details of your errata. Once your errata are verified, your submission will be accepted and the errata added to any list of existing errata. Any existing errata can be viewed by selecting your title from http://www.packtpub.com/support.

Piracy

Piracy of copyright material on the Internet is an ongoing problem across all media. At Packt, we take the protection of our copyright and licenses very seriously. If you come across any illegal copies of our works in any form on the Internet, please provide us with the location address or website name immediately so that we can pursue a remedy.

Please contact us at copyright@packtpub.com with a link to the suspected pirated material.

We appreciate your help in protecting our authors, and our ability to bring you valuable content.

Questions

You can contact us at questions@packtpub.com if you are having a problem with any aspect of the book, and we will do our best to address it.

1
Introduction to CodeIgniter

Most of us just want to write applications that work well, and to do it as simply and easily as we can. This book is about CodeIgniter—a tool for making PHP easy to use.

If you need to produce results, have better and more maintainable code, and you enjoy programming, then you should try using CodeIgniter (CI to its friends). CI is free, lightweight, and simple to install, and it really makes your life much easier. Just read this chapter to find out how:

- What CI can do for you?
- What is CI? What are Frameworks?
- Comparing CI to other open source solutions.
- What CI doesn't do?

What can CodeIgniter do for you?

If you are already writing code in PHP, CI will help you to do it in a better and easier way. It will cut down the amount of code you actually type. Your scripts will be easier to read and update—improving team work and maintainability. It will help you to give large websites a coherent structure. It will discipline your code and make it more robust, in some cases even without your knowing it.

That's quite a big claim. You have already spent some time learning PHP, HTML, CSS, a database, and so on. You need basic, not necessarily expert knowledge of PHP to benefit from CI.

CI is not for you if:

- You don't have a minimum knowledge of PHP and HTML.

- You like to write all of your code. There are people who prefer to write their code instead of using already built solutions. If you are that kind of a person, you should try CI. It is very well commented and, if you are short of time, it will help you. You won't need to reinvent the wheel again and again. CI comes with a lot of helpers, libraries, and much more for the most common tasks. Give it a try!

- You don't like PHP; but how is that possible? With a huge community and hordes of code and tools, PHP is one of the favorite languages of the Web.

- And definitely CI is not for you if you don't like to finish your projects on time, in a well-structured fashion, and without having to redo the same things again and again.

If you don't belong to any of the categories mentioned in the previous points, keep reading!

Save time

CI doesn't take long to learn, and it quickly pays for your effort in the time saved later. Let's look at a simple measure—how CI cuts down the amount of code you need to type. This is not just good for the lazy. The less you type, the fewer mistakes you make, and the less time you spend debugging your code.

Let's take two examples, (they are explained later in this book, so don't worry now about how they work!). If you are writing a database query, this is how you might write a function within your PHP program to query a MySQL database:

```
$connection = mysql_connect("localhost","fred","12345");
mysql_select_db("websites", $connection);
$result = mysql_query ("SELECT * FROM sites", $connection);
while ($row = mysql_fetch_array($result, MYSQL_NUM))
{
  foreach ($row as $attribute)
  print "{$attribute[1]}";
}
```

Now see how a CI function would handle a similar query:

```
$this->load->database('websites');
$query = $this->db->get('sites');
foreach ($query->result() as $row)
{
  print $row->url;
}
```

Compare the character count—244 for the traditional syntax and 112 for CI. Another thing that you have to take into account when using Active Record is that you can change your database from MySQL to Postgres (or any other that is supported by CI) and you won't need to change your queries—a very helpful thing.

Now let's take an example where you are writing a data entry form in HTML, and you want a drop-down query box. Let's say this drop-down query box shows three options and allows the user to select one of them. In HTML, a drop-down box can be created like this:

```
<select name="url">
<option value="this">www.this.com</option>
<option value="that">www.that.com</option>
<option value="theother" selected>www.theother.com</option>
</select>
```

CI's version is both shorter and, because it works from an array, more adapted to PHP processing:

```
$urlarray = array(
                'this' => 'www.this.com',
                'that' => 'www.that.com',
                'theother' => 'www.theother.com',
             );
$variable = form_dropdown('url', $urlarray, 'this');
```

In HTML, you need to type 154 characters, and 128 in CI. Note how easily we can define the "selected" element of the drop-down menu, putting it in the third parameter. This thing alone will save us a lot of time.

Make your site more robust

Although you don't need to write much code, CI provides a lot of the standard functionality and better security, and it remembers all those oddities and quirks. It keeps track of things you may have forgotten about (those little touches that distinguish amateur sites from professional ones).

Keep your links up-to-date automatically

Suppose you've just written a menu page, with lot of hyperlinks to other pages in your site. They are all in the traditional HTML format as shown:

```
<a href="http://www.mysite.com/index.php/start/hello/fred
">say hello to Fred</a>
```

Then, you decide to move the site to another URL. That means you have to go painstakingly through your code, looking for each URL, and rewriting it, else none of your links will work.

CI gives you a simple function to write hyperlinks like this:

```
echo anchor('start/hello/fred', 'Say hello to Fred');
```

CI also encourages you to put the URL of your site in a configuration file that the rest of your site can access. CI's anchor function that we've used here, automatically refers to that configuration file. So, when you come to move your site, you only need to change that one entry in the configuration file, and all your hyperlinks are updated automatically.

Preventing database SQL injection attacks and form prepping

Data entry is fraught with problems. There are certain limitations of HTML and databases, as a result of which data containing symbols such as apostrophes and quotation marks may not be saved correctly, or even worse, your database may be open to malicious attacks.

For example, take this query:

```
SELECT id, name FROM users WHERE user = '{$user}' AND password =
'{$password}';
```

Consider that the variables have the following values:

```
$user = "Fred";
$password = "1234";
```

Now our query would translate to:

```
SELECT id, name FROM users WHERE user = 'Fred' AND password = '1234';
```

This query will return a good result, but, what if our variables were:

```
$user = "Fred";
$password = "1234' OR '1' = '1";
```

Now our query would produce:

```
SELECT id, name FROM users WHERE user = 'Fred' AND password = '1234'
OR '1' = '1';
```

This time the variable's data contains a new "where" clause with a condition that is always true. The user inserts some characters, such as " ' " to make our query behave in a way we don't want, and give bad results. It's easy to see that with this kind of attacks more than just giving bad results can be achieved, dropping tables being one of the worse things. These problems don't always come in the shape of SQL injection attacks; most of the time not prepping data correctly would bring problems too, for example:

```
$user = "Fred";
$password = "12xWgBq'wS";
```

Our `password` variable contains a password that looks quite secure, but will produce a problem in our query:

```
SELECT id, name FROM users WHERE user = 'Fred' AND password =
'12xWgBq'wS';
```

The data will cut the query, producing some errors when executed. What can we do to prevent these problems? Well the answer to this is to prepare or "prep" our data in our data entry form, before it is submitted to the database. All this takes time and a certain amount of extra coding.

CI's form helper does this, automatically. So, when you create an input box by typing:

```
echo form_input('user', 'Fred');
```

You're also getting the hidden benefit of:

```
function form_prep($str = '')
{
  // if the field name is an array we do this recursively
  if (is_array($str))
  {
    foreach ($str as $key => $val)
    {
      $str[$key] = form_prep($val);
    }
    return $str;
  }
  if ($str === '')
  {
```

```
    return '';
  }
  $temp = '__TEMP_AMPERSANDS__';

  // Replace entities to temporary markers so that
  // htmlspecialchars won't mess them up

  $str = preg_replace("/&#(\d+);/", "$temp\\1;", $str);
  $str = preg_replace("/&(\w+);/",  "$temp\\1;", $str);
  $str = htmlspecialchars($str);

  // In case htmlspecialchars misses these.

  $str = str_replace(array("'", '"'), array("&#39;", "&quot;"),
                     $str);

   // Decode the temp markers back to entities

  $str = preg_replace("/$temp(\d+);/","&#\\1;",$str);
  $str = preg_replace("/$temp(\w+);/","&\\1;",$str);
  return $str;
}
```

This is the code that handles special characters such as "&" so that they don't cause confusion while your form is being submitted. As you can see, there is some quite tricky regex code in there.

Possibly you like typing regexes. Some people like lying on a bed of nails, some like listening to ABBA; it's a free country. If you don't like these things, you can let CI do them for you (the regexes, not ABBA), and you needn't even be aware of the code that's working in the background for you, every time you write that one simple line of code:

```
echo form_input('user', 'Fred');
```

Besides this, CI's Active Record class automatically escapes special characters in database queries; this can also be achieved with query bindings, to give some extra automatic protection to your site; without our doing anything CI is helping us to make our site more secure.

Protect your site from XSS attacks

As stated on Wikipedia (http://en.wikipedia.org/wiki/Cross-site_scripting), XSS (cross site scripting) is a kind of vulnerability that allows some unwanted code to be executed in our application, phising attacks, data theft, and more. In order to avoid this you should validate your data.

CodeIgniter helps you to do so, in all your applications if you set global XSS filter to true in your configuration file, or whenever you need it:

```
$data = $this->input->xss_clean($data);
```

You can even use it to check potential XSS attacks within image files:

```
$this->input->xss_clean($file, TRUE);
```

The second parameter tells CI that it is an image that needs validation.

Make your code bolder

CI also makes it easy to do things you might not have tried before. Of course, PHP users can always integrate libraries from **PHP Extension and Application Repository (PEAR)** and other sources. They aren't always easy to integrate, or use, and their syntax and standards differ greatly. CI has a common set of standards, and once you've mastered its syntax, all its parts work together without complication. All its code is well-written and reliable, and is tested by its user community. It puts much more sophistication in your hands.

Let's take a look at two examples to illustrate this point.

Send email attachments without hassles

Sending emails is a complex business. CI's code for doing it looks easy to follow:

```
$this->load->library('email');
$this->email->from('your@your-site.com', 'Your Name');
$this->email->subject('Email Test');
$this->email->message('Testing the email class.');
$this->email->send();
```

There are a number of issues involved in sending emails—setting word wrapping and escaping it (so that long URLs don't get wrapped and broken up). For example, when sending attachments, the standard PHP functions can get quite complex. As a result many code writers are tempted to avoid using these functions if possible.

CI's email class makes it simple to send an attachment. You write:

```
$this->email->attach('/path/to/photo1.jpg');
```

CI does the rest, working behind the scenes. There is a function that sorts out MIME types for nearly a hundred type of attachments. So it knows that your photo, photo1.jpg, is an image/jpeg MIME type. It remembers to generate boundary delimiters in the right places around your attachments. It takes care of wrapping your text, and it allows you to easily mark chunks of text you don't want wrapped.

Save bandwidth by zipping files that users need to download

To save bandwidth, it's a fairly common practice to compress or zip files before you download them. That's something you might have never done, and you wouldn't know how to go about it. On the other hand, CI has a nice facility that allows you to produce ZIP files with four lines of code:

```
$name = 'mydata1.txt';
$data = 'the contents of my file...........';
$this->zip->add_data($name, $data);
$this->zip->archive('c:/my_backup.zip');
```

Run this snippet, and you will find a ZIP archive on your `c:` drive containing one file. Your ZIP file reader will unzip it and produce the original data for you. People who use your site won't know that you've produced this impressive result so easily. They'll be impressed! Your site will save bandwidth. You did it in minutes rather than hours.

What CI doesn't do

There are some things that CI doesn't do. CI was intended to be a small and **lightweight** framework. The zipped download for version 1.7.2 is only 2.1 MB and is downloaded in seconds, whereas the Zend framework is 10 MB. It won't answer all the problems you will have. But it does:

- Make it easy and quick to program in PHP
- Structure your site and help you through the architectural decisions

As a result of being lightweight, it does not have as many features as some of its rivals. Other frameworks such as Rails, CakePHP, or Symfony have **scaffolding** and **generators**. These tools automatically write certain basic scripts for you.

Once you have set up a database, Rails creates out-of-the-box web pages to do basic **Create, Read, Update, and Delete (CRUD)** operations on the database tables. In addition, Rails allows you to write generators—pieces of code that automatically write other basic scripts. The Rails community has created quite a lot of these, so you can automatically generate scripts that do all sorts of clever things.

CI concentrates on making basic things easy. Some of the things it handles are:

- Session management and cookies (see Chapter 6)
- Database access and queries (see Chapter 4)
- Building HTML stuff, like pages and forms, and validating form entries (see Chapter 5)
- Communicating on the Internet, using FTP (Chapter 9)

Sounds familiar? All of these are basic processes, which you will have to go through if you're building a dynamic website. CI makes these processes easier, and makes your code more likely to work. Join this outstanding community; it will help you in case you need it (at the CodeIgniter forums). You can even share code at the Wiki (`http://codeigniter.com/wiki/`), and you will find why CI is so popular.

Yes, but…what is CodeIgniter? What are frameworks?

Shortly after programming was invented, it was noticed that it involved many repetitive operations. And maybe shortly after that, Ada Lovelace—spanner in hand adjusting Babbage's differential engine—or Alan Turing at Bletchley Park decided to modularize code. So, you only had to write certain chunks once, and could then reuse them. PHP programmers are used to writing separate chunks of code in functions, and then storing those functions in `include` files.

At one level, a framework is just that—lot of chunks of code stored in separate files, which simplify the coding of repetitive operations. In the previous examples, connecting to the database or building HTML form elements are abstracted and simplified for you. You call a function in the framework, which is easy to handle than the original code.

It goes beyond that. Writing code involves continuous choices between the many ways of tackling the same problem. Most frameworks impose a set of choices on you. They've started to handle the problem one way, so you have to go that way as well. If they are sensible choices, it makes your life much simpler. If not, it's like trying to write a sales brochure using Excel, or showing cash flow projections using Word. Both can probably be done, but neither is the best use of your time.

Sensible design decisions make sure that the things you need are accessible, but prevent them from spilling over into each other. A good framework makes these decisions for you—starting off with a sensible foundation for your program and guiding you through the next steps.

A framework will also improve team programming. As every developer has to adhere to the framework syntax and structure, it is an important part of software maintainability. The code you write today needs to be readable by other people in future. Imagine you arrive to a new workplace and then you inherit a couple of projects. In a perfect world those projects would be well commented, but reality usually hits... Wouldn't it be nice to have a central resource of documentation to get started with those projects?

Most frameworks will offer good documentation. CI isn't an exception; everything is well documented—functions, structures, conventions. You won't have to imagine what a certain function does, you will know it. A very good starting point, don't you think?

Nowadays there are lot of frameworks out there, not only PHP frameworks but Ruby frameworks, Python frameworks, and so on. For PHP programmers there are hundreds of options (well, may not be hundreds, but if we do search for PHP frameworks the results will be overwhelming). Of all these options there are some that are more popular; CI is among them, with others such as CakePHP, Zend Framework, Symfony, and more.

As you are reading this book, you are interested in PHP frameworks, especially CodeIgniter, so we will keep to it.

If you take a look at `http://phpframeworks.com/` and `http://www.phpframeworks.com/top-10-php-frameworks/`, you will see how well CodeIgniter is doing. CI is very popular as a PHP framework; with this book you will know, why. Also if you look at some forums and blogs you'll notice that postings get very heated about which framework is the best. The truth seems to be that each has its strengths, and none is without its own weaknesses. In time you will learn to decide which framework to use in which project. It is recommended that you should think about which tool to use, before starting your projects. Choose the one that will help you to end with a well done project, in good time, and with the best possible scalability. Most of the times CI helps achieve this.

Comparing CI to other open source solutions (CakePHP and Joomla!)

For one reason or another one should compare these three most of the time and, of course, use one of them. There are other solutions out there, as we have commented before, "few" is not the word to describe PHP frameworks.

Though you would like to have Zend Framework and Symfony in your toolbox, for now, let's use these three for comparison. For example, when Jose heard about frameworks it was all about Ruby on Rails. Before that he used to write his own code for every project. Though Ruby on Rails is a very good framework, for him—a PHP programmer at heart—that was not the solution.

Searching for a PHP framework that was similar to Ruby on Rails, but PHP made, CakePHP was one option. It was quite similar in concept to Ruby on Rails, it also had the same convention-driven architecture that you need to learn before using it. It will pay-back with lots of functionality, automation, and more. But keep in mind that the learning curve is steeper than CodeIgniter's.

Using CakePHP requires you to adhere to some strict conventions (those can be changed but the out-of-the-box software comes with them). Most of the time they are naming conventions, but there are database conventions also.

After some time, because of curiosity, in spite of incredible lack of learning time (some nearby shouting boss also helped), continuing research of PHP frameworks found CodeIgniter. The most convincing thing was the documentation (CakePHP wasn't as well documented as it is today).

CI has less conventions, and minimal configuration, also you can forget about most of them and work as you have always done. You don't want to use models, and you don't have to (though it is recommended). That said, one of the strengths of CI is just that—download it and start programming.

Joomla! is not exactly a framework, it helps you build websites faster. Also in the latest versions it has turned into the **MVC (Model-View-Controller)** pattern. The good part of Joomla! is that it is a CMS (Content Management System), but I think it is also its bad part, as sometimes you just don't need so much as Joomla! has to offer. Of course you can develop your own solution over Joomla!, but then what's the point of using Joomla!, and not using what it has to offer?

CI, usually, is the most well-balanced of the three, but let's see how we can choose one of them.

What to choose

With all those options out there, why should you go with CI? The answer—it's not that easy and involves, in most cases, personal preference. There will be projects that will be better suited to one of the other two options. Let's see some examples that will guide us.

When to choose Joomla!

- If we need a CMS (it may sound redundant, but...).

- If there is already a component, module, or some other functionality that we need, then there is something built that can help us carry out the project in no time.

- If the client asks you to use it. Joomla! is a well known software, and sometimes your client can just ask you to use it.

When to choose CakePHP

- If there are lot of relations between database tables. Cake's Active Record capabilities are slightly more powerful than CI's.

- If you need to build some admin zone quickly. Cake's bake script can read your database and build some CRUD (Create, Read, Update, Delete) pages for your tables.

When to choose CodeIgniter

- If the project doesn't have or doesn't need a very rigid structure. Also CI is good for working with legacy code.

- If you need to start programming right away, without having to learn a lot of conventions.

- If you need some software that helps you, with the confidence that it will help you in the way you really need, and learn the way something needs to be done.

- If you know PHP, you can use CI.

- The client needs some solution built specifically for him/her, and not an adapted solution (that would be in case of some Joomla! components/modules).

Most of the time we will be using CI because it is very flexible. If you like programming CI will help you in doing it. It will seem as if CI isn't even there. You realize it only when you look at the time you are gaining and the better structure of your project.

If you are new to frameworks it is recommended that you get CI, maybe later you use another one (probably both of them), but CI will always have a place in your heart.

Packt Publishing has books on some other frameworks and Joomla!.
It is recommended to read them, it will give you a broader view of things.

For books on Joomla visit `http://www.packtpub.com/`
`joomla-version-1-5/book`.

For books on CakePHP visit `http://www.packtpub.com/`
`cakephp-application-development/book`.

License

If you are building a commercial application, the license terms for any software you are using become critical. If you are raising venture capital, expect the VC's lawyers to go over them in detail. With CI this is not a problem. It has a very generous license that is downloaded with your files.

Unlike some commercial software, CI's license even fits on one screen. Here it is, in the following screenshot:

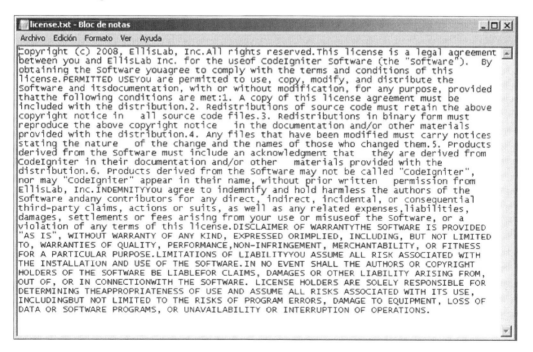

Summary

If you already know some PHP and are designing intelligent websites, the CodeIgniter framework is all about making your life easier. It helps you to:

- Save time
- Make your site more robust
- Achieve more sophisticated coding
- It makes coding fun again, rather than a chore

There are quite a lot of frameworks and all of them offer chunks of pre-written code that make the repetitive or complex processes of coding easier and not just for the PHP language. They impose a helpful structure on your site's development.

This book does not make any comparisons between frameworks. CI works for most, and we will see, how and why. It will be useful for you too, and you will be able to save much time and, as a result, enjoy the coding process more.

This book takes you through some of the framework's main features, and tries to explain some of what goes on "under the hood". We've used a real-world example for the code illustrations in this book to show that CI is a serious tool that can be quickly and easily used in a demanding environment.

Enjoy!

2
Setting up a CodeIgniter Site

Setting up the CI package on your web server or a local machine is easy. This chapter explains, what happens when you install the site and which files will be created. Let's look at:

- What software you require for your site's development
- Installing the CI files—a simple download and unzip operation
- The basic configuration of CI—which folders are there and how they are organized
- The initial controller and view that CI installs
- Some basic modifications to show how these work

Prerequisites

CodeIgniter is very flexible. It will work equally well with PHP 4.3.2 and above, or PHP 5, as there are lot of hosting providers that still don't support PHP 5, this is useful. It is suggested to search for a PHP 5 hosting. CI will work in the same way. In some cases it's not possible and you will have to go with a PHP 4 hosting. You will also need a database. CI's online user guide says:

> *Supported databases are MySQL, MySQLi, MS SQL, Postgre SQL, Oracle, SQLite, and ODBC.*

In order to develop and test a dynamic website, you need a web server. Normally, you would develop and test your site on a local server—one that runs on your own machine (with the loopback address `127.0.0.1` or `localhost`) rather than on a remote site on the Internet.

If you aren't familiar with the process of setting up a web server, it's easier to install a package such as XAMPP Lite or WAMP. It installs Apache, PHP, and MySQL on to a Windows machine with minimum configuration to be done by you. XAMPP Lite is free, it comes with comprehensive instructions, and is almost always easy to install. Alternatively, some versions of Windows come with their own web server, but it is good to use XAMPP or WAMP.

WAMP and XAMPP are very easy to install, and they provide you with a good development environment within minutes.
You can find instructions about how to install them on:

For WAMP:
`http://www.wampserver.com/en/presentation.php`

For XAMPP:
`http://www.apachefriends.org/en/xampp-windows.html#522`

Also, if you have any questions you can ask them on the forums:

For WAMP:
`http://www.wampserver.com/phorum/`

For XAMPP:
`http://www.apachefriends.org/f/`

It also helps to have a good PHP editor on your system (Notepad++ or Dreamweaver are good options; notepad++ is available for free). You can do it all in a text editor, but the syntax highlighting feature of a good editor saves you from making lot of simple mistakes with unclosed brackets or mismatched quotation marks.

Once you've reached this far, it will take you two minutes to have CI running on your system.

Installing CodeIgniter

One thing you don't need is your credit card — CI is completely free!

Once your server is set up, go to the CodeIgniter site at (`http://www.codeigniter.com/`) and download the latest version of the framework. Version 1.7.2, the latest, it is only 2.1 MB when zipped, so it doesn't take much time to download the framework.

Unzip the folder, and install the CodeIgniter files in your website's root folder. If you are using XAMPP Lite, this is usually the `htdocs` folder within the `xampplite` folder. For WAMP it is `www` inside the `wamp` folder.

The CodeIgniter `index.php` file should be in the root directory. The root folder is the folder that you would point at if you navigated to the site—in this case, by accessing `http://127.0.0.1`. If you put CodeIgniter in some other directory you will need to point to that directory. For example, if you create a folder called `codeigniter` inside your WAMP installation, you will need to put `http://127.0.0.1/codeigniter`, in order to access your CodeIgniter installation.

Included with CI is a comprehensive user guide (in the `user_guide` folder), it's the same as the one on their website. You'll use this a lot. It is usually clear, try it if you get stuck, it will save your time.

When these files are on your machine, you can access them in two ways:

- As a URL: For example, `http://127.0.0.1`
- Through the normal directory path: For example, `C:/xampplite/htdocs/index.php`

You should be able to see the CI welcome screen by simply navigating to your URL with the browser. It's that simple! The welcome page tells you, what you are seeing is built by two file—a view and a controller.

Exploring the file structure

Once you have installed the CI files, have a look at the new directories that have been created. Understanding what different type of files and folders do is critical.

The initial files and folders we can see are:

- `system`
- `user_guide`
- `index.php`
- `license.txt`

These are our main site's files and folders, the `index.php` file being the most important one, it will act as the main controller and will route application requests to the required controllers. Without this file, CodeIgniter can't work.

Next in importance is the `system` folder. The framework's base files and libraries are present in this folder. We, as programmers, won't need to modify those files for our normal usage. However, it's important to know what those files are and what they do.

The application folder is placed inside the system folder. Our site's files and code will be put here. This separation of the system and application folders has two purposes:

- We can update the CI framework without any trouble, as our files are separated from the framework's. As we don't make changes to CI base files updating those files won't do any harm.

- We can have as many application folders as we need, all of them using the same system folder. That is a great advantage, because if we need to update our framework version, we will need to do it only once.

Of course, there are more files and folders. If you have opened the system folder you would have glanced through them. We are going to see them one by one. If you've ever looked at any other PHP framework, the structure will look fairly familiar. The folder structure is similar to the following:

system

- application: This folder contains your application files. The following is the list of folders in the application folder:
  - config: This folder contains CI configuration files, such as database connection files and more.
  - controllers: This folder contains your application controller files.
  - errors: This folder contains your error documents, such as 404 error pages.
  - helpers: This folder contains helper files.
  - hooks: This folder contains files that are intended to change CI functionalities without changing CI core files. This way your changes would not be lost if you update your CI version.
  - language: This folder contains language files for your application.
  - libraries: This folder contains your own libraries and classes.
  - models: This folder contains model files.
  - views: This folder contains your application's view files.

- `cache`: This folder contains cache files that will be created if you use CI cache capabilities. This directory needs write permissions in your server.

- `codeigniter`: This folder contains CI framework files, you shouldn't need to edit those files.

- `database`: This folder contains database connection libraries and other tools, again you will rarely be editing those files.

- `fonts`: This folder contains fonts that will be used by the image library, for example, when watermarking images.

- `helpers`: This folder contains CI helpers (email helper, form helper).

- `language`: This folder contains language files for CI libraries. Your application's language files can be placed inside the `application\language` folder.

- `libraries`: This folder contains CI library files, containing the classes that will help you build your application. If you create your own libraries place them inside `application\libraries`.

- `logs`: This folder contains log files.

- `plugins`: This folder contains some CI plugins. If there is no `plugins` folder inside `application` you can make it and put your plugins there.

- `scaffolding`: This folder contains CI CRUD generation files.

`user_guide`: This folder contains help documents for CI, they are the same as those on CodeIgniter's site.

`index.php`: This file must be in the document root of your server so that CodeIgniter can work.

`license.txt`: This file is the license document, you should read it.

 If you are working on a Linux server remember that paths use the forward slash, that is: `application/language`.

Does it work?—checking our CI installation

Now that we have taken a look at our CI files and structure, we are going to check if it's working. An easy way to see if your site is working is to navigate to it using your browser. For example, if you have installed CI in a folder called `codeigniter` inside your `wamp` installation, you can see it by using the path `http://127.0.0.1/codeigniter/` in your browser. You should see something similar to the following screenshot:

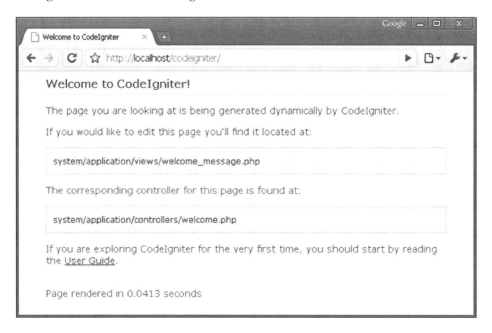

This means CI is up and running. Did you see how easy it is? We will need to make some configuration changes to adapt it to our needs, but that will be very easy.

The configuration file

Remember we were going to take two minutes to set up our site. The second minute is spent doing some basic configuration.

The `config` folder contains a group of files that set basic configurations for your site. Open the `system/application/config/config.php` file and tell the site where to find itself. The first few lines of the file should say something like:

```
/*
|--------------------------------------------------
| Base Site URL
|--------------------------------------------------
|
| URL to your Code Igniter root. Typically this
| will be your base URL, WITH a trailing slash:
|
|   http://www.your-site.com/
|
*/
$config['base_url'] = "http://127.0.0.1/";
/*
```

Notice, how well CI files are commented! Alter the values in quotes to match your own website's root. If you have a problem, more detailed set up instructions are given in the online manual. Some functions such as anchor and base_url use this configuration, so modify it carefully.

As a basic principle, use the config.php file to store information about your site rather than scattering it around your files. In the first place, it is easier to update if it's all in one place. Second, when you transfer your site from the development server to the production server, you'll have to make only one set of changes. Lastly, many CI functions assume that certain information is to be found there.

There are other config files in the config folder. The database connection file, the routes file, and the autoload file are some of the most important files we will be changing for our application to work correctly. Should your CI installation produce a 404 error, after this basic configuration, look at line 44 of the config file:

```
$config['uri_protocol'] = "AUTO";
```

This line determines which global variable will be used to retrieve the query string. This is needed to create nice URLs and know which part of the URL is our path to the file and which part contains the variables we are passing between pages. Sometimes one of those variables is not available, though usually AUTO will work, on other occasions we will have to specify which one should be used, manually.

For example, take this URL:

```
http://localhost/demo/sayhello.php?to=Fred.
```

In my server configuration, PATH_INFO and ORIG_PATH_INFO return nothing, but the others return:

- QUERY_STRING: to=Fred
- REQUEST_URI: /demo/sayhello.php?to=Fred

As we can see, they work in a different way, if PATH_INFO had been active it would have returned the values before the question mark, that is:

- PATH_INFO: /demo/sayhello.php

If the AUTO option doesn't work for you, try to change this setting with the other options, and if none of them works for you then change your index_page variable to:

```
$config['index_page'] = "index.php?";
```

The only difference is the question mark (?), which should solve your problem. As we have seen before, these methods are used to determine which part of the URL is our path to the file and which part contains the variables. For some reason the question mark (?) is not automatically appended to the URL, the reason couldn't be determined. At these times we will put the question mark manually.

Autoloading libraries, helpers, and so on

Inside the config folder you will also find the autoload.php file. This file will help you determine which libraries, helpers, and so on, should be autoloaded within your application. But at this point you may not know what libraries or helpers are. Don't worry about that, we will summarize this concept. Libraries are like classes, which contain methods that help us while working with some tasks such as, session control, database access, and a lot of other things. Helpers work in the same way but in a smaller scope.

You need to load the library first and then you can use it. Usually, to load a library you need to do something like:

```
$this->load->library('pagination');
```

Similarly for helper loading you need:

```
$this->load->helper('form');
```

After doing that you can use the library or helper. If you need to use a particular library or helper once or twice in your application there is no problem with that. But now imagine, you have to write those lines in every controller function of your site.

If you want to save some time, and forget about the repetitive task of adding the loading lines, you can put those libraries and helpers in the `autoload.php` file. For example, if you are using the `pagination` library you could add it to the `autoload` file this way:

```
$autoload['libraries'] = array('pagination');
```

Now you will have access to the functions of the `pagination` library in every function of your application, without the need to load it first. Another good candidate library to be autoloaded is the `database` library, you can add it in the same array (don't do it now, just take a look at how it works):

```
$autoload['libraries'] = array('pagination', 'database');
```

If your application is using a database, you will end up putting the `database` library in the `autoload` array, eliminating the necessity to load the library every time you need access to the database.

Helpers, plugins, and extra configuration files could be added to the `autoload.php` file the same way, in their corresponding arrays. You maybe tempted to put all libraries and helpers you will be using in this file. But remember that all the libraries and helpers you put here add to the loading time and your application will load slowly.

If your site has only a few visitors you don't need to look after these things. But as time passes by and, luckily, your site becomes popular, all these things count and you need to take everything into account.

Don't worry about this, after you have built some sites with CI, you will know which libraries, helpers, plugins, and so on should be put here and you will be doing that soon. That means CI is up and running. Did it take more than two minutes?

Mod rewrite and apache .htaccess to achieve nice URL rewrites

Earlier we saw the welcome page of CI, it is there by default, thanks to the `welcome` controller and `welcome` view. The `welcome` controller is the default controller (this is configured in the `routes.php` file of the `config` directory),
so it is loaded on the home page of our application.

 This part is a bit more technical, our CI installation can work without doing this, so you can obviate it.

If we want to see it and if the default controller isn't there, we would have to put this URL:

```
http://127.0.0.1/codeigniter/index.php/welcome
```

Note the `index.php` in the path between the base URL and the controller we want to load. If you try to put the URL like:

```
http://127.0.0.1/codeigniter/welcome
```

You will get an error page, but this can be solved, so we can get rid of the `index.php`. This, we have to admit, doesn't make our URLs easy to write. The first thing that we need to do is put an `.htaccess` file in our application's root. Of course our server needs to support the use of these files (you can ask your hosting provider about this).

We can find a sample `.htaccess` file for CI on Wiki:

```
http://codeigniter.com/wiki/mod_rewrite/
```

Create a file called `.htaccess` in your application root (where the `index.php` file was located), and copy the code you found on Wiki:

```
<IfModule mod_rewrite.c>
  RewriteEngine On
  RewriteBase /
  #Removes access to the system folder by users.
  #Additionally this will allow you to create a System.php
  #controller, previously this would not have been possible.
  #'system' can be replaced if you have renamed your system folder.
  RewriteCond %{REQUEST_URI} ^system.*
  RewriteRule ^(.*)$ /codeigniter/index.php?/$1 [L]


  #Checks to see if the user is attempting to access a valid file,
  #such as an image or css document, if this isn't true it sends
  #the request to index.php

  RewriteCond %{REQUEST_FILENAME} !-f
  RewriteCond %{REQUEST_FILENAME} !-d
  RewriteRule ^(.*)$ /codeigniter/index.php?/$1 [L]
</IfModule>
<IfModule !mod_rewrite.c>

  # If we don't have mod_rewrite installed, all 404's
  # can be sent to index.php, and everything works as normal.
  # Submitted by: ElliotHaughin

  ErrorDocument 404 /index.php
</IfModule>
```

If you cannot create the `.htaccess` file (Windows needs a file name to be put before the extension), then create it on a Linux server and download it, after that you will be able to edit it. For example, you can connect it to an FTP tool (like FileZilla), to another hosting you have, and create the file and download it to your PC.

After creating the file and copying the code from Wiki into it, you may need to change it to adapt to your hosting configuration. If we have to add our base URL **/codeigniter** at some places (it is in bold so you can recognize it), we need to change the `config.php` file, located at `system/application/config`. The only thing you need to do is change this line:

```
$config['index_page'] = "index.php";
```

To this:

```
$config['index_page'] = "";
```

After that you will be able to go to `http://127.0.0.1/codeigniter/welcome` and you won't need to put `index.php` in between your base URL and your controller. Now it is much easier to write, and for your visitors to remember, it's also better for your website's SEO.

Moving the application directory and the system directory—benefits

Here we are making the final changes to our CI installation.

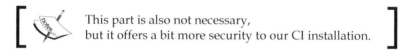

This part is also not necessary, but it offers a bit more security to our CI installation.

To make these changes, open the `index.php` file, go to the `system` folder, and move the `application` folder and all it's content to the same level as the `index.php` file (cut and paste the entire folder with all it's subfolders). Now put the `system` folder outside the document root and change the following line in `index.php` file from:

```
$system_folder = "system";
```

To:

```
$system_folder = "../CI_system";
```

We can change the name of the folder from `system` to `CI_system`, or whatever you want.

So now our structure will look similar to the following:

```
CI_system
    www (or htdocs in xampp)
        codeigniter
            application
            user_guide
            .htaccess
            index.php
            license.txt
```

This way we get some benefits. First, by moving the `system` folder outside the document root we prevent possible attacks on CI core files. In this case if some vulnerability is discovered, in one of those files, the attacker will have a difficult time trying to reach for them. Second, separating the `application` folder from the `system` folder we can have as many CI applications as we need and only one CI core folder. This way if we need to upgrade CI, we only need to do it in one directory.

Summary

In this chapter, we've seen how easy it is to install CI. Once you have a development web server set up, all you need to do is download the CI code, unzip it, and copy it over.

Then, we quickly looked at the structure of the files we've installed and did some basic configuration, and now we have a working CI site.

Other changes we made will help us have a site that is more secure and with better URLs. Those changes are really not necessary and you can develop your site without them, but we saw how easy it was to make them and achieve their benefits.

Now, if you haven't done it already, install your own copy of CI, remember, the most important steps are:

- Install XAMPP (`http://www.apachefriends.org/en/xampp-windows.html`) or WAMP (`http://www.wampserver.com/en/`)
- Download CodeIgniter (`http://codeigniter.com/`), unzip into `htdocs` (XAMPP) or `www` (WAMP), better if you do it inside it's own folder
- Edit the `system/application/config/config.php` file to suit your configuration

You are almost done by then, and you can do the other changes too. Then continue with the next chapter. Waiting for you out there!

3
Navigating Your Site

Now that we've installed CI, we need to understand how it works.

Readers familiar with design patterns would have recognized by now that CI implements the Model-View-Controller (MVC) pattern. This is a method of organizing the files that make up a website or if you like, of splitting the site into sensible parts rather than having one huge lump of code.

In this chapter, we'll briefly look at the theory behind MVC, and then at the way CI organizes itself internally. In particular, what goes in those different folders and how do they communicate?

In this chapter we will look at:

- How MVC helps to organize a dynamic website
- The process by which CI analyzes an incoming Internet request and decides which part of your code will handle it
- What the code does
- CI syntax rules
- The different type of files or classes you can find—or write for yourself—on a CodeIgniter site
- How to pass parameters to controllers using the URL
- How to write better views and pass dynamic data to them
- How a reply is returned to the surfer
- How the files or classes pass information and control to each other
- How useful code is kept inside helper and library files
- Some practical hints on site design

MVC: Model-View-Controller

What's MVC all about? For sure at this time you are very curious about this. In short, MVC is an architectural pattern, a way of structuring our application. When you were reading the previous chapters you had a glance at it; remember when we explored the file structure? At that time we saw that CodeIgniter was divided into these folders (among others):

```
system

        application

                models

                views

                controllers
```

As you can see there is a folder for each of the words (MVC); let's see what we can put into them:

- Models: The models represent our application data, be it in databases, in XML files or anywhere else. Also, interaction with databases is carried here. For example, models will allow us to fetch, modify, insert, and remove data from our database. All actions that require our application to talk to our database must be put in a model.

- Views: Files placed here are responsible for showing our data to the visitors to our site, or users of our application. No programming logic, no insert or update queries must be run here, though data access may occur in these files. They are here only to show the results of the other two. So we fetch the data in the model, and show it in the view. Now, what if we need to process the data, for example, putting it into an array? Then we do it in the controller; let's see how.

- Controllers: These act as a nexus between models and views, and programming logic occurs here.

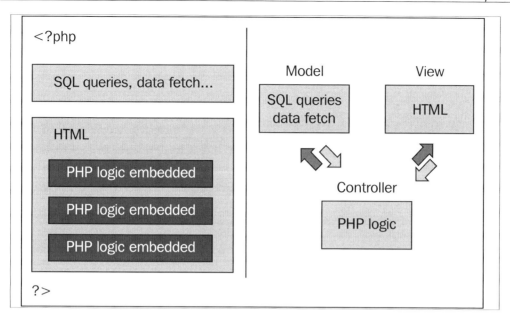

Take a look at this little diagram, in the left column we can see a "classical" way of doing things (a little outdated right now). We have a PHP file with SQL queries and HTML code in the same file and embedded into the HTML PHP logic.

It may seem, at first glance, that this way it is easier and faster to program. But in this case the code gets messed faster and becomes cluttered with SQL queries, HTML, and PHP logic. Look at the right-side column—we have **SQL queries** in the **Model**, **HTML** and other graphic elements in the **View**, and **PHP logic** in the **Controller**. Doesn't that seem organized? The **Controller** calls and fetches data from the **Model**. It then loads the data and passes it to the **Views**, and sends the results to the user.

Once we start working with this pattern we will feel how easy it is; it will keep our projects organized. If we need to come back to our project months after finishing it we will appreciate having made it in a structured fashion. No more of—*Oh my God where did I put that query, where is that include file?*—they will be in the model and the controller respectively.

But, what happens if we want to put our queries in the controller? Well, CodeIgniter allows us to do so (though it is not recommended; if you can avoid, it is better to do so). As we saw in the previous chapters CI is here to help us. Other frameworks force you to keep a particular structure, but with CI you can do programming in the way you want. Although it is recommended to keep to the structure, there will be times when we will need to do things the other way. With this structure we can accomplish two important things:

- Loose Coupling: Coupling is the degree by which the components of a system rely on each other. The less the components depend on each other, the more reusable and flexible the system becomes.

- Component Singularity: Singularity is the degree by which components have a narrow focus. In CI, each class and its functions are highly autonomous in order to allow maximum usefulness.

But how does all this work?

Now that we have seen how CI is structured, maybe you are asking yourself—how are the files in those three folders (models, views, controllers) working together? To answer this question we have another diagram, here it is:

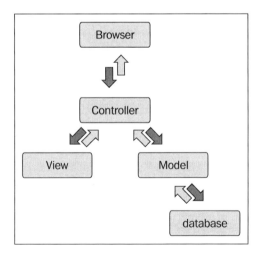

As you can see it's similar to the previous one, and a little summarized (but with a wider scope of things, this is how the MVC pattern works), but this time we can see some new elements, and if you look at it closely you will be able to distinguish the flow of data. Let's explain it. First of all there is a browser call to your site, then the index.php file in the root folder is called (because we removed it from the URL, using the .htaccess file, we don't see it). This file acts as a router and calls the controllers, as and when they are needed. The controllers, as they are called, come into action. Now, two things can happen:

- **There is no need to fetch data from the database** — in this case only the **View** is called, and loaded by the **Controller**. Then it is returned to the **Browser** for you or your visitors to see.

- **There is the need to fetch some data from the database** — in this case the **Controller** calls the **Model,** which in turn makes a query to the **database**. The **database** returns data to the **Model**, and the **Model** to the **Controller**. The **Controller** modifies the data in every necessary way. Then it loads the **View**, passing all necessary data to it, and the **View** is created and returned to the **Browser** again.

 Do not get confused with the first case; there will be times when you will need to create static pages. CI doesn't differentiate between static and dynamic pages. On those occasions simply don't create the **Models**.

Now, return to our sample site to see how all this applies to it. Remember when we put the URL as http://127.0.0.1/codeigniter, CI's welcome screen appeared in our browser. Now try this URL http://127.0.0.1/codeigniter/welcome.

If you didn't follow the last few steps of Chapter 2 (or your hosting service doesn't support .htacces files)try using this URL: http://127.0.0.1/codeigniter/index.php/welcome.

In both cases the welcome screen appears in the browser. You maybe wondering, how CI knows, if you put http://127.0.0.1/codeigniter/, that it has to load the welcome controller. Don't worry, we will see that in a moment; for now, we will go on with our example:

http://127.0.0.1/codeigniter/index.php/welcome

A request coming to your website's root is intercepted by the index.php file, which acts as a router. That is, it calls a controller — welcome controller — which then returns a view, just as in the previous diagram. But how does the controller do that? We are going to see how in the welcome controller.

The welcome controller

As we know the `welcome` controller is the default controller, configured in the `routes.php` file of the `config` directory and the code is at `./application/controllers/welcome.php`. Here's what it says:

```php
<?php
  class  Welcome extends Controller
  {
    function Welcome()
    {
      parent::Controller();
    }
    function index()
    {
      $this->load->view('welcome_message');
    }
  }
/* End of file welcome.php */
/* Location: ./system/application/controllers/welcome.php */
```

From the second line you'll learn that this file is a class. Every controller inherits from an original `Controller` class, hence `extends Controller`. The next three lines make the constructor function. Within the class there are two functions or methods—`Welcome()` and `index()`.

Though it is not necessary, naming controllers the same way as for tables is a good practice. For example, if I have a `projects` table I will create a `projects` controller. You can name your controllers the way you want, but naming them like the tables they represent keeps things organized. Also, getting used to this won't harm you, as other frameworks are stricter about this.

Notice that CI uses the older PHP 4 convention for naming constructor functions, which is also acceptable by PHP 5—it doesn't require you to use PHP 5 and is happy with either version of the language. The constructor function is used to set up the class each time you instantiate it. We can obviate this and the controller will still work, and if we use it, it won't do any harm. Inside it we can put instructions to load other `libraries` or `models`, or definitions of class variables.

So far the only thing inside the constructor is the `parent::Controller();` statement. This is just a way of making sure that you inherit the functionality of the `Controller` class. If you want to understand the parent CI `Controller` class in detail, you can look at the file `/www/CI_system/libraries/controller.php`.

One of the reassuring things about CI is that all the code is there for you to inspect, though you don't often need to.

Working with views

Let's go back to the incoming request for a moment. The router needs to know which controller and which function within that controller should handle the request. By default the index function is called if the function is not specified. So, when we put `http://127.0.0.1/codeigniter/welcome/`, the index function is called. If no error is shown, this function simply loads the view, `welcome_message` using CI's loader function (`$this->load->view`). At this stage, it doesn't do anything cool with the view, such as passing dynamic information to it. That comes in later.

The `welcome_message` it wants to load, is in the `views` folder that you have just installed at `/www/codeigniter/application/views/welcome_message.php`. This particular view is only a simple HTML page, but it is saved as a PHP file because most views have PHP code in them (no point in doing all this if we're only going to serve up plain old static HTML).

Here's the (slightly shortened) code for the view:

```
<html>
<head>
  <title>Welcome to CodeIgniter</title>
  <style type="text/css">
    body
    {
      background-color: #fff;
      margin: 40px;
      font-family: Lucida Grande, Verdana, Sans-serif;
      font-size: 14px;
      color: #4F5155;
    }
.  .  .  .  . more style information here . . . .
  </style>
</head>
<body>
  <h1>Welcome to CodeIgniter!</h1>
  <p>The page you are looking at is being generated dynamically by
     CodeIgniter.
  </p>
```

```
<p>If you would like to edit this page you'll find it located
   at:
</p>
<code>system/application/views/welcome_message.php</code>

<p>The corresponding controller for this page is found at:</p>
<code>system/application/controllers/welcome.php</code>

<p>If you are exploring CodeIgniter for the very first time, you
   should start by reading the <a href="user_guide/">User
   Guide</a>.
</p>
<p><br />Page rendered in {elapsed_time} seconds</p>
</body>
</html>
```

As you can see, it consists entirely of HTML, with an embedded CSS stylesheet. In this simple example, the controller hasn't passed any variables to the view.

 Curious about—`<p><br />Page rendered in {elapsed_time} seconds</p>`? Take a look at: `http://codeigniter.com/user_guide/libraries/benchmark.html`.

You can name the views the way you want, and don't put the `.php` extension for them. You will have to specify the extension when loading them, for example:

```
$this->load->view('welcome_message.html');
```

The default controller

A few moments ago we were wondering how it was possible that when we put `http://127.0.0.1/codeigniter/`, the welcome controller was called. Well, no magic there, it is all in `/www/codeigniter/application/config/routes.php`; open that file and take a look. Read it till you find this line:

```
$route['default_controller'] = "welcome";
```

This line tells CI which controller to call, if it is not specified in the URL. Don't misunderstand this, if you pass a wrong URL the default controller won't be called, it's only called if no other controllers are specified. Usually it is used to load the controller that contains the functions that create our index page; after that our application or website will provide our visitors with some kind of navigation.

In this case we are not specifying the function, so the index one will be called, but we could put another one if we want, such as:

```
$route['default_controller'] = "welcome/myfriend";
```

In this case we are calling the `myfriend` function inside the `welcome` controller. Can you think of more uses of the router file? Let's see one more. Suppose you have a long URL, we are going to use this as an example—`http://127.0.0.1/codeigniter/welcome/myfriend/23`.

If we add this line of code in the `routes.php` file:

```
$route['john'] = "welcome/myfriend/23";
```

From now on, if you put into your browser `http://127.0.0.1/codeigniter/john` you will end up seeing the result of the `welcome` controller, function `myfriend` with a parameter with value 23.

As we said, by default, the `index` function is called if no other is passed. You can alter this default if you like, by including a function called `_remap($function)`. Where `$function` is the function, in the controller(s), you want to intercept and redirect. The function `_remap` always gets called first, irrespective of what the URL says.

For example, if we have called `http://127.0.0.1/codeigniter/welcome/hello` and our `welcome` controller looks this way:

```php
<?php
class Welcome extends Controller
{
  function Welcome()
  {
    parent::Controller();
  }
  function _remap($method)
  {
    if ($method == 'hello')
    {
      $this->say_hello();
    }
    else
    {
      $this->$method();
    }
  }
  function say_hello()
```

```
  {
    echo "Hello";
  }
  function index()
  {
    $this->load->view('welcome_message');
  }
}
/* End of file welcome.php */
/* Location: ./system/application/controllers/welcome.php */
```

 Take this last example as a demonstration of the _remap method. But don't try to use it in a real-world application, as more work needs to be put here.

The _remap function $method will be called instead of the hello function passed in the URL. This part of the URL would instead be passed as a parameter to the _remap function. Once inside we can use this parameter in our logic, for example, this time if we receive hello, we call the say_hello function. In other case we call the function passed as a parameter, so if we have the URL http://127.0.0.1/codeigniter/welcome/hello, the function say_hello will be called. If we have http://127.0.0.1/codeigniter/welcome/index, then the index function will be called.

 Have you noticed the underscore "_" before the function name remap? You can use it in your own functions. This way they will be only accessible by other functions inside the controller, but not from outside. That said, the following won't work: http://127.0.0.1/codeigniter/welcome/remap

CodeIgniter syntax rules

Before we start, let's just summarize the syntax rules that CI uses. The framework expects files to be set up in a certain way, otherwise it may have difficulty indentifying your files properly, or using them.

Controller

This is a class (that is OO code). It is called directly by the URL, for example, `www.example.com/index.php/start/hello`. Controllers are used to call functions by name, for example, `mainpage()`. However, within a controller you cannot call functions inside another controller. If you need to do such a thing, the functions common to both the controllers can be converted into a library or helper.

Syntax:

Controllers begin with `class Start extends Controller` (where the name of the controller has the first letter in uppercase) and are saved as a `.php` file in the `/application/controllers` folder. When saved, they should not have the first letter in uppercase, as in `start.php` and not `Start.php`. Also, they can include a constructor containing at least:

```
function Start()
{
  parent::Controller();
}
```

All other code must be written as separate functions within the class, for example, a `hello()` function.

View

`Views` are HTML files that can contain PHP "islands". Here we place all the HTML code needed to create our site's pages. This is what our site's users are going to see. We place all our data, retrieved by our models and prepared by our controllers here. We can consider the views as the final stage of our data. They are loaded by `$this->load->view('testview', $data)`. Loading and using the view are done in the same action.

Syntax:

The view is written in HTML. The PHP code is included within `<?php ?>` tags, as with any HTML file. It is saved as a `.php` file in the `views` folder.

Types of files or classes on a CI site

There are several sub-folders within the `application` folder. We have already looked at the `controllers`, `config`, and `views` folders.

But what are `libraries`, `helpers`, and `plugins`? In a technical sense, these folders are treated in much the same way. Let's say that you have written a block of code called `display`, which contains a function called `mainpage`. There are four ways you might have done this—as a model, a library, a helper, or a plugin. The following table summarizes the difference between each approach, and shows you how to load and use each type.

File type	How to use it
Model	This is a class (object-oriented or OO code).
	Load it like this: `$this->load->model('display');`
	Use it like this: `$ this->display->mainpage();`
	Notes on syntax:
	It must begin with `class Display extends Model`.

	It must include a constructor containing at least:
	``
	function display()
	{
	  parent::Model();
	}
	``

	Also it should contain a separate `mainpage()` function.
	Conceptually: The user guide says, "Models are PHP classes that are designed to work with information in your database".
Library	It is present in both the `system` and the `application` folder. Again, this is a class.
	Load it like this: `$this->load->library('display');`
	Use it like this: `$this->display->mainpage();`

	Notes on syntax:
	No need to extend a base class, or for a constructor function, this is enough:
	``
	class Display()
	{
	  function mainpage()
	    {
	      //code here
	    }
	}
	``

	Conceptually: Intended to hold your own code to extend CI functionality or to create site-specific functionality.

File type	How to use it
Helper	It can be in the `system/helpers` folder or in the `application/helpers` folder. This is a script (procedural code, not an OO class).
	Load it like this: `$this->load->helper('display');`
	Use a function from it like this: `mainpage();`
	Notes on syntax:
	The file should be saved as `display_helper.php`, that is add `_helper` to the file name. The function `mainpage()` should be included in the file, which is simply a collection of separate functions, not a class. As a result you can't directly access other resources of CI any more.
	Conceptually: Helpers are intended as a collection of low-level functions to help you perform specific tasks.
Plugin	It is present in the `system/plugins` folder but can also be created in an `applications/plugins` folder. This is a script (not an OO class).
	Load it like this: `$this->load->plugin('display');`
	Use a function from it like this: `mainpage();`
	Notes on syntax:
	The file should be saved as `display_pi.php`, that is, add `_pi` to the end of the filename.
	The function `mainpage()` should be included in the file, which is simply a collection of separate functions, not a class. As a result, you can't directly access other resources of CI any more.
	Conceptually: The user guide says, "…the main difference is that a plugin usually provides a single function, whereas a helper is usually a collection of functions…"

You could put your piece of new code in any of these folders, though you'd have to write it as an object-oriented class in the first two cases, as a procedural script in the second, and in the latter cases you wouldn't be able to draw directly on other CI classes.

Though we are not able to directly draw CI resources from within helpers and plugins, there's a way in which we can achieve that, using the `get_instance();` method. Take a look at `http://codeigniter.com/user_guide/general/creating_libraries.html`. You will learn more about it, in Chapter 8.

You'll notice that CI can have two set of helpers, plugins, and libraries, though not of models. There can be one set of each in the `application` folder, and another set in the `system` folder. The difference, again, is largely conceptual as explained in the following:

- Those in the `system` folder are intended to be part of the core CI code and to be shared by all applications. If you update to a later version of CI, then you will overwrite the `system` folder and these files may be modified.

- Those in the `application` folder will only be available to that particular application. If you update to a new version of CI, the `application` folder will not be overwritten.

- When you try to load a helper, plugin, or library, CI sensibly looks in both paths. If you attempt to load a library called `display`, for example, CI will first look in your `system/application/libraries` directory. If the directory does not exist or the `display` library is not there, CI will then look in the `system/libraries` folder.

- It is possible to effectively overwrite CI's core `libraries`, `helpers`, and `plugins` by introducing your own with the same names in the `applications` folder. Don't do this accidentally. However, this flexibility is a great advantage for experienced CI users; if you want to extend the basic classes and scripts that come with CI, see Chapter 13.

Designing a better view

At this stage, you might ask: *Why are we going through so much effort to serve a simple HTML page? Why not put everything in one file?* For a simple site, that's a valid point—but whoever heard of a simple site? One of the coolest things about CI is the way it helps us to develop a consistent structure. So, as we add to and develop our site, it is internally consistent, well laid out, and simple to maintain.

At the start, we need to take these three common steps:

- Write a view page
- Write a stylesheet
- Update our `config` file to specify where the stylesheet is

After this is done, we need to update our controller to accept parameters from the URL, and pass variables to the view.

First, let's redesign our view and save it as `testview.php`, at `/www/codeigniter/` `application/views/testview.php`.

```
<html>
<head>
  <!DOCTYPE html PUBLIC '-//W3C//DTD XHTML 1.0
  Strict//EN'http:\/\/www.w3.org/TR/xhtml1/DTD/xhtml1-strict.dtd'>
  <html xmlns='http:\/\/www.w3.org/1999/xhtml'>
  <title>Web test Site</title>
    <link rel="stylesheet" type="text/css" href="<?php echo
    $base."/".$css;?>">
</head>
<body>
  <h1><?php echo $mytitle; ?> </h1>
  <p class='test'> <?php echo $mytext; ?> </p>
</body>
</html>
```

It's still mostly HTML, but notice the PHP "code islands" in the highlighted lines. You'll notice that the first bits of PHP code build a link to a stylesheet. Make a folder named css in the root folder (codeigniter/css) and save a simple stylesheet as `style.css`. It just says:

```
h1
{
  margin: 5px;
  padding-left: 10px;
  padding-right: 10px;
  background: #ffffff;
  color: blue;
  width: 100%;
  font-size: 36px;
}
.test
{
  margin: 5px;
  padding-left: 10px;
  padding-right: 10px;
  background: #ffffff;
  color: red;
  width: 100%;
  font-size: 36px;
}
```

This gives us two styles to play with, and you'll see we've used both of them in the view. Firstly, let's add an entry to the `config` file:

```
$config['css'] = 'css/styles.css';
```

This is simply to tell the name and address of the CSS file that we've just written to the site. But note that the link to the stylesheet is referenced at $base/$css: *Where do those variables,* $base *and* $css, *get their values?* And come to think of those variables $mytitle and $mytext at the end of the code? We need a new controller!

Designing a better controller

Now, we need a new controller. We'll call it `Start` and save it as `start.php`, at `/www/codeigniter/application/controllers/start.php`.

This controller has to do several things:

- Call a view
- Provide the view with the base URL and the location of the CSS file we just wrote
- Provide the view with some data—it's expecting a title ($mytitle) and some text ($mytext)
- Lastly, accept a parameter from the user (that is using the URL request)

In other words, we have to populate the variables in the view. So let's start with our `Start` controller. This is an OO class:

```
<?php
class Start extends Controller
{
    var    $base;
    var    $css;
```

Notice that here we've declared the $base and $css (the CSS filename) as variables or class properties. This saves us from having to redeclare them if we write more than one function in each class. But you can define and use them as local variables within one function, if you prefer.

The constructor function now defines the properties we've declared, by looking them up in the `config` file. To do this, we use the syntax:

```
$this->config->item('name_of_config_variable');
```

As in:

```
function Start()
{
  parent::Controller();
  $this->base = $this->config->item('base_url');
  $this->css = $this->config->item('css');
}
```

CI recovers whatever we entered in the `config` file against that name.

Using this system, no matter how many controllers and functions we write, we'll have to change these fundamental variables only once. This is true even if our site becomes so popular that we have to move it to a bigger server.

Getting parameters to a function

Now, within the `Start` controller class, let's define the function that will actually do the work:

```
function hello($name = 'Guest')
{
  $data['css'] = $this->css;
  $data['base'] = $this->base;
  $data['mytitle'] = 'Welcome to this site';
  $data['mytext'] = "Hello, $name, now we're getting dynamic!";
  $this->load->view('testview', $data);
}
```

This function expects the parameter `$name`, but you can set a default value—`myfunction($myvariable = 0)`—which it uses to build the string assigned to the `$mytext` variable. Well, as we just asked, where does that come from?

In this case, it needs to come from the URL request, where it will be the third parameter. So, it comes through the HTTP request:

```
http://127.0.0.1/codeigniter/start/hello/Jose
```

This example code doesn't "clean" the passed variable `Jose`, or check it in any way. You might want to do this while writing the code. We'll look at how to check form inputs in Chapter 5. Normally, variables passed by hyperlinks in this way are generated by your own site. A malicious user can easily add his or her own, just by sending a URL such as: `http://www.mysite.com/index.php/start/hello/ my_malicious_variable`. So, you might want to check that the variables you receive are within the range you expect, before handling them.

The last segment of the URL is passed to the function as a parameter. In fact, you can add more segments of extra parameters if you like, subject to the practical limits imposed by your browser.

Let's recap on how CI handles URLs, since we've covered it all now:

URL segment	What it does
http://www.mysite.com	The base URL that finds your site.
/index.php	Finds the CI router that sets about reading the rest of the URL and selecting the correct route into your site. If you have added the .htaccess file in the previous chapter, this part will not be visible, but will still work as expected.
/start	The name of the controller that CI will call (if no name is set, CI will call whichever default controller you've specified).
/hello	The name of a function that CI will call, inside the selected controller (if no function is specified, it defaults to the index function, unless you've used _remap).
/Jose	CI passes this to the function as a variable.
If there is a further URL segment, for example, /bert	CI passes this to the function as the second variable.
More variables	CI will pass further URL segments as subsequent variables.

Passing data to a view

Let's go back to the hello function:

```
function hello($name)
{
   $data['css'] = $this->css;
   $data['base'] = $this->base;
   $data['mytitle'] = 'Welcome to this site';
   $data['mytext'] = "Hello, $name, now we're getting dynamic!";
   $this->load->view('testview', $data);
}
```

Notice how the hello() function first creates an array called $data, taking a mixture of object properties set up by the constructor and text. Then it loads the view by name, with the array it has just built as the second parameter.

Behind the scenes, CI makes good use of another PHP function—extract(). This takes each value in the $data array and turns it into a new variable in its own right. So, the $data array that we've just defined is received by the view as a series of separate variables; $text (equal to "Hello, $name, now we're getting dynamic"), $css (equal to the value from the config file), and so on. In other words, when built, the $data array looks like this:

```
Array
    (
        [css] => 'mystyles.css';
        [base] => 'http://127.0.0.1/packt';
        [mytitle] => 'Welcome to this site';
        [mytext] => 'Hello, fred, now we're getting dynamic!';
    )
```

But on its way to the view, it is unpacked, and the following variables are created in the view to correspond to each key/value pair in the array:

```
$css = 'mystyles.css';
$base = 'http://127.0.0.1/packt';
$mytitle = 'Welcome to this site';
$mytext = 'Hello, fred, now we're getting dynamic!';
```

Although you can only pass one variable to a view, you can pack a lot of information into it. Each value in the $data array can itself be another array, so you can pass pieces of information to the view in a tightly structured manner.

Now navigate to http://127.0.0.1/codeigniter/start/hello/jose (note that the URL is different—it is looking for the start function we wrote in the index controller) and you'll see the result—a dynamic page written using MVC architecture (well, VC at least! We haven't really used the M yet).

You can see that the parameter jose is the last segment of the URL. It has been passed into the function, and then to the view. Please remember that your view must be written in parallel with your controller. If the view does not expect and make a place for a variable, it won't be displayed. If the view is expecting a variable to be set and it isn't, you are likely to get an error message (your view can of course accept variables conditionally).

Also, a controller can use more than one view; this way we can separate our pages into sections such as the header, the menu, and so on. Each of these views can be nested one inside the other. Child views can even inherit variables passed by the controller to their parent view.

Loading a view from inside another view is very easy; just put something like the following PHP snippet in your HTML code:

```
<body>
  <div id="menu">
  <?php $this->load->view('menu'); ?>
```

This way we can load a view inside a view, with all variables in the first one also available into the nested one. We will see more about this in Chapter 5.

How CI classes pass information and control to each other

As you write your controllers, models, and so on, you will need to pass control and data between them. Let's look at some of the ways in which we can do this.

Calling views

We have seen how the controller calls a view and passes data to it.

First it creates an array of data ($data) to pass to the view, loads it, and calls the view in the same expression:

```
$this->load->view('testview', $data);
```

Calling functions directly

If you want to use code from libraries, models, plugins, or helpers, you have to load them first, and then call them as described in the previous table. So, if display is a model and I want to use its mainpage function, my controller might call:

```
$this->display->mainpage();
```

If the function requires parameters, we can pass them to the function like this:

```
$this->display->mainpage('parameter1', $parameter2);
```

Interacting with controllers

You can call libraries, models, plugins, or helpers from within any controller, or model; libraries, plugins, and helpers can also call each other.

However, you can't call one controller from another, or a controller from a model or library. There are only two ways in which a model or a library can refer back to a controller:

- It can return data if the controller assigns a value such as this:

  ```
  $fred = $this->mymodel->myfunction();
  ```

  Using this, the function is set to return a value, which will be passed to the variable $fred inside the controller.

- Your model or library can create (and send to a view) a URL, which allows a human user to call the controller functions. Controllers are there to receive human interactions.

You can't, of course, hyperlink directly to a model or library. Users always talk to controllers, never to anything else; however, you can write a calling function in the controller. In other words, your view might contain a hyperlink to a controller function:

```
echo anchor('start/callmodel', 'Do something with a model');
```

The callmodel function would exit only to call a function in the model:

```
function callmodel()
{
  $this->load->model(mymodel);
  $this->mymodel->myfunction();
}
```

An example of a CI helper—the URL helper

As an example you can split your code into neat, focused chunks. CI's URL helper contains a set of functions that help you to manipulate URLs. You load it like this:

```
$this->load->helper('url');
```

You can also use it to find and return the site and/or base URLs that you set in your config file:

```
echo site_url();
echo base_url();
```

You can also use it to create hyperlinks. In the last section, we saw how to access the hello function in the start controller and pass the parameter fred to it, with a URL such as:

```
http://www.mysite.com/index.php/start/hello/fred
```

If you want your code to create a hyperlink to a URL, you can use the URL helper to do it. The syntax is:

```
echo anchor('start/hello/fred', 'Say hello to Fred');
```

This generates a hyperlink to the same URL, and displays the words `Say hello to Fred` for the user to click on. In other words, it's an equivalent of:

```
<a href="http://www.mysite.com/index.php/start/hello/fred ">Say hello to Fred</a>
```

Remember, there are two advantages to using the CI helper. Firstly, less typing required—49 characters as opposed to 82, both including spaces. If you include another 27 characters loading the URL helper, which you have to do once per controller, it still comes to 76 rather than 82.

Secondly, the URL helper automatically looks up the site URL in the `config` files (and the index file name). This means that if you change your site location, you only need to alter the `config` file once. You don't have to hunt through your code for hyperlinks that don't work any more.

The URL helper has other useful functions. For instance, it can create a `mailto` hyperlink such as:

```
echo mailto('me@example.com', 'Click Here to Email Me');
```

It has the same effect as typing this HTML:

```
<a href="mailto:me@example.com">click here to email me</a>
```

If you are worried about robots harvesting the email addresses from your website and using them for spamming, change `mailto` in the CI code to `safe_mailto`. What appears on your viewer's screen is exactly the same, and works the same way.

However, if you examine the actual HTML code, this has now become a complex heap of JavaScript, which the robot cannot (easily) read:

```
<script type="text/javascript">
//<![CDATA[
var l=new Array();
l[0]='>';l[1]='a';l[2]='/
';l[3]='<';l[4]='|101';l[5]='|109';l[6]='|32';l[7]='|108';l[8]='|105'
;l[9]='|97';l[10]='|109';l[11]='|101';l[12]='|32';l[13]='|111';l[14]=
'|116';l[15]='|32';l[16]='|101';l[17]='|114';l[18]='|101';l[19]='|72
';l[20]='|32';l[21]='|107';l[22]='|99';l[23]='|105';l[24]='|108';l[25
]='|67';l[26]='>';l[27]='"';l[28]='|109';l[29]='|111';l[30]='|99';l[3
1]='|46';l[32]='|101';l[33]='|108';l[34]='|112';l[35]='|109';l[36]='|
97';l[37]='|120';l[38]='|101';l[39]='|64';l[40]='|101';l[41]='|109';
```

```
l[42]=':';l[43]='o';l[44]='t';l[45]='l';l[46]='i';l[47]='a';l[48]='m'
;l[49]='"';l[50]='=';l[51]='f';l[52]='e';l[53]='r';l[54]='h';l[55]='
';l[56]='a';l[57]='<';
for (var i = l.length-1; i >= 0; i=i-1){
if (l[i].substring(0, 1) == '|') document.write("&#"+unescape(l[i].
substring(1))+";");
else document.write(unescape(l[i]));}
//]]>
</script>
```

You and your users need never see this code. It's only there to confuse the robots and keep your email addresses safe from spam. You put it there by adding four letters and an underscore, where you wrote `safe_mailto` instead of `mailto`, and CI did the rest.

There are several other useful functions in the URL helper. Take a look at the user guide, where you will find some helpful ones:

`http://codeigniter.com/user_guide/helpers/url_helper.html`

Just consider the URL helper as a whole. Let's go back to the touchstones for coding, which we discussed earlier in this chapter:

- This code has high "component singularity". It does a limited range of things, and it's clear what they are.

- It is "loosely coupled"—it has a simple interface and no dependency on any code that's calling it. You can use the URL helper in any CI project you're writing. Most of your projects will need some sort of hyperlinks. You can use this helper over and over again to create them.

If you look at the URL helper's code in `/www/codeigniter/application/helpers/url_helper.php`, you'll see that it is procedural code, that is, it is simply a set of functions, not an OO class. It doesn't load any other CI classes or helpers (not being an object it can't do this directly).

A simple library example—creating a menu

Now let's look at some code that uses the CI classes. For instance, here is a simple library file that creates a menu with three choices. You can save it in `/www/codeigniter/application/libraries/menu.php`:

```
1 <?php
2 class Menu{
3 function show_menu()
4   {
5   $obj =& get_instance();
6   $obj->load->helper('url');
```

```
7   $menu  = anchor("start/hello/fred","Say hello to Fred |");
8   $menu  .= anchor("start/hello/bert","Say hello to Bert |");
9   $menu  .= anchor("start/another_function","Do something else |");
10  return $menu;
11  }
12  }
13  ?>
```

For the moment, don't worry about the unusual syntax—`$obj->` rather than `$this->`, on line 6. This is explained in Chapter 7.

Note that this code is now OO code, in which the function `show_menu()` is contained in a single class, that is `Menu`. It can access other CI classes and helpers; in this case it is using the URL helper, which we just examined.

First it loads the URL helper and then it creates a string (`$menu`), consisting of HTML code for hyperlinks to the three controllers and functions specified. Then it returns the `$menu` string.

You might call it from a controller like this:

```
$this->load->library('menu');
$mymenu = $this->menu->show_menu();
```

The controller can then use the `$menu` variable to call a `view`:

```
$data['menu'] = $mymenu;
$this->load->view('myview', $data);
```

After that you will only have to put `echo $menu` in your view file, which will produce a site-specific menu. For this reason, we have saved it in the `/www/codeigniter/application/libraries`, rather than the `/CI_system/libraries` folder. It's not as loosely coupled as the URL helper, which I can use on any site.

It does have high singularity—it creates a menu, and that's all it does. It can be called from any controller in the site and it will show the standard menu in the view.

Summary

The MVC pattern is a widely used and is a very effective way of organizing a complex website. CI uses it to help you sort your own code, but it is also fairly flexible about how it does so.

The crucial thing is to understand what the different type of files are, and how they relate to each other. Then, you can decide whether to write your code in library or model files, or as helpers or plugins.

We've looked at the CI file structure, and seen how you can, if you want, inspect all the CI code, but (thankfully!) you don't have to. We did tinker with one of the original files—the `config` file, which holds critical site information in one place to make it easy for us to upgrade or change later.

We've seen the basic object structure of a controller, and used a simple constructor to get some data from our `config` file and put it into a class property. We've dynamically passed information from a new controller we wrote, to a new view. So far, the main thing CI has done for us is to encourage us to use a basic structure as we start to define our site. As we go on, it will become clear just how important that structure is.

Also, we looked at the way in which CI's components pass data and control between themselves. It's useful to understand this when you start to write your code.

Lastly, we looked at CI's own URL helper as a good example of a chunk of code, and we wrote our own rudimentary `menu` library class. Now continue to Chapter 4, where we will see how CodeIgniter will help us improve the way we work with databases, don't wait!

4
Using CI to Simplify
Databases

You're looking at CI because you want to make coding easier and more productive. This chapter is about CI's **Active Record** class. If CI offered nothing more than its Active Record class, it would still be worth every penny of the purchase price. All right, it's free! Let's rephrase that—it would still be a major tool to increase your productivity.

Active Record allows you to handle databases with a minimum of fuss and maximum of clarity. It's simple to use and maintain.

This chapter looks at how you set up a database to work with CI, and then how you use the Active Record class to manipulate the database. You'll see:

- How Active Record code compares with "classic" PHP/MySQL interface code
- How to write "read" queries, and display the results
- How to do create, update, and delete queries

CI allows you to write queries in the traditional "classic" PHP style as well, but let's not get into details of that. It's fully covered in the online user guide. Jose started off by doing it the traditional way, but once he tried Active Record, he never looked back.

Configuration settings

As for the other configuration settings you have done for CodeIgniter, the file you need to modify is in `/www/codeigniter/application/config`. This time, the file you need to update is `database.php`. This file contains all the information necessary for CodeIgniter to connect to your database. Open the file, you will see the options that you must set along with a few other options that you can leave at the default, for now.

```
$active_group = "default";
$active_record = TRUE;
$db['default']['hostname'] = "localhost";
$db['default']['username'] = "";
$db['default']['password'] = "";
$db['default']['database'] = "";
$db['default']['dbdriver'] = "mysql";
$db['default']['dbprefix'] = "";
$db['default']['pconnect'] = TRUE;
$db['default']['db_debug'] = TRUE;
$db['default']['cache_on'] = FALSE;
$db['default']['cachedir'] = "";
$db['default']['char_set'] = "utf8";
$db['default']['dbcollat'] = "utf8_general_ci";
```

The options you must fill in are:

- `hostname`: The location of your database, for example, `localhost` or an IP address.

- `username` and `password`: The username and password of a database user with sufficient permissions to do whatever you may want your site to do. This is not (usually) the same username and password as of your site or your ISP's control panel.

- `database`: The name of your database, for example, `websites`.

- `dbdriver`: The type of database you're using. At the time of writing, the options CI offers are MySQL, MySQLi, Postgre SQL, ODBC, and MS SQL.

From experience, it can be said that one of the most difficult things to set up on a new CI site can be a link to the database. You may need to consult your ISP if in doubt—sometimes their database runs at a different address than their web server's. If you are using MySQL, they may offer phpMyAdmin, which usually tells you the hostname—this may be `localhost` or it may be an IP address.

If you are new to phpMyAdmin you can find all you need in this Packt book:

`http://www.packtpub.com/`
`mastering-phpmyadmin-3-1-fourth-edition/book`

It is strongly recommended!

You'll note that this part of the `config` file is actually a multi-dimensional array. Within $db is an array called `default`, and you're adding key/variable pairs like `hostname = 127.0.0.1` to that array. Because of this you can set up other databases, as secondary arrays. You can swap between them easily by simply changing the `$active_group` setting to the name of another array.

This makes it possible to run a site with several database options—for instance, a test database and a production database—and to swap between them easily. Or you might need to draw information from two separate databases.

Designing the database for our site

We are going to build an example application, so that you will be able to give all this a try. In this case we are going to build a website monitoring program, to help you test websites, keep reports of what has been done in each one, and so on. Firstly, let's set some objectives. These are:

- To manage one or more remote websites with a minimum of human intervention
- To run regular tests on the remote sites
- To generate reports on demand, giving details of the site and of tests conducted

So, the first thing you will need is a database of websites to check. Set up a database called `websites` in MySQL or whatever RDBMS you're using. You can get all the SQL necessary to create the tables needed in your application in the chapter appendix. Copy it and execute the SQL into your database in order to generate the database structure.

Summarizing it a little you will have a **site** table, to keep information about your sites, a **hosts** table associated to a **domains** table, and of course a **people** table. Don't worry about all the structure for now, just copy it and generate the structure executing the queries.

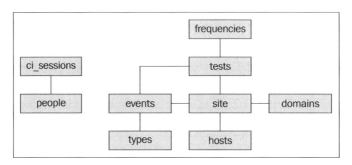

After creating the database structure take a look at the preceding diagram, it will help you know which tables relate to other tables. You will need a simple flexible way of accessing all this. So, let's turn to what CI offers, and in particular to its Active Record class.

Active Record

Active Record is a "design pattern"—another of those highly abstract systems like MVC, which provide templates for solving common coding problems. In itself, it isn't code, it is just a pattern for code. There are several different interpretations of it. At its core is the creation of a relationship between your database and an object, every time you write a query. Typically, each table is a class (represented by our models), and each single row becomes an object. All the things you might want to do with a table row, for example, create it, read it, update it, or delete it, become "methods", which that object inherits from its class. CakePHP is built around the Active Record pattern, and so is CI—although the exact implementation in the two frameworks seems to have differences.

For example, `models` in CakePHP are associated to `tables`, every table has a corresponding model representing it. CodeIgniter gives you a little more freedom here; your models don't need to be associated directly to tables. Though by experience we can say, most of the times that association simply happens to occur. But enough theory for now—what does it mean? Well, simple and clear code statements, if you don't mind putting arrows in them.

Advantages of using the Active Record class

Active Record saves your time, brings in automatic functionality that you don't have to think about, and makes SQL statements easy to understand. One thing you should take into account, should you need to change your RDBMS (database management system) from MySQL to Postgres (or another of the databases supported by CodeIgniter) is that you wouldn't need to rewrite your Active Record queries as CodeIgniter translates them for your choice of RDBMS. This will save us time and code rewrites.

Saving time

When you write a normal database query in PHP, you must write a connection to the database each time. With CI, you connect once to the database, by putting the following line in the constructor function of each controller or model:

```
$this->load->database();
```

 Remember, you can autoload the database library in order not to have to write that line of code in every function of every controller. If you are building an application that uses the database intensively, it would be a good idea to do so. It is very easy, you only need to add the database library to the libraries array in /www/codeigniter/ application/config/autoload.php, like this:

```
$autoload['libraries'] = array('database');
```

 Before autoloading the database library update the file /www/codeigniter/application/config/database.php with the correct configuration. Otherwise CodeIgniter will only return an error screen, even if you are not querying the database.

Once you've done this, however, many queries you make in that controller or model, you don't have to repeat the connection. You set up the database details in the config files as we saw earlier in this chapter. Once again, this makes it easier to update your site, if you ever change the database name, password, or location.

Automatic functionality

Once you've connected to the database, CI's Active Record syntax brings hidden code with it. For instance, if you enter the following `insert` query:

```
$data = array(
            'title' => $title,
            'name' => $name,
            'date' => $date
          );
$this->db->insert('mytable', $data);
```

The values you insert escape behind the scenes by using this code:

```
function escape($str)
{
  switch (gettype($str))
  {
    case 'string':
    $str = "'".$this->escape_str($str)."'";
    break;
    case 'boolean':     $str = ($str === FALSE) ? 0 : 1;
    break;
    default      :      $str = ($str === NULL) ? 'NULL' : $str;
    break;
  }
  return $str;
}
```

In other words, the CI framework is making your code more robust. Now, let's look at how it works. Firstly, connecting to the database is very simple. In classic PHP, you might say something like this:

```
$connection = mysql_connect("localhost","fred","12345");
            mysql_select_db("websites", $connection);
$result = mysql_query ("SELECT * FROM sites", $connection);
while ($row = mysql_fetch_array($result, MYSQL_NUM))
{
  foreach ($row as $attribute)
  print "{$attribute[1]} ";
}
```

In other words, you have to restate the host username and password, make a connection, and then select the database from that connection. Only then do you get to the actual query. CI replaces the connection stuff with one line:

```
$this->load->database();
```

You need to put it once in each controller, model, and class constructor that you write. If you feel it's necessary, autoload it. After that, in each function within those controllers, and so on, you go straight into your query. The connection information is stored in your `database.php` file in the `config` folder, and CI goes and looks it up there, each time.

So, in each CI function, you go straight to your query. The previous query written in CI comes out as:

```
$query = $this->db->get('sites');
foreach ($query->result() as $row)
  {
    print $row->url
  }
```

Simple, isn't it?

But as always, in CodeIgniter there are many hidden functionalities in case you need them. For example, if you need to connect to another database instead of the default one, you could do it very easily as:

```
$this->load->database('name');
```

Where `name` equals to what you have in the `database.php` config file:

```
$db['name']['hostname'] = "localhost";
$db['name']['username'] = "root";
$db['name']['password'] = "root";
$db['name']['database'] = "websites";
$db['name']['dbdriver'] = "mysql";
$db['name']['dbprefix'] = "";
$db['name']['pconnect'] = TRUE;
$db['name']['db_debug'] = TRUE;
$db['name']['cache_on'] = FALSE;
$db['name']['cachedir'] = "";
$db['name']['char_set'] = "utf8";
$db['name']['dbcollat'] = "utf8_general_ci";
```

What if you want to connect to two or more databases, you can do that very easily too:

```
$database1 = $this->load->database('name', TRUE);
$database2 = $this->load->database('name2', TRUE);
```

The TRUE parameter indicates to the function to return the database object. Once you have done so you will be able to query both databases, but in a slightly different way, instead of using:

```
$this->db->query();
```

You will use:

```
$database1->query();
```

In the rest of this chapter you will see ways of making different queries, making them more specific.

Read queries

The most common query that we'll write simply retrieves information from the database according to our criteria. The basic instruction to perform a read query is:

```
$query = $this->db->get('sites');
```

This is a SELECT * query on the sites table—in other words, it retrieves all the fields. If you prefer to specify the target table (sites) in a separate line, you can do so in this way:

```
$this->db->from('sites');
$query = $this->db->get();
```

If you want to select or limit the number of fields retrieved, rather than get them all, use this instruction:

```
$this->db->select('url,name,clientid');
$query = $this->db->get('sites');
```

You may want to present the results in a particular order, say by the site name, in which case you insert (before the $this->db->get line):

```
$this->db->orderby("name", "desc");
```

The parameter desc means in descending order. You can also choose asc (ascending) or rand (random).

You may also want to limit the number of results your query display. Say you want only the first five results. In this case insert:

```
$this->db->limit(5);
```

Of course, in most queries, you're not likely to ask for every record in the table. The power of databases depends on their ability to select—to pick out the one piece of data you want from the piles of stuff you don't. This is usually done by a `where` statement that CI expresses in this way:

```
$this->db->where('clientid', '1');
```

This statement would find all websites linked to the client whose ID is 1. But that's not of much help to us. We don't want to remember all the IDs in our `people` table. As humans, we prefer to remember human names, so we need to link in the `people` table:

```
$this->db->from('sites');
$this->db->join('people', 'sites.peopleid = people.id');
```

For each `peopleid` in the `sites` table, look up the information against that ID in the `people` table as well.

> Note the SQL convention: If a field name may be ambiguous between two tables, you reference it with the table name first, then a period, and then the field name. So, `sites.peopleid` means the `peopleid` field in the `sites` table. It's a good habit to make your meaning explicit, and CI syntax happily accepts the full names.

You can play around with the syntax of `where` statements. For instance, you can:

- Add negation operators

  ```
  $this->db->where('url !=','www.mysite.com' );
  ```

- Add comparison operators

  ```
  $this->db->where('id >','3' );
  ```

- Add combine statements ("WHERE... AND...")

  ```
  $this->db->where('url !=','www.mysite.com');
  $this->db->where('id >', '3');
  ```

 The two `where` statements behave as an `and` statement.

You can also use `$this->db->or_where()` to search for alternatives ("WHERE ... OR"):

```
$this->db->where('url !=','www.mysite.com' );
$this->db->or_where('url !=','www.anothersite.com' );
```

So let's say we've built a query like this:

```
$this->db->select('url,name,clientid,people.surname AS client');
$this->db->where('clientid', '3');
$this->db->limit(5);
$this->db->from('sites');
$this->db->join('people', 'sites.clientid = people.id');
$this->db->order_by("name", "desc");
$query = $this->db->get();
```

The previous snippet should give you the first five websites (ordered by name) belonging to client number 3, and fetch the client's surname, as well as his/her ID number!

A hidden benefit of using Active Record is that data coming in from users is automatically escaped, so you don't have to worry about putting quotes around it. This applies to functions such as `$this->db->where()`; and also to the data creation and update statements described in the sections that follow.

Security warning

This is not the same thing as preventing cross-scripting attacks—for that you need CI's `xss_clean()` function. It's also not the same as validating your data—for this you need CI's validation class.

If you don't use Active Record, it is advisable that you escape your data before sending it to your database. When using Active Record this is done automatically for you, but if you aren't using it, you have to do it manually, using the `escape` function:

```
$this->db->escape();
```

For example:

```
$sql = "SELECT * FROM people WHERE uname = '".$this->db-
>escape($uname)."'";
$this->db->query($sql);
```

It's an easy way of giving your queries more security if you can't or don't want to use Active Record. There is another way of doing so—query binding. Query binding will escape your data before it is passed to the database. Let's see an example of query binding:

```
$sql = "SELECT * FROM people WHERE id = ? AND uname = ? AND status =
?";
$this->db->query($sql, array(1, 'Jose', 1));
```

Now it is for you to decide which method to use. At least you can't say CodeIgniter doesn't gives you choices!

Displaying query results

Showing database query results in CI is quite simple. Define your query as you did previously, ending in:

```
$query = $this->db->get();
```

Then, if there are multiple results, they can be returned as an array of `$row` objects, through which you iterate with a `foreach` loop:

```
foreach ($query->result() as $row)
{
  print $row->url;
  print $row->name;
  print $row->client;
}
```

If you only want a single result, it can be returned as an object or as a `$row` array, as in the following example:

```
if ($query->num_rows() > 0)
{
  $row = $query->row_array();
  print $row['url'];
  print $row['name'];
  print $row['client'];
}
```

Personally, I prefer the object syntax to the array — less typing!

When you follow the MVC pattern, you will usually want to keep your queries and database interactions in models, and display the information through views.

Create and update queries

Active Record has three functions that help you to create new entries in your database. They are `$this->db->insert()`, `$this->db->update()`, and `$this->db->set()`.

Let's see the difference between a "create" and an "update" query. When you create a new record, there is no reference to any existing record, you write a new one. When you update, there is an existing record and you are changing it. So, in the second case you have to specify, which record you are changing. In both cases you have to set the values that you want to keep in the database after your query. Values you don't set will be left unaltered. If they didn't exist before, they will still be "null" after your query.

CI allows you to set the values either using an array or `$this->db-set()`. The only difference is the syntax. So, let's add a line to your `sites` table in the `websites` database. We've already connected to this database in our controller. The controller's constructor function included the line:

```
$this->load->database();
```

You want to add a new site, which has a URL, a name, a type, and a client ID number. As an array, this can be written as:

```
$data = array(
            'url' => 'www.mynewclient.com',
            'name' => 'BigCo Inc',
            'clientid' => '33',
            'type' => 'dynamic',
        );
```

To add that to the `sites` table, we follow it with:

```
$this->db->insert('sites', $data);
```

Alternatively, you could set each value using `$this->db->set()`:

```
$this->db->set('url', 'www.mynewclinet.com');
$this->db->set('name', 'BigCo Inc');
$this->db->set('clientid', '33');
$this->db->set('type', 'dynamic');
$this->db->insert('sites');
```

Of these two, we prefer the first one as it seems clearer. However, there is no difference between them, use the one you are comfortable with.

If you are updating an existing record, then again you can either create an array, or use `$this->db->set()`. But there are two differences. Firstly, you have to specify the record you want to update. Second, you need to use `$this->db->update()`. If you want to update a record (say the record with its `id` field set to 1) in your `sites` table, using the data set in your `$data` array as you did earlier, the syntax is:

```
$this->db->where('id', '1');
$this->db->update('sites', $data);
```

You can also set the information using `$this->db->set()`, as you saw earlier. CI gives you several functions to check what the database has done. Most usefully:

```
$this->db->affected_rows();
```

This should return "1" after the insert or update statement—it might show more rows if we were to alter several rows of data at one time. You can use it to check that the operation has done what you expected.

You've noticed that we didn't set an ID field when we created a new record. That's because you set the database to populate the ID field automatically when a new record is added. You have to specify an ID when you update an existing record, otherwise the database doesn't know which one to alter.

However, if you're generating a new record, you don't know the ID number until you've generated it. Then, if you need to refer to the new record, you can get the new ID number using:

```
$new_id_number = $this->db->insert_id();
```

 This code has to go as soon as possible after the operation where you generated the record, or it may give a misleading result.

For a little more peace of mind remember that CI's Active Record functions, including `$this->db->insert()` and `$this->db->update()`, automatically escape data passed to them as input.

From version 1.5, CI also includes support for transactions—linking two or more database actions together so that either all succeed or all fail. This is essential in double-entry book keeping applications and many commercial sites. For instance, if you are selling theatre tickets you can record receiving a payment in one transaction, and then allocate a seat to the customer in another. If your system fails, after doing the first database operation and before doing the second, you may end up with an angry customer—who has been charged, but has not had a seat reserved.

CI, now makes it much simpler to link two or more database operations into one transaction. So, if they all succeed, the transaction is "committed". If one or more fails, the transaction is "rolled back". Transactions are enabled by default; you only have to indicate to CodeIgniter that you want to use them:

```
$this->db->trans_start();
$this->db->query('first sql query');
$this->db->query('second sql query');
$this->db->query('third sql query');
$this->db->trans_complete();
```

These three queries need to be executed correctly, or all three of them will be rolled back. This is useful for shopping carts, or any query that needs another one to be successful.

More information about CodeIgniter transactions can be found at: `http://codeigniter.com/user_guide/database/transactions.html`

Delete queries

Delete queries are perhaps the simplest to describe. All you need is the name of the table and the ID number of the record to delete. Let's say, you want to delete a record in the `sites` table with the `id` number 2:

```
$this->db->where('id', '2');
$this->db->delete('sites');
```

Please remember to make sure that there is a valid value in the `where` clause, or you may delete the whole table! Neither the authors nor Packt Publishing will accept any liability if....

Mixing Active Record and "classic" styles

CI doesn't insist that you use Active Record. You can also use CI to issue straight SQL queries. For instance, assuming you loaded the database in your constructor, you can still write queries such as:

```
$this->db->query("SELECT id, name, url FROM sites WHERE `type` =
                  'dynamic'");
```

Active Record is easy to use. Conceptually, setting a query in an array makes it easier to see and manipulate it as an entity than writing it in SQL syntax. It's slightly more verbose, but clearly structured. It automatically escapes data and may be more portable. It also minimizes typing errors with commas and quotes.

However, there are a few cases where you may have to resort to the original SQL. For example, you might want to do complex joins or need to use multiple WHERE conditions. If you want to find the websites associated with client 3, but only those of two specific types, you may need to put brackets around the SQL, to make sure the query is correctly interpreted.

In cases like these, you can always write the SQL as a string, put it in a variable, and use the variable in CI's `$this->db->where()` function, as follows:

```
$condition = "client ='3' AND (type ='dynamic' OR type='static')";
$this->db->where($condition);
```

Without the brackets this is ambiguous. Do you mean:

```
(client='3' AND type = 'dynamic') OR type = 'static'
```

Or:

```
client='3' AND (type = 'dynamic' OR type = 'static')
```

Well, of course it's obvious, but the machine usually guesses wrong. Be careful with the syntax of `$condition`. The actual SQL query is:

```
client='3' AND (type = 'dynamic' OR type = 'static')
```

The double quotes come from the variable assignment:

```
$condition = "     ";
```

It's easy to get your single and double quotes confused. Some of the CI expressions quoted earlier, such as `$this->db->affected_rows()`, are not a part of its Active Record model. But they can be mixed up easily.

Dealing with complex queries

There will be some queries that will need some extra effort to translate to Active Record, let's see this one:

```
SELECT `M`.`name`, `S`.`brand_id`, count(S.brand_id) as votes
FROM (`selections` as S, `brands` as M)
WHERE `M`.`id` = S.brand_id
AND `S`.`id_usu_facebook` IN ('1704982171', '1428056700')
GROUP BY `S`.`brand_id`
ORDER BY count(S.brand_id) DESC
LIMIT 0,6
```

If you start translating this query to an Active Record one, you may come across errors. But how can you solve them, if you are not seeing the SQL query that is being generated?

There is a way in which you can see the SQL queries that are generated and run when our application is executed. In order to do so, you need to enable the CI profiler, such as:

```
$this->output->enable_profiler(TRUE);
```

 The profiler doesn't need to be initialized, as it is loaded by the output class.

Now, when you load your application, all queries and generated SQL are output to your browser's screen. You will then be able to see what SQL your Active Record query is generating, making it easier for you to check errors. Following with the example, you can create this Active Record query:

```
$this->db->select('M.name, S.brand_id, count(S.brand_id) as votes');
$this->db->from('selections as S, brands as M');
$this->db->where('M.id = S.brand_id');
$this->db->where_in('S.id_usu_facebook ', $users);
$this->db->group_by('S.brand_id');
$this->db->order_by('count(S.brand_id)', 'desc');
$this->db->limit(0, 6);
$query = $this->db->get();
```

This looks correct, but it is not. The SQL query that it will generate is this one:

```
SELECT `M`.`name`, `S`.`brand_id`, count(S.brand_id) as votes
FROM (`selections` as S, `brands` as M)
WHERE `M`.`id` = S.brand_id
AND `S`.`id_usu_facebook`  IN ('1704982171', '1428056700')
GROUP BY `S`.`brand_id`
ORDER BY count(S.brand_id) desc
LIMIT 6,0
```

See the difference? In our starting query we had the limit 0,6 and the generated one has limit 6,0. This query won't generate any errors, but it will produce bad results that would be very difficult to trace without the help of the profiler. Now, if we change this:

```
$this->db->limit(0, 6);
```

To:

```
$this->db->limit(6, 0);
```

Our query will be correct this time. With the help of the profiler you will notice this earlier than without it. So if you are having problems with your queries don't forget to use the profile in order to see what SQL your Active Record is generating.

Another method that can help you while working with databases is `last_query`, which can be called using `$this->db->last_query()`. This method will return the SQL for the last query, the SQL string, not the result. This works somewhat like the profiler, showing the SQL equivalent to the Active Record but only for the query you want, and not for all, unlike the profiler.

Take our last query, for example:

```
$this->db->select('M.name, S.brand_id, count(S.brand_id) as votes');
$this->db->from('selections as S, brands as M');
$this->db->where('M.id = S.brand_id');
$this->db->where_in('S.id_usu_facebook ', $users);
$this->db->group_by('S.brand_id');
$this->db->order_by('count(S.brand_id)', 'desc');
$this->db->limit(0, 6);
$query = $this->db->get();
$last_query = $this->db->last_query();
```

If you "echo" the `$last_query` variable you will get:

```
SELECT `M`.`name`, `S`.`brand_id`, count(S.brand_id) as votes
FROM (`selections` as S, `brands` as M)
WHERE `M`.`id` = S.brand_id
AND `S`.`id_usu_facebook`  IN ('1704982171', '1428056700')
GROUP BY `S`.`brand_id`
ORDER BY count(S.brand_id) desc
LIMIT 6,0
```

It is useful if you don't want to use the profiler, but you need to check one query in particular.

 There are more useful methods you can use; check them here.

http://codeigniter.com/user_guide/database/helpers.html

Summary

We've looked at CI's Active Record class and seen how easy it is to:

- Set up connections to one or more databases
- Do standard SQL read, update, create, and delete queries
- Perform other functions that we need to use a database properly

CI's Active Record function is clean and easy to use, and makes coding much clearer to read. It automates database connections, allowing you to abstract the connection information to one `config` file.

Now, before going to the next chapter, you may want to take a look at some other functions the database class has to offer:

http://codeigniter.com/user_guide/database/active_record.html.

If you feel like going deeper into the intricacies of CodeIgniter you must take a look at "database caching" (not view caching):

http://codeigniter.com/user_guide/database/caching.html.

Chapter appendix: MySQL query to set up the website's database

```
DROP TABLE IF EXISTS `ci_sessions`;
CREATE TABLE IF NOT EXISTS `ci_sessions` (
  `session_id` varchar(40) NOT NULL default '0',
  `peopleid` int(11) NOT NULL,
  `ip_address` varchar(16) NOT NULL default '0',
  `user_agent` varchar(50) NOT NULL,
  `last_activity` int(10) unsigned NOT NULL default '0',
  `left` int(11) NOT NULL,
  `name` varchar(25) NOT NULL,
  `status` tinyint(4) NOT NULL default '0'
) ENGINE=MyISAM DEFAULT CHARSET=latin1;

DROP TABLE IF EXISTS `domains`;
CREATE TABLE IF NOT EXISTS `domains` (
  `id` int(10) NOT NULL auto_increment,
  `url` varchar(100) NOT NULL,
  `name` varchar(100) NOT NULL,
  `registrar` varchar(100) NOT NULL,
```

```
  `dateregd` int(11) NOT NULL default '0',
  `cost` float NOT NULL default '0',
  `regdfor` int(11) NOT NULL default '0',
  `notes` blob NOT NULL,
  `pw` varchar(25) NOT NULL,
  `un` varchar(25) NOT NULL,
  `lastupdate` int(11) NOT NULL default '0',
  `submit` varchar(25) NOT NULL,
  PRIMARY KEY  (`id`)
) ENGINE=MyISAM DEFAULT CHARSET=latin1 AUTO_INCREMENT=10 ;

DROP TABLE IF EXISTS `events`;
CREATE TABLE IF NOT EXISTS `events` (
  `id` int(10) NOT NULL auto_increment,
  `name` varchar(50) NOT NULL default 'not set',
  `type` enum('test','alert','report') NOT NULL,
  `testid` int(10) NOT NULL,
  `siteid` int(10) NOT NULL,
  `userid` int(10) NOT NULL,
  `reported` int(11) NOT NULL,
  `result` blob NOT NULL,
  `time` int(11) NOT NULL,
  `timetaken` float NOT NULL,
  `isalert` varchar(2) NOT NULL,
  `emailid` int(11) NOT NULL,
  `submit` varchar(25) NOT NULL,
  PRIMARY KEY  (`id`)
) ENGINE=MyISAM DEFAULT CHARSET=latin1 AUTO_INCREMENT=69 ;

DROP TABLE IF EXISTS `frequencies`;
CREATE TABLE IF NOT EXISTS `frequencies` (
  `id` int(10) NOT NULL,
  `name` varchar(16) NOT NULL,
  `submit` varchar(25) NOT NULL,
  PRIMARY KEY  (`id`)
) ENGINE=MyISAM DEFAULT CHARSET=latin1;

DROP TABLE IF EXISTS `hosts`;
CREATE TABLE IF NOT EXISTS `hosts` (
  `id` int(11) NOT NULL auto_increment,
  `cost` float NOT NULL,
  `name` varchar(100) NOT NULL,
  `hosturl` varchar(100) NOT NULL,
  `un` varchar(50) NOT NULL,
```

```
  `pw` varchar(50) NOT NULL,
  `ns1url` varchar(36) NOT NULL,
  `ns1ip` varchar(36) NOT NULL,
  `ns2url` varchar(36) NOT NULL,
  `ns2ip` varchar(36) NOT NULL,
  `ftpurl` varchar(100) NOT NULL,
  `ftpserverip` varchar(36) NOT NULL,
  `ftpun` varchar(50) NOT NULL,
  `ftppw` varchar(50) NOT NULL,
  `cpurl` varchar(36) NOT NULL,
  `cpun` varchar(36) NOT NULL,
  `cppw` varchar(36) NOT NULL,
  `pop3server` varchar(36) NOT NULL,
  `servicetel` varchar(50) NOT NULL,
  `servicetel2` varchar(50) NOT NULL,
  `serviceemail` varchar(100) NOT NULL,
  `webroot` varchar(48) NOT NULL,
  `absoluteroot` varchar(48) NOT NULL,
  `cgiroot` varchar(48) NOT NULL,
  `booked` int(11) NOT NULL,
  `duration` int(11) NOT NULL,
  `lastupdate` int(11) NOT NULL default '0',
  `submit` varchar(25) NOT NULL,
  PRIMARY KEY  (`id`)
) ENGINE=MyISAM DEFAULT CHARSET=latin1 AUTO_INCREMENT=6 ;

DROP TABLE IF EXISTS `people`;
CREATE TABLE IF NOT EXISTS `people` (
  `id` int(11) NOT NULL auto_increment,
  `uname` varchar(25) NOT NULL,
  `pw` varchar(25) NOT NULL,
  `status` smallint(3) NOT NULL default '1',
  `name` varchar(50) NOT NULL,
  `firstname` varchar(50) NOT NULL,
  `surname` varchar(50) NOT NULL,
  `email` varchar(120) NOT NULL,
  `lastupdate` int(11) NOT NULL default '0',
  `submit` varchar(25) NOT NULL,
  PRIMARY KEY  (`id`)
) ENGINE=MyISAM DEFAULT CHARSET=latin1 AUTO_INCREMENT=5 ;

DROP TABLE IF EXISTS `sites`;
CREATE TABLE IF NOT EXISTS `sites` (
  `id` int(10) NOT NULL auto_increment,
  `name` varchar(100) NOT NULL,
  `url` varchar(100) NOT NULL,
  `un` varchar(50) NOT NULL,
```

```
    `pw` varchar(50) NOT NULL,
    `client1` int(10) NOT NULL default '0',
    `client2` int(10) NOT NULL default '0',
    `admin1` int(10) NOT NULL default '0',
    `admin2` int(10) NOT NULL default '0',
    `domainid` int(10) NOT NULL default '0',
    `hostid` int(10) NOT NULL default '0',
    `webroot` varchar(50) NOT NULL,
    `files` text NOT NULL,
    `filesdate` int(11) NOT NULL default '0',
    `lastupdate` int(11) NOT NULL default '0',
    `submit` varchar(25) NOT NULL,
    PRIMARY KEY  (`id`)
) ENGINE=MyISAM DEFAULT CHARSET=latin1 AUTO_INCREMENT=15 ;

DROP TABLE IF EXISTS `tests`;
CREATE TABLE IF NOT EXISTS `tests` (
    `id` int(11) NOT NULL auto_increment,
    `siteid` int(11) NOT NULL default '0',
    `name` varchar(250) NOT NULL,
    `type` varchar(25) NOT NULL,
    `url` varchar(120) NOT NULL,
    `regex` varchar(250) NOT NULL,
    `p1` varchar(250) NOT NULL,
    `p2` varchar(250) NOT NULL,
    `p3` varchar(250) NOT NULL,
    `p4` varchar(250) NOT NULL,
    `p5` varchar(250) NOT NULL,
    `p6` varchar(250) NOT NULL,
    `frequency` int(10) NOT NULL default '0',
    `lastdone` int(10) NOT NULL default '0',
    `isalert` varchar(2) NOT NULL,
    `setup` int(10) NOT NULL default '0',
    `lastupdate` int(10) NOT NULL default '0',
    `notes` varchar(250) NOT NULL,
    `submit` varchar(25) NOT NULL,
    PRIMARY KEY  (`id`)
) ENGINE-MyISAM DEFAULT CHARSET=latin1 AUTO_INCREMENT=11 ;

DROP TABLE IF EXISTS `types`;
CREATE TABLE IF NOT EXISTS `types` (
    `id` varchar(7) NOT NULL,
    `name` varchar(50) NOT NULL,
    PRIMARY KEY  (`id`)
) ENGINE=MyISAM DEFAULT CHARSET=latin1;
```

5
Simplifying HTML Pages and Forms

This chapter covers yet another way in which CI helps save your time and makes your coding more rigorous and logical. Firstly, we'll cover various ways of building views—the pages that control the way you see the results prepared by your controllers and models. Next, you'll see how to create HTML forms quickly, with built-in safeguards, and you'll also see how to validate your forms.

We assume that the readers of this book are familiar with HTML and CSS. The following examples are very simplified, so we can focus on the CI code. We have assumed that you have already written a CSS file and tucked it away somewhere on your site.

Writing a view

A view controls how the user sees your website. Views make it easy for you to present a consistent interface, and to change it if you need to. One of the advantages of MVC is that you separate presentation from logic, keeping everything much cleaner.

So far, all we've done is look at the very simple `welcome` view that installs out-of-the-box when you first load CI (See Chapter 3). Now let's see how to make it more elaborate.

A view is just a set of HTML shelves to hold your content. The shelves may be in any color. There may be lot of little ones or just a few widely-spaced elegant ones. But the view doesn't know or care what data is on those shelves, it is only interested in presentation.

As we saw in the previous chapters, views are created in `./application/views` and usually they have a `.php` extension (but you can put whatever extension you want, only remember to write the extension when loading the view if it is not `.php`).

First, to create a view, you need to create a skeleton HTML web page as a PHP file. Let's call it `basic_view.php`. Save it in your `application/views` folder (the reason for saving it in this folder is simply because the loader looks for it, there).

```html
<html>
<head>
</head>
<body>
  <p>Hello world!</p>
</body>
</html>
```

You load it from a controller when you want to use it, using `$this->load->view()`, inside an appropriate function:

```php
function index()
{
  $this->load->view('basic_view');
}
```

Note, if this were a model or a helper, you'd load it first, and call it separately when you want to use it. With a view, when you call it, it loads as well. So, you only need one line of code. Of course, that's an empty view. To make it useful, you need content. Say we want to add a title and some text. First we define them in the controller:

```php
function index()
{
  $data['mytitle'] = "A website monitoring tool";
  $data['mytext'] = "This website helps you to keep track of the
                     other websites you control.";
}
```

Notice how we have defined them as elements of the array `$data` (or any other name we care to give it), and not as separate scalar variables. For the first array entry, the "key" is `mytitle` and the "value" is `A website monitoring tool`.

Next, we call the view loading function:

```
function index()
{
  $data['mytitle'] = "A website monitoring tool";
  $data['mytext'] = "This website helps you to keep track of the
                     other websites you control.";
  $this->load->view('basic_view', $data);
}
```

We have the $data array as the second parameter of the $this->load->view() function, after the name of the view itself. Once the $data array reaches the view, CI uses PHP's extract() function to turn each element of the $data array into a separate variable, with the "key" as the variable name, and the "value" as the variable value. These variables can then be referenced directly in our view:

```
<html>
<head>
</head>
<body>
  <h1 class='test'><?php echo $mytitle; ?> </h1>
  <p class='test'><?php echo $mytext; ?> </p>
</body>
</html>
```

You can pass, one variable's data to a view, but by building up an array of arrays, you can pack a large amount of information neatly into that one variable. It seems complicated, but it is a tightly structured and an elegant way of passing information.

Long and short PHP syntax and other CodeIgniter style guidelines

Before we go on, a note about different forms of PHP syntax. The usual way to include a PHP "code island" in the midst of HTML code is like this:

```
<?php echo $somevariable ?>
```

However, CI also supports a shorter version:

```
<?=$somevariable?>
```

In this case, the external brackets delimiting the code island have lost the letters php (they are just `<?` `?>`) and echo (replaced by `=`). You can also use shorter syntax for `if`, `for`, `foreach`, and `while` loops.

It is preferable to stick to the standard format and it is also recommended in the CodeIgniter style guide. If you use the short format, note that some servers won't interpret the abbreviated format correctly. If you still wish to use the short tags, then go to your `config` file, and alter the following line to TRUE:

```
$config['rewrite_short_tags'] = FALSE;
```

CI will then rewrite short tags to the normal form before it sends them to the server. However, if there is a PHP error, using this rewriting function makes the error messages less meaningful. So, debugging may be more difficult. Using the standard format will also make your code more portable. You can take a look at other CI guidelines here:

```
http://codeigniter.com/user_guide/general/styleguide.html
```

But let's look at some of them that are important and helpful too!

File format

The file format should be UTF (Unicode Transformation Format), without **BOM** (**Byte Order Mark**, which is a kind of signature used to define the byte order and form of files). *Why don't we use the BOM?* Well, the BOM can be sent as output to the browser and the following things can happen:

- The application can send its own headers; imagine you want to change your headers to image headers, in order to show an image from the database. If BOM is shown, the header change won't be possible because the header would have already been sent.

- The BOM is represented as white space at the top of the file (as a `<br/>`), and sometimes this white space can be troublesome. For example, if you are loading two views, like this:

  ```
  $this->load->view('header');
  $this->load->view('menu');
  ```

  In the header file (`/www/codeigniter/application/views/header.php`) we have:

  ```
  <div style="height: 100px; background-color: blue;">
  </div>
  ```

And in the menu file (`/www/codeigniter/application/views/menu.php`) we have:

```
<div style="height: 100px; background-color: red;">
</div>
```

If these two views are encoded as UTF, with BOM, a white space will be created between the two. Take a look at the following screenshot:

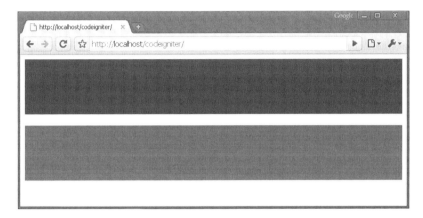

What is this blank space – a break or a margin? No, it's the BOM, and the best way to remove it is by encoding the file as UTF without BOM. By doing this we will get a screen that looks like this:

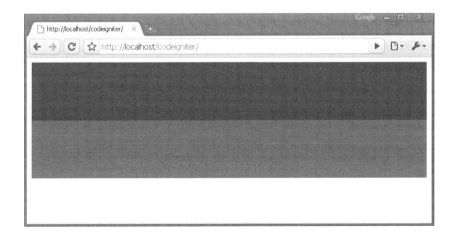

That little white space can give you some headaches, so if it is not expected to be there, look at your encoding. Most file editors have options that let you change the file encoding.

PHP closing tag

The CI style guide recommends not to use the PHP closing tag `?>`, that is the last one, and only at the end of a PHP file (think of the controllers). This is because you can put a white space after the PHP closing tag, and that can give errors similar to the file format errors. Instead CI uses a comment to indicate the end of the file.

For example, instead of ending a file with:

```
?>
```

We can write something like:

```
/* End of file welcome.php */
```

Thus avoiding such errors, without losing the ability to tell where the file ends.

Other guidelines are more style related and you can choose to adhere to them or not. If you work in a team it is recommended to adhere to these (or other) guidelines, so all the teams work and write code in the same style.

Nesting views

So far, irrespective of whether we use long or short PHP formats, this is pretty crude HTML. It would be nice, for instance, to put more information in the `<head>` section of the page. Better still, if this could be a standard chunk of each page. Once again, something we have to write (or alter) only once, and can reuse it, by nesting this view inside other views whenever we need the boring HTML header stuff.

Let's create a page header "view" for our site, which displays a standard page header, as well as HTML declarations and meta-information.

First, we type the code for our "nested" header view:

```
<!DOCTYPE html PUBLIC '-//W3C//DTD XHTML 1.0 Strict//EN'http://www.
w3.org/TR/xhtml1/DTD/xhtml1-strict.dtd'><html xmlns='http://www.
w3.org/1999/xhtml'>
<title><?php echo $mywebtitle ?></title>
""
<?php echo $myrobots ?>
<link rel="stylesheet" type="text/css" href="<?php echo
"$base/$css";?>">
```

Save this as `views/header_view.php`. It introduces new variables:

- `$mywebtitle`: This is the page title, you can send a different page title to every page on your site, which is better from an SEO point of view.

- `$myrobots`: We are using this for the standard instructions to robots. It tells them that this site is not to be indexed.

- `$base` and `$css`: This describes the base URL and the extra URL for our `.css` file—that we're pretending we've already written. Let's apply formatting consistently. These variables will be generated from data we have already stored in CI's `config` file (I could have also used the CI config variable `site_url` instead of `base`).

Now, what we need to know is:

- How do we call the second "nested" view?

- How do we assign values to its variables?

There are two options. Firstly, calls to views can be made from within other views. So our main view, `basic_view.php`, just needs a new line:

```
<html><head>
<?php $this->load->view('header_view'); ?>
</head><body>
<?php echo $mytitle; ?>
<?php echo $mytext; ?>
</body>
</html>
```

As for the variables, they can be assigned by two new lines in the original controller:

```
function index()
{
  $data['mytitle']    = "A website monitoring tool";
  $data['mytext']     = "This website helps you to keep track
                         of the other websites you control.";
  $data['myrobots']   = '<meta name="robots" content="noindex
                                   ,nofollow">';
  $data['mywebtitle'] = 'Web monitoring tool';
  $data['base']       = $this->config->item('base_url');
  $data['css']        = $this->config->item('css');
  $this->load->view('basic_view', $data);
}
```

Here the new variables $myrobots, $css, $base, and $mywebtitle are created as new elements of the existing $data array. They are passed to basic_view, which unpacks them, and makes them available to header_view, when it is called by basic_view.

 Remember not to use the same variable name in two views that you are nesting, or one will overwrite the other.

The second way is to add the view from inside the controller, by assigning it to a variable:

```php
<?php
class Welcome extends Controller
{
  function Welcome()
  {
    parent::Controller();
  }
  function index()
  {
    $data_h['myrobots']   = '<meta name="robots" content="noindex
                                      ,nofollow">';
    $data_h['mywebtitle'] = 'Web monitoring tool';
    $data_h['base'] = $this->config->item('base_url');
    $data_h['css'] = $this->config->item('css');
    $data['header'] = $this->load->view('header_view', $data_h,
                                    TRUE);
    $data['mytitle']    = "A website monitoring tool";
    $data['mytext']      = "This website helps you to keep track
                          of the other websites you control.";
    $this->load->view('basic_view', $data);
  }
}
/* End of file welcome.php */
```

This is probably more correct from a strict MVC perspective. There are actually three parameters you can pass with the load->view function.

- First is the header_view, which is the name of the view to be loaded. This is essential.

- Second, which is optional, is the data to load into it.

- Third is a Boolean value. If you don't specify the value, it defaults to FALSE, and the view is sent to the browser. However, if you are nesting the view this way, you want it to be returned as a string. This creates a nest inside the variable you are passing to the host view. Setting the third parameter to TRUE you can achieve this.

Now we've got a reference to the built-in stylesheet, we can update the view to use display classes that we might have defined there:

```
<html><head>
<?php $this->load->view('header_view'); ?>
</head>
<body>
  <h1 class='test'><?php echo $mytitle; ?> </h1>
  <p class='test'><?php echo $mytext; ?> </p>
</body>
</html>
```

Notice again, how CI's MVC system allows you to separate display from content. The views only provide "shelves" for the content, and even the styling of those shelves is derived from a .css stylesheet.

The view doesn't care about what $mytext says, it just displays it on the right shelf with the right formatting. The controller that defines $mytext doesn't even know (or care) how the information it generates is displayed.

So, if we need to change the look of our pages, or display them on a different system (say WAP), then we only need to change one view and one CSS stylesheet. We don't need to mess around inside the code of several controllers.

If we want to change the information displayed on the page, we don't need to touch the views, and remind ourselves to change some variable on each page we've written. We just change what the controller pushes out. Remember the "loose coupling" principle? Once again, this makes it easy to design, upgrade, and maintain your sites.

Practical issues of site architecture

Wait a moment, you generated the CSS stylesheet address dynamically in your header_view:

```
<link rel="stylesheet" type="text/css" href="<?php echo
"$base/$css";?>">
```

This means that the controller had to produce this data, which is only relevant to how the information is displayed. But we've just said the controller shouldn't know or care about that. Isn't that going right in the face of the "loose coupling" principle, we just set? What's more, generating this information dynamically requires several operations:

1. The controller has to look it up in the `config` file.

2. The controller has to package it in the `$data` array and pass it to the view.

3. The view has to extract the single variables `$base` and `$css` and look up their values.

Seems like a roundabout way of doing things. Why not just embed the data statically in the view?

```
<link rel="stylesheet" type="text/css" href="http://www.mysite.com/
mystylesheet.css";">
```

The advantage of building this variable dynamically, despite breaking the MVC "rule", and the overhead of creating variables and passing them around, is that the code is much more portable. If you move the site, or move your CSS file, you have to change the code only once in the `config` file, and every controller and view will reflect the change at once. If you hard-code the address in to each view, you'll have to spend time hunting through them for all those absolute URLs you wrote months ago. So, which is best?

There isn't a correct answer. It depends on what your priorities are. The key is to apply MVC principles sensibly — as a tool rather than a straitjacket. CI gives you a lot of freedom to do this.

A third option is to use CI HTML helper, like this (in the controller):

```
function index()
{
  $this->load->helper('html');
  $data_h['myrobots'] = '<meta name="robots" content="noindex
                        ,nofollow">';
  $data_h['mywebtitle'] = 'Web monitoring tool';
  $data['header'] = $this->load->view('header_view', $data_h, TRUE);
  $data['mytitle'] = "A website monitoring tool";
  $data['mytext'] = "This website helps you to keep track of the
                    other websites you control.";
  $this->load->view('basic_view', $data);
}
```

Our view (`header_view.php`) will look this way:

```
<!DOCTYPE html PUBLIC '-//W3C//DTD XHTML 1.0 Strict//EN'http://www.
w3.org/TR/xhtml1/DTD/xhtml1-strict.dtd'><html xmlns='http://www.
w3.org/1999/xhtml'>
<title><?php echo $mywebtitle ?></title>
<?php echo $myrobots ?>
<?php echo link_tag('application/css/styles.css'); ?>
```

The `link_tag` function of the HTML helper will produce a link tag, like this one:

```
<link href="http://localhost/codeigniter/application/css/styles.css"
rel="stylesheet" type="text/css" />
```

CI's form helper—entering data

Let's move on to see how you use your HTML pages. One of the most important parts of any dynamic site is interaction with the users, and this usually means HTML forms.

The CI form helper is a very useful piece of code. It introduces a slightly different syntax, which makes form creation easier. Let's build a form that allows you to enter data on your site about a new website. In the `sites` table, we want to enter the name, type, and URL of the website, and the date when it was updated.

You can build the form as a simple HTML file, or you can build it inside a controller, then pack it into a variable, call a view, and pass the variable to the view. We will do it the second way. You can also write it entirely in the view if you want.

First, you have to load the form helper into the controller where you need to use it. Then, you put the following line in the controller's constructor function:

```
$this->load->helper('form');
```

Now, you have to start the form.

Now, for the form fields, instead of typing:

```
<input type='text' name='name' value=''>
```

CI allows you to enter:

```
form_input('name', '');
```

Remember that name is the title of the field, value is what you want to put into it. Putting something in here gives you a default value, or you can dynamically fetch the existing value from the table.

But, what benefits do you get using the form helper?

Form helper advantage one: Clarity

The first advantage of using the CI form helper is sheer clarity in your code. If you want a more elaborate input box, then type the following HTML:

```
<input type="text" name="url" id="url" value="www.mysite.com"
maxlength="100" size="50" style="yellow" />
```

Just for a quick review:

- type is the sort of box you want—text, hidden, and anything you like
- name is the key used for this value in the POST array
- id is used to refer a box on the page, if you're doing neat things with JavaScript
- value is the existing or default value that you want the box to show when it comes up on the page
- maxlength and size are obvious; style can be a set of HTML formatting or a reference to a .css style defined in your stylesheet

CI uses an array instead:

```
$data = array(
            'name' => 'url',
            'id' => 'url',
            'value' => 'www.mysite.com',
            'maxlength' => '100',
            'size' => '50',
            'style' => 'yellow',
          );
echo form_input($data);
```

It looks longer than the simple HTML. However, it is clearer and easier to understand and maintain. As you can see, each of the parameters in the HTML input has its equivalent in the array, well organized. This would be of great help when we generate some of the values dynamically.

Hidden form fields are very simple. Let's say we want to automatically record the date when our database is updated. We put the date in a `$date` variable, such as:

```
form_hidden('updated', $date);
```

If you want a "text area" box, to give your user more than one line to enter data, say for URLs, which may be quite long, use CI's `form_textarea()` function. If you're happy with a default size, this would simply read:

```
$data = array(
                'name' => 'url',
                'id' => 'url',
                'value' => 'www.mysite.com',
                );
echo form_textarea($data);
```

CI's `form` helper is of great help when you write drop-down boxes, checkboxes, or radio boxes. Let's say we want to change our `url` field to a drop-down box, to allow the reader to select one URL from a list of several. First, list the options in an array, then use the `form_dropdown()` function:

```
$urlarray = array(
                    '1' => 'www.this.com',
                    '2' => 'www.that.com',
                    '3' => 'www.theother.com',
                );
echo form_dropdown('url', $urlarray, '2');
```

The first value passed to the form, `url`, is the field name in the `site` table that we intend to update. The second is an array of options. The third one is the key of the option you want to set as default. In other words, if the user accepts the default value, your `$_POST` array will contain the value `url => 2`, but your user will see the option `www.that.com`. Compare this to the plain vanilla HTML that you would otherwise have to write:

```
<select name="type">
<option value="1" >www.this.com</option>
<option value="2" selected>www.that.com</option>
<option value="3" >www.theother.com</option>
</select>
```

Now CI's code is shorter, and much easier to follow. If you store your list of possible URLs in a separate database table (say it's called `urls`), then generating a dynamic drop-down box is easy. First generate an array of all possible values:

```
$urlarray = array();
$this->db->select('id, url');
$query = $this->db->get('urls');
if ($query->num_rows() > 0)
{
  foreach ($query->result() as $row)
  {
    $urlarray[$row->id] = $row->url;
  }
}
```

Now, repeat the CI `form_dropdown()` function we used earlier:

```
echo form_dropdown('type', $urlarray, '1');
```

Only the contents of `$urlarray` have changed, the line of code remains the same. If you are updating an entry rather than creating a new one, you don't want to show the default value to the user. You want to show an already existing value for that entry. You should already know the `id` number of the entry you want to update, so you need to do a database look up of the `sites` table first. Make sure you use a different variable name for the second query and the second `row` variable, or they may overwrite the first set you wrote:

```
$this->db->select('id, url, name');
$this->db->where('id','$id')
$sitequery = $this->db->get('sites');
$siterow = $sitequery->row();
```

Then your CI form drop-down function will read:

```
echo form_dropdown('url', $urlarray, $siterow->url);
```

It looks easier and very neat this way. There are other options in the `form` helper, all of them are very useful, for example:

- `form_password()`: This is the same as `form_input()` but will produce a "password" input
- `form_upload()`: This is used to produce inputs of "file" type
- `form_submit()`: This is used in order to generate a "submit" button
- `form_reset()`: This is used to generate a "reset" button

It is suggested to take a look at all the options of the form helper, at http://codeigniter.com/user_guide/helpers/form_helper.html.

You will discover how to build checkboxes, radio boxes, and so on.

Form helper advantage two: Automation

The second advantage of using the form helper to create your HTML forms is that it automates some things you would otherwise have to script yourself. Firstly, it intercepts HTML and characters such as quotes, which the user may enter, and escapes them to avoid breaking the form. Secondly, it automates links. When you open a form, you have to specify the target page, which will receive the form's data and process it. In CI, this is a function within a controller rather than an actual static page.

Let's say it is the update function of the websites controller. So, if you were using plain HTML code, you'd write:

```
<form method="post" action="http:/www.mysite.com/index.php/websites/
update" />
```

Whereas, if you open your form with CI, you only need to use:

```
form_open('websites/update')
```

CI automatically works out the base URL from the value in your config file and points the form there. Once again, if you move your site, your forms will not break. So, you don't have to hunt for hard-coded URLs to update.

By default, CI assumes your forms will always send POST data rather than GET data. CI makes extensive use of the URLs, so this avoids confusion.

> If you want to upload files, thanks to your form, you need to create the form_open this way:
>
> ```
> form_open_multipart(websites/update)
> ```
>
> This will generate something like this:
>
> ```
> <form action="http://localhost/codcigniter/
> websites/update" method="post" enctype="multipart/
> form-data">
> ```

Also if you would like to create a hidden input at the very moment of opening the form—very useful when you need to use forms for editing previous values in the database—you can do it this way:

```
echo form_open('email/send', '', array('id' => $row->id ));
```

You have to pass it in the third parameter, and you can pass any value you want to.

My display model

As promised, here is our display model (slightly simplified):

```
<?php
class Display extends Model
{
    /*create the array to pass to the views*/
  var $data = array();

    /*two other class variables*/
  var $base;
  var $status = '';

    /*the constructor function: this calls the 'model' parent class,
    loads other CI libraries and helpers it requires, and
    dynamically sets variables*/
  function Display()
  {
    parent::Model();
    $this->load->helper('form');
    $this->load->library('user_agent');
    $this->load->library('menu');
    $this->load->library('session');

     /*now set the standard parts of the array*/
    $this->data['css']  = $this->config->item('css');
    $this->data['base'] = $this->config->item('base_url');
    $this->base         = $this->config->item('base_url');
    $this->data['myrobots'] = '<meta name="robots"
                                content="noindex,nofollow">';

     /*note that CI's session stuff doesn't automatically recall the
     extra variables you have added, so you have to look up the
     user's status in the ci_sessions table*/
    $sessionid = $this->session->userdata('session_id');
    $this->db->select('status');
```

```
      $this->db->where('session_id', $sessionid);
      $query = $this->db->get('ci_sessions');
      if ($query->num_rows() > 0)
      {
        $row = $query->row();
        $this->status = $row->status;
      }
    }

      /*function to assemble a standard page. Any controller can call
       this. Just supply as $mydata an array of key/value pairs for
       the contents you want the view to display. Available variables
       in this view are:
        mytitle. menu, mytext, diagnostic */
    function mainpage($mydata)
    {
      $this->data['mytitle'] = 'Monitoring website';
      $this->data['diagnostic'] = $diagnostic;
      foreach($mydata as $key => $variable)
      {
        $this->data[$key] = $variable;
      }
       /*here's the menu class we looked at in Chapter 3*/
      $menu = new menu;
      $this->load->library('session');
      $mysess = $this->session->userdata('session_id');
      if(isset($this->status) && $this->status > 0)
      {
        $this->data['menu'] = $menu->show_menu($this->status);
      }
      $this->load->view('basic_view', $this->data);
    }
  }
  ?>
```

You can call the main page from any controller with the lines:

```
$this->load->model('display');
$this->display->mainpage($data);
```

You then know that your view is being assembled dynamically, exactly as you want it.

CI's form validation class: Checking data easily

One task, when you write HTML forms, is validating user input. We all know that we should do it, but so far we've written a simple form, which will trustingly accept any data the user enters. You should always assume that a minority of your users are malicious, and the others could make some mistakes too. Validating your form tests the information they submit, to make sure it fits rules you specify.

You can do it on the client side, using JavaScript, but this is of limited value as a security precaution, as the user can easily circumvent it. Validating the data on the server side means an extra round trip to the server, but it's worth it, for the added peace of mind.

It's also quite complex to write the code, but—you guessed it—CI has a form validation class that works hand-in-glove with the `form` helper to make validation easier. Let's change our own form submission process to reflect this. You need to make some changes in the form, and also in the function to which it points.

If your form begins with `form_open('sites/update')`, you need to modify the `update` function in the `sites` controller. If you aren't using the CI `form` helper, the HTML equivalent is:

```
<form method="post" action="http:/www.mysite.com/index.php/sites/
update" />
```

You need to do three things:

- Set up validation
- Set up the controller
- Set up the forms

Setting up validation

In the function to which your form points, load the validation library and declare your validation rules:

```
$this->load->library('form_validation');
$this->form_validation->set_rules('url', 'url', 'required');
$this->form_validation->set_rules('name', 'Name', 'required');
$this->form_validation->run();
```

The pattern in which we write those rules is:

```
$this->form_validation->set_rules('field', 'label', 'rules');
```

In this example, each entry must have something in the `url` and `name` fields. CI gives various options for specifying what that something should be, and the user guide explains them in detail.

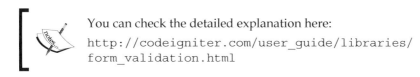

You can check the detailed explanation here:
`http://codeigniter.com/user_guide/libraries/form_validation.html`

They're fairly self-evident—`min_length[6]`, obviously means a valid entry in the field must have six characters or more. Numeric means it must not contain letters, and so on. You can also combine rules, using the "pipe" character to separate them:

```
$this->form_validation->set_rules('username', 'Username',
'required|min_length[5]|max_length[12]');
```

This would require a `name`, having `five` to `twelve` characters. You can even write your own rules.

Setting up the controller

In the same function, create an `if-else` loop:

```
if($this->validation->run() == FALSE)
{
    $this->load->view('myform');
}
else
{
    $this->load->view('success');
}
```

You run the validation test, and if the entries don't pass the test, you go back to the entry form. If you're generating your view in a function inside a controller, and it has dynamic drop-down fields, point back to that function instead—`$this->myfunction` rather than `$this->load->view('myform')`.

If your validation run is successful, create another view (`success`) to tell the user that the entry has been accepted, and give whatever navigation options you want him/her to have to move on.

Setting up forms

The entry form that we have built also needs to be tweaked. Simply returning the user to the form each time, when an entry doesn't pass the validation tests, will make your users really cross! You have to say which field failed, and why. So, you have to `echo` an extra line somewhere in the form:

```
<?php echo validation_errors(); ?>
```

This prints the appropriate messages, and saves you from users' frustration. You also need to arrange for the form fields that were correctly entered to be repopulated with the correct values, otherwise, the user will have to reenter all the fields each time he/she makes a mistake in one of them. Another way to get the user really cross!

Repopulating form fields is quite easy, in our `name` field example, we may have something similar to:

```
Name: <?php echo form_input('name', ''); ?>
```

If we want this field to be repopulated, we just need to change it this way:

```
Name: <?php echo form_input('name', set_value('name')); ?>
```

The `set_value` function, along with the field name, will put the field's value in it, without you having to do anything more.

Of course, the first time the form appears, there will be nothing in this value. But once you submit it, this value will be populated, and if the form is to be shown again, it will fill the form field. Sounds complicated? Don't worry let's see a simple working example.

Let's pack it all together

Now try to make an example with all we have learned to recap it. Firstly create the view. For example, take the file at `/www/codeigniter/application/views/basic_view.php`.

```
<html>
<head>
</head>
<body>
  <?php echo form_open('welcome/mail') ?>
  Name: <?php echo form_input('name', ''); ?> <br/>
  Phone: <?php echo form_input('phone', ''); ?> <br/>
  Message: <?php echo form_textarea('message', ''); ?> <br/>
  <?php echo form_submit('submit', 'Send'); ?>
```

```php
    <?php echo form_close(); ?>
  </body>
</html>
```

Now, in the controller put this:

```php
<?php
class Welcome extends Controller
{
  function Welcome()
  {
    parent::Controller();
    $this->load->helper('html');
    $this->load->helper('form');
  }
  function index($data = '')
  {
    $this->load->view('basic_view', $data);
  }
  function mail()
  {
    $this->load->library('form_validation');
    if ($this->form_validation->run() == FALSE)
    {
      $this->load->view('basic_view');
    }
    else
    {
      //Here we should place the code to send the email.
      //CI will also help us with that, we will see how in a few
      //chapters.
      $this->load->view('success');
    }
  }
}
/* End of file welcome.php */
```

Now you can navigate to the controller, in order to see what happens. Go to `http://localhost/codeigniter/welcome`. You will see the form we have just written, and if you try to send it you will be redirected to `http://localhost/codeigniter/welcome/mail`. *Why we have been redirected to mail and not to success?* Well this is because we haven't established any validation rules.

Now we are going to add a line to the view:

```php
<?php echo validation_errors(); ?>
<?php echo form_open('welcome/mail') ?>
Name: <?php echo form_input('name', ''); ?> <br/>
```

This will show the messages we are about to define. *How are validation rules defined?* Very easily, we will modify our controller:

```php
function mail()
{
  $this->load->library('form_validation');
  $this->form_validation->set_rules('name', 'Name', 'required');
  $this->form_validation->set_rules('phone', 'Phone', 'required');
  $this->form_validation->set_rules('message', 'Message field',
                                'required');
```

The first parameter will be the form field name, the second is the field name as it will appear in the error message (the Name field is required), and the third is the validation type.

If you try to send the form, with empty fields, you will see the error message, and if the fields are filled the form will be sent to the success page. But, if it fails, it will return back to the form, with the fields empty. If you want to repopulate them you need set_value(). Take a look at how to use it, modifying our view:

```html
<html>
<head>
</head>
<body>
  <?php echo validation_errors(); ?>
  <?php echo form_open('welcome/mail') ?>
  Name: <?php echo form_input('name', set_value('name')); ?> <br/>
  Phone: <?php echo form_input('phone', set_value('phone')); ?> <br/>
  Message: <?php echo form_textarea('message', set_value('message'));
  ?> <br/>
```

This way when you return to the form the fields will be repopulated; looks easy doesn't it? Now, if you want to delve into the intricacies of the `form_validation` you can see the CI user guide (`http://codeigniter.com/user_guide/libraries/form_validation.html`). Several other things you can do with `form_validation`, are to use it to:

- Automatically prepare your data, for example, by trimming it or removing potential cross-site scripting attacks
- Write your own complex validation criteria, for example, the value that the user has entered must not already exist in your database
- Write your own error messages

The form validation class is a very useful and powerful part of CI and well worth the time it takes to understand. If you would like to take a deeper look at it, you can go through the user guide.

Summary

We've looked at ways in which CI generates "views", and how it allows you to create "mini-views", which you can nest inside other views. This means, you can set up a title page or a part of your display once and use it over and over again, keeping your display separated from your content.

We've also seen how CI helps you in the task of writing HTML forms, with a set of helpers that simplify the process and cut down on actual coding.

Lastly, we've looked at CI's validation class, which is a powerful tool for keeping an eye on what your users actually try to enter. Nothing's perfect, but this goes a long way towards stopping users form entering rubbish, or trying to exploit security holes in your site. It also looks much more professional when your site politely but firmly catches out users' mistakes, rather than silently accepting meaningless entries.

On the way, we've also looked at the MVC process again, and made a choice between the strict application of MVC principles and deliberately breaking the "rules" to make life easier. CI has a very flexible philosophy — use the tools if you want to, provided you understand the issues — feel free to do it some other way if that suits your priorities better.

6

Simplifying Sessions and Security

In this chapter, we'll continue with the application we are building, and we'll look at one of the basic questions affecting any website, that is, session management and security.

In this chapter, you'll see:

- How to make your pages secure
- How to use CI's `session` class

Continuing with our practical site using CI

Until now you have seen how CI is structured and how the MVC pattern works. You have also seen how to work with databases, HTML, and forms. Looking at some of the CI helpers and libraries, you know how CI can help you in the site development process.

Now you will continue developing your application and see other great tools of CI. But first, recap what you are building—a site that will help you:

- Test and keep track of your other sites
- Manage them with a minimum of human intervention
- Generate detailed reports of the sites and tests conducted
- If possible it will run on a Cron job, in case that's not possible you can run it manually when you need or want to do it
- If something goes wrong the application will send an email telling exactly what happened and where, allowing you to print those reports

With an application like that you can show the reports to your client, to impress them with the regular and comprehensive checks you are doing, and the (hopefully!) flawless performance of their sites.

 Avoid making the code too long and repetitive, the code in this book is not very secure, so please bear that in mind if you use it for real. This chapter covers a basic means of securing your site's pages against unauthorized users. Other PHP security issues, which aren't unique to CodeIgniter, are outside the scope of this book.

At this stage, we're going to look at CI's approach to things that are generic to most dynamic websites. So, we'll leave the detailed design of our site until later. Let's start with some of the basic items.

Moving around the site

Any website is a collection of separate files. It's essential for them to be able to talk to each other. As we saw in Chapter 3, CI links them by using their URLs. Typically, URLs take the pattern:

base url	This is the plain vanilla address that everyone uses to access your site. Readers don't need to know all the URL structures because the site builds them as it needs to. For example, `http://www.mysite.com`.
index file	Segment 1: `index.php`
	This is the main file that CI starts off with, every time the site is hit. As we saw in Chapter 2, we can remove this (from the URL) using the `.htaccess` file.
class (or controller)	Segment 2: `start`
	If no controller is set, CI defaults to the controller you specified in the `config` file.
method (or function)	Segment 3: `assessme`
	If no method is set, CI defaults to the index function of the controller, if there is one. If not, you get a 404 error page.
plus any parameters	Segment 4: `fred` (and Segment 5: `12345`, Segment 6: `hello`, and so on.)

To call the `assessme` method in the `start` controller with the parameters `fred` and `12345`, your URL will be:

```
http://www.mysite.com/.index.php/start/assessme/fred/12345"index.php/
start/assessme/fred/12345
```

This code expects your site to contain a controller called start.php that includes a method assessme, which expects two parameters. A URL like this will call any function in any controller on your site.

As we have been testing CI, making changes, creating files, and so on, we will go from the start again, to have a solid foundation for the application. This way we will also have the same code, so you can follow with the example.

First, we'll set up a controller called start. Let's make it our default controller, and edit the /application/config/routes.php file like this:

```
$route['default_controller'] = "start";
```

 Just remember, from the previous table, if your default controller doesn't have a default index method, anyone who visits your plain vanilla base URL will get a 404 error, which is not a good idea!

Now we need to write our new start controller. Remember the basic format:

```php
<?php
class Start extends Controller
{
  function Start()
  {
    parent::Controller();
  }
  function assessme($name = '', $password ='')
  {
    if($name == 'fred' && $password == '12345')
    {$this->mainpage();}
  }
}
```

Save this in the /system/application/controllers folder as start.php.

 Note the letter cases: Start has an uppercase letter in the class name and constructor function, but not in the saved file name.)

The second line tells you that this is a controller. Then the constructor function starts and loads the parent controller class methods. The `assessme` function expects two variables `$name` and `$password`. CI (from version 1.5 onwards) automatically assigns any URL segments after the second as parameters, so `fred` and `12345` will become the `$name` and `$password` parameters, respectively.

Also, if those parameters are not received we give them a default value, which is empty for the following example, but at least the variables are initialized. Why do that? To prevent some errors, for example, if you go to:

`http://localhost/codeigniter/start/assessme`

Without the parameters at the end, you would get this error:

```
Severity: Warning
Message: Missing argument 1 for Start::assessme()
```

But with the variables initialized with a default value that won't happen. So, if we type the URL on the previous page, the function `mainpage()`, in the controller, will be called. We'll set this method later, in the `start` controller (if not, the code will just die).

For those who are more used to procedural PHP than OO classes, please note that a function within a class has to be addressed as `$this->xxxx`. So, if we are calling the `mainpage()` function of the start controller from another function within the `start` controller, we have to call `$this->mainpage()`. Otherwise, CI won't be able to find it.

Of course, it's unlikely that anyone would type in a URL such as:

`http://www.mysite.com.index.php/start/assessme/fred/12345.`

They will just enter `http://www.mysite.com`, and expect the site to sort out all the internal navigation. So, let's start that now.

Often, the first thing you see on a site is a login form. So let's prepare one of those. First, add a new function to your start controller. You want the site to default to this function, so you'll call it `index()`:

```
function index()
{
  $this->load->helper('form');
  $data['mytitle'] = "My site";
  $data['base'] = $this->config->item('base_url');
  $data['css'] = $this->config->item('css');
  $data['mytitle'] = "A website to monitor other websites";
```

```php
$data['text'] = "Please log in here!";
$this->load->view('entrypage', $data);
}
```

This is calling the `entrypage` view. The view includes a form, and the form allows the user to submit a password and username. HTML forms must point to a page that will handle the data in the `$_POST` array. We've already written the function in our `start` controller to receive it — `assessme()`. Our `views/entrypage.php` may be like this:

```php
<?php
echo form_open('start/assessme');
echo form_label('Name: ', 'username');
echo form_input('username', '');
echo form_label('Password: ', 'password');
echo form_password('password', '');
echo form_submit('submit', 'Send!');
echo form_close();
```

Of course, it needs some styling, but for now, it will help us continue with our site's development. We will also have to change the `assessme()` function a little, in order to take the variables from the `$_POST` array:

```php
function assessme()
{
  $name = $_POST['username'];
  $password = $_POST['password'];
  if($name == 'fred' && $password == '12345')
  {
    $this->mainpage();
  }
}
```

But there's little point in having a function that has only one username/password combination. We need some way to look it up in a database. To make the structure more modular, we are going to hand it over to another function — `_checkme()`.

So, as you will see, `assessme()` will call `_checkme()`. The `_checkme()` function does some sort of test on the password and username (we haven't written that yet) and returns TRUE or FALSE to `assessme()`. If it's TRUE, `assessme()` calls another function, `mainpage()`, which returns a view.

Notice the advantage of the modular approach. Each function has a role. If we need to alter the way in which the system checks a password, we will only have to alter the `_checkme()` function. If we need to alter the page it displays on a correct response, then we go to the `mainpage()` function.

Let's just look at the structure of the code and the way the sections interact. Note that in order to make the example simple to follow, we are not cleaning the input from our form. Of course, this leaves your code open to problems, but at least CI's form class automatically escapes entered data.

```
//receives the username and password from the POST array
function assessme()
{
  $username =      $_POST['username'];
  $password =      $_POST['password'];
  //calls the checkme function to see if the inputs are OK
  if($this->_checkme($username, $password)==TRUE)
  {
    //if the inputs are OK, calls the mainpage function
    $this->mainpage();
  }
   //if they are not OK, goes back to the index function, which re-
    presents the log-in screen
  else
  {
    $this->index();
  }
}
//called with a u/n and p/w, this checks them against some list. For
the moment, there's just one option. Returns TRUE or FALSE
function _checkme($username='', $password='')
{
  if($username == 'fred' && $password == '12345')
  {
    return TRUE;
  }
  else{return FALSE;}
}
```

On lines four and five, `assessme()` receives the output of the form from the `$_POST` array. This will contain something like:

```
[username] => fred [password] => 12345
```

The `assessme()` function passes these two variables to the `_checkme()` function. This simply tests if they are `fred` and `12345` respectively, and if they are, it returns TRUE. Obviously, on a real site this would be more complex. You would probably do a database lookup for valid username/password pairs. Making it a separate function means you can test the rest of the code now, and improve the `_checkme()` function later, at your leisure.

If the username and password are a valid combination, the `assessme()` function calls the `mainpage()` function, which lets you in to the site. Otherwise, it goes back to the `index()` function, that is, the login form again.

The next problem we have is how to manage states. In other words, how to recognize the logged in user, when he/she makes another page request.

Security/Sessions: Using another CI library class

If we want to build a session mechanism that will keep unwanted users from accessing our site, how many lines of code will it take?

The Internet works by a series of requests. Your browser makes a request to a server to view a particular page. The server passes the page back to your browser and you can view it. Now you need to make another request, so you click on a hyperlink, which makes a request to the server, and so on.

The Internet is stateless, that is, each request made by your browser to another website is treated as a separate event. The HTTP protocol, which underlies the Internet, has no direct way of linking your request to any other requests made by you. It's as if you were in a restaurant—the waiter takes your order and brings you the meal, but then forgets all about you. That's fine, until he needs to bring you a bill, give you a special discount, or simply remember that you wanted him to ring for a taxi for you after you've finished your meal.

If you want your website to connect one page request with another, you have to manage the state of the relationship. Somehow you need to let the website know that some requests are coming from the same browser, and should be treated as special.

PHP offers two ways of managing state—using cookies or a specially generated session ID. The PHP session function automatically checks if the browser is accepting cookies; if not it uses the session ID method, which is passed using the URL.

Cookies are small strings of data that websites pass back to any browser that accesses the site. The browser automatically stores it. Once the cookie is there the website can check for it, when the browser attempts to access the site next time. If it finds the right cookie, it can use the information in it to configure itself appropriately. This may include blocking certain pages from unauthorized users or adding personal information. In our restaurant analogy, the waiter will leave your bill on the table, and next time he sees you, it will remind him that you are entitled for 15% discount, so he can take that into account when working out your bill.

Some people set their browser such that it does not accept cookies. PHP offers an alternative approach. Each time a browser requests access, the site generates a random string called the "session ID", and returns it to the browser. Browsers then add this to the URL when they make their next request so that the site can recognize the browser. (Instead of the waiter leaving the bill on your table, you make him carry it back and forth with him to the kitchen.)

CI has a `session` class that handles much of the same stuff. In fact, it reduces a lot of code to one line. We saw in the previous chapter that CI has a wide range of "library classes", which simplify most of the common tasks that a website deals with. If you want to use the functionality inside a class from within your controller or model, you must remember to first load the class into the controller or model.

A few classes, such as `config` are always automatically loaded, which is why we haven't loaded it in any of our code so far.

You load a library class simply using:

```
$this->load->library('newclass');
```

Put the above line in the constructor of your controller or model. If you think you will use a `library` class in every controller, you can load it automatically just as the `config` class is loaded. Go to the `/application/config/autoload` file, and add the name of the class you want in the following line:

```
$autoload['libraries'] = array();
```

Now, it looks like this:

```
$autoload['libraries'] = array('newclass','anotherclass');
```

The library class that we're going to use first is the `session` class, which helps you to maintain state, and identify users. It's quite simple to do this. Here's our enlarged `assessme()` function from the `start` controller with the new line highlighted:

```
function assessme()
{
  $this->load->library('session');
  $username  =    $_POST['username'];
  $password  =    $_POST['password'];

  if($this->_checkme($username, $password)==TRUE)
  {
    $this->mainpage();
  }
  else{$this->index();}
}
```

> We've loaded the `session` library at the start of the function, but normally, you should load it in the controller's constructor so that it is loaded for all the other functions in this class.

Loading the session class immediately gives you a huge chunk of functionality in exchange for the one line of code. It will automatically read, create, and update sessions. Well, to be frank, it's not quite one line of code. You have to make some changes to the `config` file first to tell the `session` class what you want it to do.

Check your `applications/config/config.php` file, and you'll find a section like this:

```
----------------------------------------------------------------
-----
| Session Variables
|---------------------------------------------------------------
------
|
| 'session_cookie_name' = the name you want for the cookie
| 'encrypt_sess_cookie' = TRUE/FALSE (boolean).  Whether to encrypt
                          the cookie
| 'session_expiration' = the number of SECONDS you want the session
                         to last.
|   by default sessions last 7200 seconds (two hours).  Set to zero for
no expiration.
'time_to_update' = how many seconds between CI refreshing Session
                   Information
|
```

```
*/
$config['sess_cookie_name'] = 'ci_session';
$config['sess_expiration'] = 7200;
$config['sess_encrypt_cookie'] = FALSE;
$config['sess_use_database'] = FALSE;
$config['sess_table_name'] = 'ci_sessions';
$config['sess_match_ip'] = FALSE;
$config['sess_match_useragent'] = TRUE;
$config['sess_time_to_update'] = 300;
```

For now, make sure `sess_use_database` is set to FALSE. Now, every time your users connect, the site will save a cookie on their machine, containing the following information:

- A unique Session ID generated by CI — not to be confused with a PHP session ID string, which isn't generated in this instance — is a random string created by CI for this session
- The user's IP address
- The user's user agent data (the first 50 characters of the browser data string)
- Timestamps for "last activity"

If you set `sess_encrypt_cookie` to FALSE, you can read the cookie on your browser and see what has been saved (it's partly encoded, but you can make out). For example, `ip_address%22%3Bs%3A9%3A%22127.0.0.1%22%3Bs%3A10%3A%22`, includes the user's URL, in this case it is `127.0.0.1`. If you set it to TRUE, the cookie is encrypted with a string of random characters. Your browser can't even distinguish between sections of the cookie, which means the user can't meaningfully alter or even read it .

In order to store confidential information — for example , user passwords — we should set `sess_encrypt_cookie` to TRUE.

If you want to learn more about encryption, you can check:
`http://www.codeigniter.com/user_guide/libraries/sessions.html`
And, of course: `http://www.codeigniter.com/user_guide/libraries/encryption.html`.

When the user makes another page request, the site can check whether the session ID has been saved on the user's browser as part of the cookie. If it has, you know they are part of an existing session. If not, you know they are a new session. Provided you remember to load the CI `session` class on all the other controllers as well, CI will make the same checks for them too. All you have to do is tell each controller how to behave if there isn't a cookie.

Turning sessions into security

This in itself doesn't make a security system. Anyone who visits the site starts a session. The code just records whether they are a new visitor or not. One way of preventing unauthorized access to some pages involves adding something else to the cookie if they are logged in, so we can test for it. Then, if they enter the correct username and password once, it will be recorded in the cookie. The session mechanism will find it when it checks for cookies, as each new request comes through. We can then test for their authorization, and if authorized, the site will let them in to protected pages for the rest of the session. They won't have to keep on logging in.

Adding something to the cookie is easy. In my `assessme()` controller, once I have decided that the password and username are acceptable, I add:

```
if($this->_checkme($username, $password)==TRUE)
{
    $this->session->set_userdata('status','OK');
    $this->mainpage();
}
```

This way we are adding one single value. If we need to add more, we can add them one-by-one in the same way or by using an array, for example:

```
$data = array(
            'status' => 'OK',
            'othervalue' => 'value',
            'anotherone' => 'value'
            );
$this->session->set_userdata($data);
```

Now, whenever the password/username combination is acceptable, `assessme()` will add the `status` field with the value `OK` to the cookie, and we can start each controller with this code:

```
//remember to load the library!

$this->load->library('session');

//look for a 'status' variable in the contents of the session cookie
```

```
$status = $this->session->userdata('status');

//if it's not there, make the user log in

if( $status != 'OK')
{
   //function to present a login page again…
}

//otherwise, go ahead with the code
```

Also we can separate that, and create a check method, for example:

```
function _checksession()
{
  $this->load->library('session');
  $this->load->helper('url');
  $status = $this->session->userdata('status');
  if( $status != 'OK')
  {
    redirect('start/index');
  }
}
```

As you see it's preceded by a "_" so it can only be called from other class methods and not from a URL. How would we use it? Very easily, using:

```
function demo()
{
  $this->_checksession();
  echo "Function code would be here";
}
```

This would call the check method, and if you are not logged in you will be redirected to the login page. Otherwise the method will continue.

We have used `redirect('start/index');` instead of `$this->index();`. So, you can copy and paste this code to other controllers; it would continue to work without the need to be edited. Here, you have the basis of a security fence around your site. You can easily make it more elaborate. For instance, if some users have higher access levels than others, you can store a level in the status variable rather than OK—you can use this in conditional tests to control access to functions.

Saving this sort of data in a cookie is frowned upon, because the user can easily read the cookie on their machine between visits to your site. Given that CI's session class encrypts it, you're fairly safe. However, an alternative is to create a database of users, and after you have logged in, write OK to the database against that session ID. For subsequent accesses, you check the session ID (in the cookie) against the database, to check whether it has OK or a level against it.

It is very simple to save the session data in your database. We are going to do it. First, create the database table. If you're using MySQL, use the following SQL query:

```
CREATE TABLE IF NOT EXISTS  `ci_sessions` (
session_id varchar(40) DEFAULT '0' NOT NULL,
ip_address varchar(16) DEFAULT '0' NOT NULL,
user_agent varchar(50) NOT NULL,
last_activity int(10) unsigned DEFAULT 0 NOT NULL,
user_data text NOT NULL,
PRIMARY KEY (session_id)
);
```

Then, alter the connection parameters in the `system/application/config/database.php` file to tell CI where the database is. See Chapter 4, for more details on databases.

If all works, you will see the data build up in your database table, as you connect and disconnect. If you have sessions stored in a database table, as each user connects to your site, the site tests for a cookie. If it finds one, it reads the session ID, and matches it against the session IDs stored in the database.

You now have a robust session mechanism and all of this came from one line of code! Just one caveat—the native PHP session class can cope with users who turn off cookies on their browsers. Instead of storing a cookie, it adds session data to the URL string. The CI class does not do this. If the user has turned off cookies, then he/she can't log on to your site. Whether this is a problem for you or not depends on the people you expect to use your site.

But what about logout?

That's very easy to achieve too, to destroy a session we have to write only:

```
$this->session->sess_destroy();
```

What if we don't want to destroy the complete session, and we want to remove certain variables from the session, then use:

```
$this->session->unset_userdata('status');
```

Want to know more about CodeIgniter sessions? Take a look at this:

http://codeigniter.com/user_guide/libraries/sessions.html

Isn't there anything already built?

Of course, there is. In fact there are various libraries out there ready to be used, for example:

- http://codeigniter.com/wiki/auth/
- http://codeigniter.com/wiki/EasyAuth/
- http://codeigniter.com/wiki/SimpleLoginSecure/

The SimpleLoginSecure is very easy to use, and is the one we are going to see in this example. First download it from the Wiki, unzip it, and copy the unzipped contents to the application/libraries folder. We need to do just one more thing in order to use the library, we need to create this table:

```
CREATE TABLE `users` (
                `user_id` int(10) unsigned NOT NULL
                auto_increment,
                `user_email` varchar(255) NOT NULL default '',
                `user_pass` varchar(60) NOT NULL default '',
                `user_date` datetime NOT NULL default '0000-00-
                00 00:00:00',
                `user_modified` datetime NOT NULL default
                '0000-00-00 00:00:00',
                `user_last_login` datetime NULL default NULL,
                PRIMARY KEY (`user_id`),
                UNIQUE KEY `user_email` (`user_email`)
                )
DEFAULT CHARSET=utf8;
```

 This library makes use of the CI session and database libraries, so we will need to load them in order to use them.

We can also modify the application/config/autoload.php file. This change is not required, but if we are going to use the library quite often it's a good idea:

```
$autoload['libraries'] = array('database', 'SimpleLoginSecure',
                               'session');
```

If you don't want the library to be autoloaded, you can also load it as usual, using:

```
$this->load->library('SimpleLoginSecure');
```

 The first time we use the library there won't be any users, and as the password is encrypted and stored it's not that easy to insert a user with the help of phpMyAdmin. One thing we can do is run the following line of code in any of our controller's functions that has loaded the library:

```
$this->simpleloginsecure->create('demo_user', 'demo_password');
```

This will create a user, and if we don't pass the third parameter as false, it will also log in the created user.

Our next step, after creating at least one user, would be to prepare our `application/views/entrypage.php` file, which will look this way:

```php
<?php
echo form_open('start/assessme');
echo form_label('Name: ', 'username');
echo form_input('username', '');
echo form_label('Password: ', 'password');
echo form_password('password', '');
echo form_submit('submit', 'Send!');
echo form_close();
```

Once we have the view prepared, we need to work in the controller. We only need to change the `assessme()` function of our `start` controller:

```php
function assessme()
  {
    $this->simpleloginsecure->logout();
    if(!empty($_POST['username']) && !empty($_POST['password']))
    {
      $this->simpleloginsecure->login($_POST['username'],
                                      $_POST['password']);
    }
    if($this->session->userdata('logged_in'))
    {
      $this->mainpage();
    }
    else
    {
      $this->index();
    }
  }
```

Let's see what we are doing. First we call the logout method of the `simpleloginsecure` library:

```
$this->simpleloginsecure->logout();
```

This way we make sure that, if there is some active session it will be destroyed. If we don't do this, there is a possibility of failing to log in a user; the `if` statement can be true, if there is a previous active session. Next we try to log in the user, with the data sent from our form:

```
$this->simpleloginsecure->login($_POST['username'],
$_POST['password']);
```

After this is done, we need to check if the user was logged in:

```
if($this->session->userdata('logged_in'))
```

This way we know if the user was logged in or not, so we can send him/her to our restricted area, or back to the login page. Now, we can make some changes to inform our users about their log status, for example, we can change our controller's `assesme()` function this way:

```
if($this->session->userdata('logged_in'))
{
  $this->load->helper('url');
  $this->session->set_flashdata('login', 'You have logged into the
                                restricted area');
  redirect('start/mainpage', 'refresh');
}
```

Instead of calling the `mainpage()` function we are doing three things. First, we load the `url` helper, then we create a `flashdata` variable, then redirect the page, and call the `mainpage` method in the `start` controller. This method can be expressed like this:

```
function mainpage()
{
  $this->load->view('success');
}
```

For example, in our `success.php` file, in the view, we place:

```
<?php
echo $this->session->flashdata('login');
```

This will present the `flashdata` value to our visitors screen, showing them a message about their log status.

If we don't redirect, and try to load the success view in the `assessme()` function, the `flashdata` variable won't show as `flashdata` variables are not available until the next server request after creating them, as you can see here:

`http://codeigniter.com/user_guide/libraries/sessions.html`

Now you may think that, although the `assesme()` function is helping us log in our users, it's not really protecting other functions. Any one can point his/her browser to `http://localhost/codeigniter/start/mainpage` and get the page even if they are not logged in. Don't worry, we are going to correct that in a moment. We are going to create another function in our start controller:

```
function _check_status()
{
  if(!$this->session->userdata('logged_in'))
  {
    $this->load->helper('url');
    redirect('start/assessme', 'refresh');
  }
}
```

This function checks the user's log status and, if not logged in redirects the user to the `assessme()` function, where he/she will be presented with the login form.

Remember that the "_" means, this function will be only available to the other functions in the controller, and cannot be called from the browser.

Now, every time we need to know if a user is logged in, we only need to call the `check_status` function. If the user is not logged in, he/she will be redirected to the login form. For example:

```
function mainpage()
{
  $this->_check_status();
  $this->load->view('success');
}
```

As you can see this is our `mainpage()` function, with the `check_status` call. Now, we have seen almost all the functions that this login library offers; the only one that is left is the `delete` function:

```
$this->simpleloginsecure->delete($user_id);
```

With this line of code we can delete the user reference by the number passed as the first parameter, that's all. You can get more info about the library looking at this page:

```
http://codeigniter.com/wiki/SimpleLoginSecure/
```

And, of course, by taking a look into its code.

Security

Notice that the `session` class automatically stores information about the IP address and user agent of the user making a page request. You can use these to give additional security.

There are two settings you can change in your `config` file for additional security:

- `sess_match_ip`: If you set this to `true`, CI will attempt to match the user's IP address when it reads the session data. This is to prevent users from "hijacking" a log in. However, some servers (both ISPs and large corporate servers) may issue requests from the same end user over different IP addresses. If you set this value to `true`, you may exclude them unintentionally.

- `sess_match_useragent`: If you set this to `true`, CI will try to match the user agent when reading the session data. This means that someone who tried to hijack a session would have to ensure that the `user_agent` setting returned by his/her system matched with that of a genuine user. It makes hijacking a little more difficult.

CI also has a `user_agent` class, which you load like this:

```
$this->load->library('user_agent');
```

Once loaded, you can ask it to return various information about any agent who is browsing your site. For instance, the type of browser and operating system, and in particular whether it is a browser, mobile, or robot. If you want to list the robots that visit your site, you might do it like this:

```
$fred = $this->agent->is_robot();
if ($fred == TRUE)
  {
    $agent = $this->agent->agent_string();
    //add code here to store or analyze the name the user agent is
    //returning
  }
```

The class works by loading and comparing against the array of user agents, browsers, and robots, contained in the other `config` files: `system/application/config/user_agent`.

If you wished, you could easily develop this to enable your site to lock out certain types of browsers or robots. However, remember that it is easy for an attacker to write robot user agents, and have them return whatever `user_agent` string they want. So, they can easily masquerade as common browsers. Many robots, including ones like Googlebot listed in CI's `user_agent` array are well-behaved. This means that if you set your `robots.txt` file to exclude them, they won't trespass. There is no easy way of excluding robots that don't obey this file, unless you know their names in advance.

In CI, the session mechanism stores the IP address of the requesting site. You can use this to operate a blacklist of sites and retrieve the IP address from the session like this:

```
//look for an 'ip_address' variable
$ip = $this->input->ip_address();
```

Then you can test the `$ip` variable against the blacklist. You can also develop CI's session mechanism to limit the damage from repeated requests. For example, denial of service attacks, where a robot is set to overload your site by repeatedly asking for pages. You could use this mechanism to handle "dictionary attacks", where a robot is set up to call your login form repeatedly. It tries hundreds or thousands of password/username combinations until it finds the right one.

You can do this because CI's sessions class stores the `last_activity` time for each session. Each time a page is requested, you can check when the last request was made by this user. One time interval doesn't tell you much, but you can set the system to store more data and develop usage patterns. A dictionary attack relies on getting a speedy reply, otherwise it will take too long. If you detect too many requests in rapid succession, you could either end the session or slow down the response.

Summary

We've outlined an application that we'd like to build, and attacked the first issues that almost any application raises—session management and (if we want to protect parts of our site from unauthorized users) security.

To do this, we've looked at the CI `sessions` class in detail: how it creates session records, and leaves cookies on the visitor's browser. It can then look for cookies when subsequent requests are made. You can use the response to control the way your site responds.

We have also taken a look at some CodeIgniter community libraries. Why don't you go and take a look at the others that there are in the Wiki?

`http://codeigniter.com/wiki/Special:Titles`

See you in the next chapter!

7
CodeIgniter and Objects

In this chapter we will see how CodeIgniter actually works, "under the hood". This chapter will help us understand why things happen in certain ways, as opposed to just knowing that they do.

Objects confused us, when we started using CodeIgniter. Coming to CodeIgniter through PHP 4, which is a procedural language, and not an object-oriented (OO) language. We duly looked up objects and methods, properties and inheritance, and encapsulation, but our early attempts to write CI code were plagued by the error message "Call to a member function on a non-object". We saw it so often that we were thinking of having it printed on a T-shirt.

To save the world from a lot of boring T-shirts, this chapter covers the way in which CI uses objects, and the different ways you can write and use your own objects. Incidentally, we've used "variables/properties", and "methods/functions" interchangeably, as CI and PHP often do. You write "functions" in your controllers, for instance, when an OO purist would call them "methods". You define class "variables" when the purist would call them "properties".

Object-oriented programming

We assume that you have basic knowledge of OOP. You may have learned it as an afterthought to "normal" PHP 4. PHP 4 is not an OO language, though some OO functionality has been stacked on to it. PHP 5 is much better, with an underlying engine that was written from the ground up with OO in mind.

You can do most of the basics in PHP 4, and CI manages to do everything it needs internally in either language. The key thing to remember—when an OO program is running, there is always one current object (but only one). Objects may call each other or hand over control to each other, in which case the current object changes, but only one of them can be current at any time. The current object defines the **scope**, in other words, the variables (properties) and methods (functions) that are available to the program at that moment. So it's important to know and control the current object.

PHP, being a mixture of functional and OO programming, also offers the possibility where no object is current. You can start off with a functional program, call an object, let it take charge for a while, and then return control to the program. Luckily, CI takes care of this for you.

The CI super-object

CI works by building one **super-object**—it runs the entire program as one big object, in order to eliminate scoping issues. When you start CI, a complex chain of events occurs. If you set your CI installation to create a log (in `/codeigniter/application/config/config.php` set `$config['log_threshold'] = 4;` value. This will generate a log file in `/www/CI_system/logs/`), you'll see something like this:

```
 1 DEBUG - 2006-10-03 08:56:39 --> Config Class Initialized
 2 DEBUG - 2006-10-03 08:56:39 --> No URI present. Default controller
                                   set.
 3 DEBUG - 2006-10-03 08:56:39 --> Router Class Initialized
 4 DEBUG - 2006-10-03 08:56:39 --> Output Class Initialized
 5 DEBUG - 2006-10-03 08:56:39 --> Input Class Initialized
 6 DEBUG - 2006-10-03 08:56:39 --> Global POST and COOKIE data
                                   sanitized
 7 DEBUG - 2006-10-03 08:56:39 --> URI Class Initialized
 8 DEBUG - 2006-10-03 08:56:39 --> Language Class Initialized
 9 DEBUG - 2006-10-03 08:56:39 --> Loader Class Initialized
10 DEBUG - 2006-10-03 08:56:39 --> Controller Class Initialized
11 DEBUG - 2006-10-03 08:56:39 --> Helpers loaded: security
12 DEBUG - 2006-10-03 08:56:40 --> Scripts loaded: errors
13 DEBUG - 2006-10-03 08:56:40 --> Scripts loaded: boilerplate
14 DEBUG - 2006-10-03 08:56:40 --> Helpers loaded: url
15 DEBUG - 2006-10-03 08:56:40 --> Database Driver Class Initialized
16 DEBUG - 2006-10-03 08:56:40 --> Model Class Initialized
```

At start up, that is, each time a page request is received over the Internet—CI goes through the same procedure. You can trace the log through the CI files:

1. The `index.php` file receives a page request. The URL may indicate which controller is required, if not, CI has a default controller (line 2). The `index.php` file makes some basic checks and calls the `codeigniter.php` file (`\codeigniter\codeigniter.php`).

   ```
   require_once BASEPATH.'codeigniter/CodeIgniter'.EXT;
   ```

2. The `codeigniter.php` file instantiates the `Config`, `Router`, `Input`, `URL`, and other such, classes (see lines 1, and 3 to 9). These are called the **base** classes—you rarely interact directly with them, but they underlie almost everything CI does.

```
/*
 * ---------------------------------------------------------
 *   Instantiate the base classes
 * ---------------------------------------------------------
 */
$CFG =& load_class('Config');
$URI =& load_class('URI');
$RTR =& load_class('Router');
$OUT =& load_class('Output');
```

3. The file `codeigniter.php` tests to see the version of PHP it is running on, and calls `Base4` or `Base5` (`/codeigniter/Base4.php` or `codeigniter/Base5.php`).

```
if (floor(phpversion()) < 5)
{
    load_class('Loader', FALSE);
    require(BASEPATH.'codeigniter/Base4'.EXT);
}
else
{
    require(BASEPATH.'codeigniter/Base5'.EXT);
}
```

4. The above snippet creates an object—one which ensures that a class has only one instance. Each has a public `&get_instance()` function. Note the `&`—this is assignment by reference. So, if you assign using `&get_instance()` method, it assigns to the single running instance of the class. In other words, it points to the same **pigeonhole**. So, instead of setting up lot of new objects, you start building one super-object, which contains everything related to the framework.

```
function &get_instance()
{
    return CI_Base::get_instance();
}
```

5. A security check,

```
/*
 * ----------------------------------------------------
 *   Security check
 * ----------------------------------------------------
 *
 *   None of the functions in the app controller or the
 *   loader class can be called via the URI, nor can
 *   controller functions that begin with an underscore
 */
$class = $RTR->fetch_class();
$method = $RTR->fetch_method();
if ( !class_exists($class)
    OR $method == 'controller'
    OR strncmp($method, '_', 1) == 0
    OR in_array(strtolower($method), array_map('strtolower',
                get_class_methods('Controller')))
    )
{
  show_404("{$class}/{$method}");
}
```

6. The file, `codeigniter.php` instantiates the controller that was requested, or a default controller (line 10). The new class is called `$CI`.

```
$CI = new $class();
```

7. The function specified in the URL (or a default) is then called and life, as we know it, starts to wake up and happen. Depending on what you wrote in your controller, CI will initialize the classes you need, and "include" functional scripts you asked for. So, in the log, the `model` class is initialized (line 16). The `boilerplate` script, which is also shown in the log (line 13), is the one we wrote to contain standard chunks of text. It's a `.php` file, saved in the folder called `scripts`. It's not a class — just a set of functions. If you were writing pure PHP you might use `include` or `require` to bring it into the namespace — CI needs to use its own `load` function to bring it into the super-object.

The concept of **namespace** or scope is crucial here. When you declare a variable, array, object, and so on, PHP holds the variable name in its memory and assigns a further block of memory to hold its contents. However, problems might arise if you define two variables with the same name. (In a complex site, this is easily done.) For this reason, PHP has several set of rules. Some of them are as listed:

- Each function has its own namespace or scope, and variables defined within a function are usually **local** to it. Outside the function, they are meaningless.

- You can declare **global** variables, which are held in a special global namespace and are available throughout the program.

- Objects have their own namespaces—variables exist inside the object as long as the object exists, and can only be referenced by using the object.

So, `$variable`, `global $variable`, and `$this->variable` are three different things.

 Remember, `$variable` and `global $variable` can't be used in the same scope. So, inside a function you will have to decide if you want to use `$variable` or `global $variable`.

Particularly before OO, this could lead to all sort of confusions—you may have too many variables in your namespace (so that conflicting names overwrite each other). You may also find that some variables are just not accessible from whatever scope you happen to be.

Copying by reference

You may have noticed the function `&get_instance()` in the previous section. This is to ensure that, as the variables change, the variables of the original class also change. As assignment by reference can be confusing, so here's a short explanation. We're all familiar with simple copying in PHP:

```
$one = 1;
$two = $one;
echo $two;
```

The previous snippet produces 1, because `$two` is a copy of `$one`. However, suppose you reassign `$one`:

```
$one = 1;
$two = $one;
$one = 5;
echo $two;
```

This code still produces $two = 1$, because changes made to $one after assigning $two have not been reflected in $two. This was a one-off assignment of the value that happened to be in variable $one at that time, to a new variable $two. Once that is done, the two variables lead separate lives (in just the same way if we alter $two, $one doesn't change).

In effect, PHP creates two pigeonholes—called $one and $two. A separate value lives in each. You may, on any occasion, make the values equal, but after that each does its own work. PHP also allows **copying by reference**. If you add just a simple & to line 2 of the snippet as shown:

```
$one = 1;
$two =& $one;
$one = 5;
echo $two;
```

The code now echoes 5, the change we made to $one is reflected in $two. Changing the = to =& in the second line means that the assignment is "by reference". It looks as if there was only one pigeonhole, which has two names ($one and $two). Whatever happens to the contents of the pigeonhole is reflected in both $one and $two, as if they were just different names for the same variables.

The principle works for objects as well as simple string variables. You can copy or clone an object using the = operator in PHP 4. Or you can clone keyword in PHP, in which case you make a simple one-off new copy, which then leads an independent life. You can also assign one to the other by reference, so the two objects point to each other. Any changes made to one will also happen to the other. Again, think of them as two different names for the same thing.

Adding your own code to the CI super-object

You contribute to the process of building the super-object, as you write your own code. Suppose you have written a model called status, which contains two class variables of its own, $one and $two. It also consists of a constructor that assigns the values to $one and $two respectively. Let's examine what happens when you load this model.

The instance class includes a variable load, which is a copy (by reference) of the object ci_load. So, the code you write in your controller is:

```
$this->load->model($status)
```

In other words, take the class variable `load` of the current CI super-class (`this`) and use its method `model`. This actually references the `model` function in the `loader` class (`/CI_system/libraries/loader.php`) and that says:

```
function model($model, $name = '')
{
  if ($model == '')
  return;
  $obj =& get_instance();
  $obj->_ci_load_model($model, $name);
}
```

 The `$name` variable in this code is there in case you want to load your model under an alias.

As you can see, the model is loaded by reference into the `instance` class. As `get_instance()` returns an instance to the CI super-object, we're always using the same CI object, instead of creating copies of it.

 Note that if you use `get_instance()` inside class constructors and you are using PHP 4, you may have problems, as PHP 4 can't reference the CI super-object until the class is completely instantiated.

If you run the controller again the CI super-object will include an object called `$status` that includes the class variables you defined in your original `status` model, assigned to the values we set.

So we are gradually building one big CI super-object, which allows you to use any of its methods and variables without worrying much about where they come from and what namespace they are in.

To use the methods of (say) a model, you must first load the model in your controller:

```
$this->load->model('model_name');
```

This makes the model available in our controller, and we can use it through the pseudo-variable `$this->`. We then call a function of that `model_name` class from the controller, like this:

```
$this->model_name->function();
```

And off you go.

Problems with the CI super-object

PHP 4 handles objects less elegantly than PHP 5. You may have problems trying to call `get_instance()` inside class constructors, as PHP 4 will have trouble referencing the CI super-object before the class is fully instantiated. Also you can find yourself trying to work with an object that isn't available.

Let's look at these problems in turn. You remember the T-shirt we mentioned earlier—"Call to a member function on a non-object". This annoying error message often means that you tried to use a function from a class (say `model_name` class) that you wrote, but forgot to load. In other words, you wrote:

```
$this->model_name->function();
```

But forgot to precede it by:

```
$this->load->model('model_name');
```

Or some variation of this—for instance, you loaded the model inside one function of a class; this loads the model, but only inside that function. If you try to use its methods from inside another function, albeit in the same class, you get the error. It's usually best to load models, and so on, from the class constructor function so that they are available to all the other functions in the class.

The problem can also be more subtle. If you write your own classes you may wish to use them to access the database, or look up something in your `config` files, in other words, give them access to something that is a part of the CI super-object. Unless, your new class is a controller, a model, or a view, it doesn't get built into the CI super-object. So, you can't write things inside your new class like this:

```
$this->config->item('base_url');
```

This just won't work, because to your new class, `$this->` means itself, not the CI super-object. Instead, you have to build your new class into the super-class by calling the `instance` class (sounds familiar?), using another variable name (usually `$obj`).

```
$obj =& get_instance();
```

Now you can call the CI super-class as:

```
$obj->config->item('base_url');
```

This time it works.

However, as you write your new class, remember that it still has its own identity. Let's use a short outline example to make this clear.

You want to write a library class that prepares a URL based on the location of the server that requests the page. So, you write some code to look up the geographic location of the IP address that is calling your page (using a library like the NetGeo class available at http://www.phpclasses.org/browse/package/514.html). Then, using a switch function, you select one of the several alternative functions, and you serve up an English page to US or British requests, a German page to German or Austrian requests, and so on. Now, the full URL to your country-specific page will be made up of two parts—the base URL of your site (www.mysite.com/index.php/), plus the URL of the individual page (mypage/germanversion).

You need to get the base URL of the site from CI's config file. The second half of the URL is being generated by a switch statement in the constructor of your new class—if this client is in Germany, serve up the German page function, and so on. As this is being done in the constructor calls, you need to put the result into a class variable, so it can be used in other functions within the same class. This means:

- The first half of your URL comes from the CI config file, which can only be referenced through the super-object, to which you have linked using $obj =& get_instance(). In other words, you call it using $obj->config->item('base_url');.

- But the second half of your URL is generated inside the constructor of your new class and assigned to a class variable, $base. It has nothing to do with the CI super-object; it belongs to your new class, and is referenced as $this->base.

This can lead to using both $this-> and $obj-> references in the same line, for example:

```
class my_new_class
{
  var $base;
  My_new_class()
  {
    $obj =& get_instance();
    // geolocation code here, returning a value through a switch
    statement
    //this value is assigned to $local_url
    $this->base = $obj->config->item('base_url');
    $this->base = $local_url;
  }
```

Getting these confused is another fruitful source of, "Call to a member function on a non-object". In our example, you'd get this error message if you tried to call either `$obj->base`, or `$this->config->item()`.

Turning to the remaining problem, you can't call methods of one controller from inside another. *Why would you want to do this?* Well, it depends, in one application, we wrote a series of self-test functions inside each controller. If we called `$this->selftest()` inside the controller, it did various useful tests. But it seems against the principle of programming—the virtue of laziness—to have to repeatedly call the self-test method in each controller separately. We tried to write a function, in one controller that would go through all the controllers, call the self-test method in each, and amalgamate all the results, while we stared out of the window. After all that it would give you a comprehensive report in exchange for one click. Alas, no. It can't be done that way, we have to think of another way to do it.

As a general rule, if you have a piece of code that maybe needed by more than one controller, put it in a helper, plugin, or library so you can load and use it wherever you need. Also we have the option of extending CI base `libraries`, so you can add functions you need to these `libraries`. It is very easy to achieve this—you have to create a file with the same name as that of the class you want to extend, in the `libraries` folder, with `MY_` preceding the filename. So, to extend a base class we would go to `application/libraries/MY_Baseclass.php`.

Inside the file we would create the class this way:

```
class MY_Baseclass extends CI_Baseclass
{
}
```

In the constructor, however, we will make reference to the base class:

```
class MY_Baseclass extends CI_Baseclass
{

  function My_Baseclass()
  {
    parent::CI_Baseclass();
  }
}
```

This way we can easily add functions that we need to CI base classes. You may think that this is very useful but doesn't help us in the problem of having functions available throughout our application. No problem, we can achieve this by extending the base controller class—the class from which all of our controllers are extended. This is quite easy, but has a few steps; these steps are fully covered here:

```
http://codeigniter.com/wiki/MY_Controller_-_how_to_extend_the_CI_
Controller/
```

Summary

We've looked at the way CI builds up one super-object to make sure that all the methods and variables you need are automatically available to you without you having to manage them and worry about their scope.

CI makes extensive use of assignment by reference, instantiating one class after another and linking them all together so that you can access them through the super-class. We've also looked at how you can write your own classes and still have access to the CI framework.

Also, we looked at a few problems that can arise, particularly if you're not used to OO programs, and seen a few solutions to them. Lastly we looked at how we can extend core classes and even the controller class.

If you want to go deeper into extending CI it is recommended to take a look at these links, they will be of great help:

- `http://codeigniter.com/user_guide/general/
  creating_libraries.html`
- `http://codeigniter.com/user_guide/general/hooks.html`
- `http://codeigniter.com/wiki/PEAR_integration/`

8
Improving Our Application with Third-Party Code

In this chapter, we have something different for you; we are going to see some examples of code from other programmers that you can use in your application. We hope it's a very entertaining chapter, so we can get some rest from theory before going ahead.

We've found these examples in CodeIgniter's Wiki at `http://codeigniter.com/wiki`, and other sources. We recommend you to take a look at the Wiki from time-to-time, you will find useful things and, who knows, maybe one day you could contribute too!

We are going to see:

- How to use meta tags
- A sitemap generator

Also we are going to see; how to use a Google charts plugin inside our CodeIgniter application, don't miss it!

Creating a helper

The easiest way in which we can reuse our own code, or other's code, is by creating a helper and functions inside it. For example, take this code:

```
$user = "demo_user";
preg_match('/^[a-z\d_]{6,12}$/i', $user);
```

This is a useful piece of code, a regular expression it will check that a string has between 6 and 12 alphabetic characters, decimal numbers, or underscores. With this expression we could, for example, check usernames.

If we would like to have this code available for every controller of our site, we could put it into a helper. Our helpers are placed inside `application/helpers`. We can call the file `common_helper.php`. Place this code into it:

```php
<?php if ( ! defined('BASEPATH')) exit('No direct script access
                                        allowed');
if ( ! function_exists('validate_user'))
{
  function validate_user($user)
  {
    if (preg_match('/^[a-z\d_]{6,12}$/i', $user))
    {
      $validate = "Ok";
    }
    else
    {
      $validate = "Ko";
    }
    return $validate;
  }
}
```

In addition to the code we have seen before, there are some other things, for example:

```php
<?php if ( ! defined('BASEPATH')) exit('No direct script access
                                        allowed');
```

The BASEPATH is a variable defined in the `index.php` file, and like all other site parameters that are loaded inside it, this variable is available. If we tried to call a file with a direct URL access, this variable wouldn't be available, thus preventing file access. If called directly, using a URL, it will produce the message "No direct script access allowed" and exit. This way the file is protected from being directly loaded.

After that, `function_exists` checks if the function is already defined, and if not, defines it. Inside our function we can see pretty much the same code, with the only difference being that of the `if`, which checks the result and prepares a variable that will be returned after all operations are finished.

Now we are done. In future we could add more functions, or create other helpers, and so on. Let's remember how we would use this one. We are going to check this in our `Start` controller, as this is not used in the sample application that any controller will have.

Open the `application/controllers/start.php` file, and add a new function, `create_user`:

```
function create_user()
{
  $this->load->helper('common');
  $check = validate_user('correctname');
  echo $check;
}
```

As we can see, to load our newly created helper we only need to call the `load` class, using the helper method and passing the helper name as a parameter. After this is done, we can call the functions inside the helper file as usual.

The difference between libraries and helpers is that if we have loaded a library we can't call its functions directly. For example, if `common` was a library instead of a helper, we would need to call it using something like:

```
$this->common->validate_user('correctname');
```

Everything else would mostly remain the same. You can try this function using the following path:

```
http://localhost/codeigniter/start/create_user
```

Of course this example can be greatly extended, and our helper can contain more functions. As an example, we can see the way in which we can create our own helpers, be it from the previous code we have made, for other projects, office partners, and so on.

Creating a library

Creating a CodeIgniter library is an easy task, for example, take this PHP library:

```
http://code.google.com/p/php-excel/
```

The `php-excel` library created by Oliver Schwarz is used to generate Excel files—a task that is needed from time to time. Again, this example is not one of our main examples, but it's a good way to see how a library is created. Now, you will be able to create your own and use them.

First, download the library. It comes in a ZIP file, with four files:

- `license.txt`: Here we can see the license under which the library is shipped
- `readme.txt`: Here we can see the change log and some instructions about how to use the library

- `test.php`: Here we can see an example
- `php-excel.class.php`: Here the library is stored; it is the class file that contains all the methods we need to generate Excel files

CI libraries are placed inside the `application/libraries` folder, and we are going to create a new one there. Call this new library `excel.php`, open it, and copy all the code that is inside the `php-excel.class.php` library file.

We have named our library `excel.php`. So, we need to rename the class from `Excel_XML` to `Excel`; that's the only change we will need.

Open `start.php`, which is in `application/controllers`, and create a new function called `generate_excel` — we will load our new library there:

```
function generate_excel()
{
  $this->load->library('excel');
}
```

Our example is similar to the one provided in the ZIP we downloaded; it is:

```
function generate_excel()
{
  $this->load->library('excel');
  $data = array(1 => array ('Site', 'Owner'),
                array('demosite1', 'Owner1'),
                array('demosite2', 'Owner2'),
                array('demosite3', 'Owner3'),
             );
  $xls = new Excel('UTF-8', false, 'Demo sheet');
  $xls->addArray($data);
  $xls->generateXML('demo1');
}
```

As you can see, there's nothing strange about this example We load the library, and then we are able to use `if` methods as usual. In this case we can see that first we prepare an array of data, this data being the columns and rows of our XML file. Then we call the new `Excel` method with some parameters:

- The first one is the encoding of the file (UTF-8)
- In the second one we specify if we want to convert variables to field specification
- The last one will be the title for the worksheet

These examples are just to show how we can reuse code to create helpers and libraries that help us in our work.

Sitemap

This library will help us with our site SEO; keep reading, and don't miss this `Sitemap` library! Firstly, take a look at the Wiki `http://codeigniter.com/wiki/Sitemap/`.

This library has been made available to the community by Jonathon Hill, and will help us build sitemaps of our site with ease. It is very easy to prepare it for use, as in the previous example, we need to create some files in our `application/libraries` folder. We just need to copy the contents of the `Sitemap.php` file and the `MY_Parser.php` file and create two files with the same names in the `libraries` folder.

We will need to do some tweaking to the `Sitemap.php` library (just some changes that were pointed out in the forums at `http://codeigniter.com/forums/viewthread/86534/`). Change line 142 from:

```
if(is_array($this->ignore[$controller])) $pages = array_merge($this-
>ignore[$controller], (array) $pages);
```

To:

```
if(isset($this->ignore[$controller]) AND is_array($this-
>ignore[$controller])) $pages = array_merge($this-
>ignore[$controller], (array) $pages);
```

And line 171 from:

```
if(in_array(strtolower($method->name), (array) $this-
>ignore[strtolower($class)])) continue;
```

To:

```
if(isset($this->ignore[strtolower($class)]) AND in_
array(strtolower($method->name), (array) $this-
>ignore[strtolower($class)])) continue;
```

And lastly line 209 from:

```
if($this->ignore[strtolower($class)] == '*') continue;

// skip controllers marked as 'ignore'
```

To:

```
if(isset($this->ignore[strtolower($class)]) AND $this-
>ignore[strtolower($class)] == '*') continue;

// skip controllers marked as 'ignore'
```

Done, you don't need to change anything else, you can now create your controller and start enjoying your sitemap. You can just copy the sample controller from the Wiki.

 Just remember to name your controller something other than Sitemap—the class itself is called sitemap—this could drive in some errors.

Let's take a look at the controller's code:

```php
<?php
class Site extends Controller
{
  function Site()
  {
    parent::Controller();
    $this->load->library('sitemap');
  }
  function index()
  {
    // Show the index page of each controller (default is FALSE)
    $this->sitemap->set_option('show_index', true);
    // Exclude a list of methods from any controller
    $this->sitemap->ignore('*', array('view', 'create', 'edit',
                                      'delete'));
    // Exclude this controller
    $this->sitemap->ignore('Site', '*');
    // Show the sitemap
    echo '<h1>Sitemap</h1>';
    echo $this->sitemap->generate();
  }
}
```

By default all controllers and methods are included in the sitemap. We will see, in a moment, how to change that, but for now let's see the results of loading that controller. Check `http://localhost/codeigniter/site` and you will see something like this:

What if we want to remove the **Logout** link? It doesn't make sense, so let's get rid of it:

```
$this->sitemap->ignore('Start', 'logout');
```

This will prevent showing the **Start** controller's **Logout** method. If there was a method in every controller that we didn't want to show, we could add that method to this line:

```
$this->sitemap->ignore('*', array('view', 'create', 'edit',
                                  'delete'));
```

We could add as many as we need. We can also remove the entire controller in an easy way using:

```
$this->sitemap->ignore('Site', '*');
```

This library allows us to create sitemaps of our site the way we want.

 Remember, it only works in a PHP 5-enabled server.

Explanation for My_Parser.php

In the previous example, we have created a file called MY_Parser.php, but why have we named it that way? Could we have simply called it Parser.php, or not?

Well, in fact there are two answers to this question. The Parser.php file, which we can find in CI_system/libraries, is a core CodeIgniter library. Depending on the option we choose, one of the following two commented options will happen:

- If we create a file, in our application/libraries folder, called Parser.php, it will substitute the CI core file. Whenever CI needs to use the Parser library it will take the newly created one. But take care, all methods inside the CI one can't be used.

- The other option is to create a file, inside our application/libraries folder, and call it My_Parser.php. This time we are not replacing the CI core class, we are extending it. This way we keep all the functionality of the CI class, and add any function we need.

If we are not going to do major changes, it is more reasonable to use the second option, and create only the functions we need.

 Keep in mind that if we create any function in our My_Parser.php file, that has the same name as one in the core Parser.php one, our function, the one in My_parser.php, will be used instead of the core one.

Importantly, when creating our class, inside My_parser.php file, we have to make it extend the core CI one:

```
class MY_Parser extends CI_Parser
{
```

And if we need a constructor, we will extend the parent constructor:

```
function MY_Parser()
  {
    parent::CI_Parser();
  }
```

As you can see, in this way we can extend CI core functionalities without the need to change any core files. Thus, we can update CI easily, without losing any functionalities or changes we have added.

> If you extend the core controller, remember to extend it when creating your controllers, for example:
>
> class Start extends MY_Controller
>
> ```
>     {
>         function Welcome()
>         {
>             parent::MY_Controller();
>         }
> ```

Finally, if you don't like to use the MY_ prefix you can change it, just open application/config/config.php file and search for this line:

```
$config['subclass_prefix'] = 'MY_';
```

We can change it for anything we want, except for CI, as this is used by CodeIgniter's own libraries.

Google charts plugin

This is not a library from the Wiki, it's a PHP plugin that I've used in the past and thought it could be of help to you. Also, we will see through an example how we can virtually get any PHP code and put it inside our CodeIgniter application.

The bad news is that it is a paid plugin; the good news is that it costs USD 5 only. You can check it at http://themeforest.net/item/google-charts-plugin/47082. Doesn't it look good? It's also very easy to use.

After downloading it, unpack and copy the entire googlechart folder in our application/libraries folder. You can call the index.php file from this, but check it first as it has some examples.

Also, we are going to rename GoogleChart.class.php to googlechart.php and open it, as we are going to make some modifications:

```
define("_GOOGLECHART_URL","http://dev.freekrai.net/");
define("_GOOGLECHART_CACHE",true);
class GoogleChart
{
```

We are going to change that a little:

```php
<?php
define("_GOOGLECHART_URL","http://localhost/codeigniter/application/
libraries/");

//define("_GOOGLECHART_CACHE",true);

define("_GOOGLECHART_CACHE",false);
class Googlecharts
{
```

We are changing the class name to match the file name (there is also another instance to the name on line 46; change `GoogleChart` to `Googlecharts` there too), also we need to change the URL to the one of our application.

 While in development change `GOOGLECHART_CACHE` to `false`, otherwise we won't see the changes we are doing.

We now have our `googlecharts` CodeIgniter library, quickly and easily. Let's see it in action. For that purpose we are going to create a new controller, name it `Charts`, for example, `application/controllers/charts.php`:

```php
<?php
class Charts extends Controller
{
  function index()
  {
    $this->load->library('googlecharts');
  }
}
```

When we have the library loaded, working with it differs a little from the examples that are shown in the `index.php` file that came in the ZIP file. We are going to take one of the examples and rebuild it inside our controller. First, we are going to create the data array, which is the data that we will show in our chart:

```php
$values = array(
                'IE7' => 22,
                'IE6' => 30.7,
                'IE5' => 1.7,
                'Firefox' => 36.5,
                'Mozilla' => 1.1,
```

```
                           'Safari' => 2,
                           'Opera' => 1.4,
                      );
```

When the data is prepared we need a title, a colors array with a color for each data item, a chart type, and the size of the chart. They are sent to the library in this way:

```
$gtitle = "Browser trends";
$color = array('#AFD8F8','#F6BD0F','#8BBA00','#FF8E46','#008E8E');
$chart = $this->googlecharts->setChartAttrs(array(
                                        'type' => 'pie',
                                        'title' => $gtitle,
                                        'data' => $values,
                                        'size' => array(
                                                450, 200),
                                        'color' => $color
                      ));

echo $this->googlecharts;
```

The last line is the one that actually generates the chart. If all has gone smoothly, when we go to http://localhost/codeigniter/charts, we will see this chart:

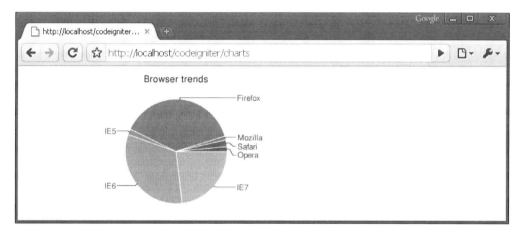

A very neat chart. We are sure that you are already thinking about adding it to your projects! But continue reading for now, we have more things we want you to see. Let's say we need two graphs on the same page, add the following after the code we already have:

```
$gtitle = "Ice cream sales";
$color = array('#AFD8F8');
$values = array(
                'strawberry' => 43,
                'mint' => 3,
```

```
                            'vanilla' => 15,
                            'chocolat' => 20,
                            'cream' => 8,
                            );
    $chart = $this->googlecharts->setChartAttrs(array(
                                                'type' => 'pie',
                                                'title' => $gtitle,
                                                'data' => $values,
                                                'size' => array(
                                                        450, 200),
                                                'color' => $color
                                                ));
        echo $this->googlecharts;
```

After loading the page again, another chart will be added next to the one you already have. As you can see, if only one color is passed, the googlecharts API will range it, not to have repeating colors.

That done, you have two graphs on your site. You may be thinking, though, that this is not fully MVC as we are making echos in the controller. Why not do it in a view? Nice idea, let's do it, it will be pretty easy. First, where we had:

```
        echo $this->googlecharts;
```

Now put:

```
        $data['chart_1'] = $this->googlecharts;
```

And in the second one, put:

```
        $data['chart_2'] = $this->googlecharts;
```

After that we load a view and pass the data to it:

```
        $this->load->view('charts', $data);
```

Our application/views/chart.php would be something like this:

```
    <?php
    echo $chart_1;
    echo $chart_2;
```

Now refresh your browser and you will see the same chart twice. *Why is that happening?* Well we have missed something; in our previous example we were working with one instance of the library. The first time it wasn't a problem, we passed the data to the library and echoed it, after that we changed the data and echoed it. But, instead of echoing the data, if we save it to a variable:

```
        $data['chart_2'] = $this->googlecharts;
```

We are, in fact, putting the instance into the variable when we change the data, and pass the new data array. We will be changing the value in the two `$data[...]` values, as they are referencing the same instance.

But then what can we do? Create two instances of the library. We have not seen that before, but it's pretty straightforward, just check it:

```php
<?php
class Charts extends Controller {
  function index()
  {
    $this->load->library('googlecharts');
    $chart1 = new googlecharts();
    $values = array(
                  'IE7' => 22,
                  'IE6' => 30.7,
                  'IE5' => 1.7,
                  'Firefox' => 36.5,
                  'Mozilla' => 1.1,
                  'Safari' => 2,
                  'Opera' => 1.4,
                  );
    $gtitle = "Browser trends";
    $color = array('#AFD8F8','#F6BD0F',
                  '#8BBA00','#FF8E46','#008E8E');
    $chart1->setChartAttrs( array(
                                  'type' => 'pie',
                                  'title' => $gtitle,
                                  'data' => $values,
                                  'size' => array( 450, 200 ),
                                  'color' => $color
                                  ));
    $data['chart_1'] = $chart1;
    //The other chart
    $chart2 = new googlecharts();
    $gtitle = "Ice cream sales";
    $color = array('#AFD8F8');
    $values = array(
                  'strawberry' => 43,
                  'mint' => 3,
                  'vanilla' => 15,
                  'chocolat' => 20,
                  'cream' => 8,
                  );
    $chart2->setChartAttrs( array(
                                  'type' => 'pie',
                                  'title' => $gtitle,
                                  'data' => $values,
                                  'size' => array( 450, 200 ),
```

```
                                    'color' => $color
                                ));
        $data['chart_2'] = $chart2;
        $this->load->view('charts', $data);
    }
}
```

It's basically the same, the only difference is that we instantiate the class:

```
$chart2 = new googlecharts();
```

And after that we use it in the same way as we have been doing before.

Now, to end with the charts plugin I'm going to give you this URL:

```
http://code.google.com/intl/es/apis/chart/#chart_type
```

Here you can check for other chart types and a lot more information on Google charts. When using the library don't forget that the library types are equal to these Google chart types:

Chart library type	Google chart type	Result
pie	p	Pie chart
pie3d	p3	3D pie chart
line	lc	Line chart
sparkline	ls	The same as the line chart but without the axis
bar-horizontal	bhg	Horizontal bar chart with grouped bars
bar-vertical	bvg	Vertical bar chart with grouped bars
bhs	bhs	Horizontal bar chart with stacked bars
bvs	bvs	Vertical bar chart with stacked bars
lc	lc	The same as line
lxy	lxy	Line chart with points
pc	pc	Concentric pie chart

All these chart types are supported by the library, but it would be quite easy to extend the library, or modify it.

Summary

We hope you have enjoyed this chapter. We have seen quite a lot of things here, the `meta_tags` library, the `sitemap` library, and the `googlecharts` one. But, most important of all, we have seen how we can add third-party code to our CodeIgniter application, making it possible for us to use already built functionalities in our applications.

We can take those functionalities from the Wiki `http://codeigniter.com/wiki/`, or other third-party code, and it is quite usual to do so. We can take our code from previous applications and put it into a CodeIgniter library, this way we won't lose any of our work.

Before going into the next chapter, you may want to take another look at the Wiki; may we recommend two things?

- `http://codeigniter.com/wiki/Excel_Plugin/`
- `http://codeigniter.com/wiki/PDF_generation_using_dompdf/`

We think those two could be quite useful, but of course there are a lot of other libraries in the Wiki. Have a nice time checking them.

9
Using CI to Communicate

The main strength of the Internet is its ability to communicate. In this chapter, we will look at three ways in which CI makes communication easy. First, we'll add to our testing toolkit by using CI's FTP class, to access remote files directly. Then, we'll use the `email` class to make our site automatically send emails when certain conditions are met.

Lastly, we'll venture into Web 2.0 territory—using **XML-RPC (XML Remote Procedure Call)** to create a private "web service" that allows our remote sites to take action, and return information on a request from our test site. We will also take a look at a twitter library that will help us stay in contact with our clients at every moment. Don't miss it!

Using the FTP class to test remote files

File Transfer Protocol (FTP) is a method of transferring files over the Internet. It's normally used to move files from and to your website, using a special FTP program. It's something most of us use occasionally, especially when we are putting up a new site.

You can, however, automate the whole process painlessly with CI. One use is to test the integrity of your remote site—are the files still there? As a website owner, you always face the possibility that someone will tamper with the files on your site. It may just be your ISP or server admin, deleting or overwriting something by mistake. This happened to David once, when his ISP rebuilt their server and forgot to reload one of his application files. The file concerned wasn't used very often, but mattered a lot when it wasn't there. This led to an interesting error that took some time to track down!

As an example, to show the power of the `ftp` class, let's build a regular test program, to check the files on a remote site. A few lines of code are all we need:

```
function getremotefiles($hostname, $username, $password)
{
  $this->load->library('ftp');
  $config['hostname'] = $hostname;
  $config['username'] = $username;
  $config['password'] = $password;
  $config['debug'] = TRUE;
  $this->ftp->connect($config);
  $filelist = $this->ftp->list_files('/my_directory/');
  $this->ftp->close();
  return $filelist;
}
```

First, load the `ftp` library if you haven't done so. Then, define the configuration parameters—hostname (for example, `www.mysite.com`), `username`, and `password` for your FTP access.

If you think you are going to need the same configuration all over your application, you can put it in a `config` file. All we need to do is create a file called `ftp.php` inside `application/config`, with the `config` array in it:

```
<?php
$config['hostname'] = 'ftp.demosite.com';
$config['username'] = 'anonymous';
$config['password'] = '';
$config['port'] = 21;
$config['passive'] = FALSE;
$config['debug'] = TRUE;
```

Now, we can connect to the FTP site without needing to create or pass the `config` array:

```
function index()
{
  $this->load->library('ftp');
  $this->ftp->connect();
  $list = $this->ftp->list_files('/');
  print_r($list);
}
```

After that, if we need, we can override it by passing a `config` array to the connect method.

Once connected, CI's `ftp` class gives you several options. In this case, we've used `list_files()` to return a list of files in the `/my_directory/` folder. The function returns an array, and you can easily check this against an array of the files that you expect to find there. As before, we're trying to list all our tests in a database. So, this time we need to list the FTP URL (or `hostname`), the `username` and `password`, and instead of a regex use an array of files to check against. To maintain the integrity of this array—if you store it inside your database—you will need to serialize it before you put it in, and unserialize it when you take it out again.

Then it's easy to compare the `$remotearray` returned by the `getremotefiles()` function, with the unserialized `$referencearray` returned by your database:

```
function comparefiles($remotearray, $referencearray)
{
  $report = "<br />On site, not in reference array: ";
  $report .= print_r(array_diff($remotearray, $referencearray), TRUE);
  $report .= "<br />In reference array, not on site: ";
  $report .= print_r(array_diff($referencearray, $remotearray), TRUE);
  return $report;
}
```

The PHP `array_diff` function compares the second array to the first, so it will list files present only in the first, but not the ones in the second. So, run the function twice, reversing the order of the array parameters—that way you get two lists, one of which isn't on your site (but should be), and second which is on your site (but shouldn't be). The first should show any files that your ISP has accidentally deleted, and the second shows the files that may be added.

The CI `ftp` class also allows you to upload, move, rename, and delete files. Suppose, that your test reveals that one of the files in your reference array (let's call it `myfile.php`) is missing from your site. You can use the `ftp` class to upload it:

```
$this->ftp->upload('c:/myfile.php', '/public_html/myfile.php');
```

In this example, the local path is given first and then the path on the remote server. Optionally you can specify, as a third parameter, how the file should be uploaded—ASCII or binary. If you don't, CI makes its own decision based on the file extension, which will usually be correct. If you are running PHP 5, you can add a fourth parameter to set the file permissions, assuming you are uploading to a Linux server:

```
$this->ftp->upload('c:/myfile.php', '/public_html/myfile.php',
                   'ascii', 0775);
```

Don't forget to close the FTP connection after you have finished uploading files:

```
$this->ftp->close();
```

CI has two delete options now, one for files, and another for folders. Use the second one very carefully as it will delete folders recursively. So, if there are some subfolders, they will be deleted too. Let's see the difference. First, the `delete_file` function:

```
$this->ftp->delete_file('/public_html/images/image023.jpg');
```

This will effectively delete the `image023.jpg` file, and nothing more. Have a look at this now:

```
$this->ftp->delete_dir('/public_html/images/');
```

It will delete everything inside the folder, even subfolders and their contents. It maybe very useful sometimes, but use it with care.

Using a combination of the FTP `delete` and `upload` functions, you could automatically update the files on your remote sites. List the files you need to update, and visit each site in turn. First, delete the old ones and then upload the new ones.

There is also an interesting `mirror` function, which allows you to set up a complete duplicate website on another server. It's also very straightforward:

```
$this->ftp->mirror('c:\wamp\www\codeigniter', '/public_html/');
```

The entire structure of our site will be uploaded to the folder specified in the second parameter. If you are running PHP 5, you will also be able to change file permissions with the `ftp` class:

```
$this->ftp->chmod('/public_html/images/', DIR_WRITE_MODE);
```

This is the same as:

```
$this->ftp->chmod('/public_html/images/', 0777);
```

We can set permissions using an octal value, which should be the preferred method. CI provides us with some constants, these constants are:

```
FILE_READ_MODE  => 0644
FILE_WRITE_MODE => 0666
DIR_READ_MODE   => 0755
DIR_WRITE_MODE  => 0777
```

These constants are defined in the `constants.php` file found in the `config` folder of our application.

These can be used, when creating a folder with the `mkdir` function:

```
$this->ftp->mkdir('/public_html/images/user23/', DIR_WRITE_MODE);
```

This command will create a new folder with write permissions, but it's better to use the octal format, as it is more readable. But as always, it's better to have a choice.

As you can see, there's plenty of scope for expanding your application from testing your remote websites to actually maintaining or updating them. You could, for instance, write code to distribute updates automatically.

Don't forget to take a look at the `directory_helper`, it's a nice complement to the `ftp` class:

`http://codeigniter.com/user_guide/helpers/directory_helper.html`

Machines talking to machines again: XML-RPC

The Web 2.0 revolution is largely built on machine-to-machine interfaces, which allow mashups and APIs and all those good things.

This is the basis of "web service". You can offer an interface to your site that allows other people to use it to do something for them. To give a simple example, if you set up a "web service" that converts temperature values in Centigrade to Fahrenheit, the client sends in a request with one parameter (the temperature to be converted) and the server returns the converted value. So, anyone can add a temperature conversion function that appears to be on his/her own site, but is actually calling yours.

XML-RPC allows two machines to talk directly. The receiving site creates a simple API. Anyone who wants to talk to it needs to know that API—which methods are available, which parameters they take, and what is the syntax for addressing them. Many major sites use this system, for instance, Google allows you to make direct calls to its search engine or to Google Earth using a published API.

Setting up your private API is relatively easy, thanks to CI. You need two websites to set up and test it, which makes it a little more complex than most things. One site (let's call it the "receiving" site) offers the API, listens for requests, and answers them. In our example, this is one of the remote sites that we are trying to test and manage. The other site makes the request using the API and gets an answer. In our example, this is the test site.

In the XML-RPC protocol, the two sites talk by means of highly structured XML, hence the name. The client sends an XML packet to the receiving site's server, stating the function it wants to use and any arguments or parameters to be passed. The server decodes the XML and if it fits the API, calls the function and returns a response, also structured as XML, which the client decodes and acts on.

Your API consists of the functions that the receiving site offers, and instructions for using them, for example, what parameters they take, what data type should be used, and so on.

On the receiving site, we create an XML-RPC server, which makes the selected internal methods available to external sites. These internal methods are normal functions within one of your controllers. The server's role is to handle the interface between the external call and the internal function.

There are two set of problems when you set up an XML-RPC process:

- Getting the two sites to talk to each other
- Making sure that the data is transmitted in a suitable format

Both rely heavily on multi-dimensional arrays, which machines can take in their stride, even humans need to puzzle a bit over them. CI makes it much easier, though it's still quite tricky to get it right.

Getting the XML-RPC server and client in touch with each other

First, you have to set up a server on the remote site and a client on the requesting site. This can be done with a few simple lines of code. Let's say we are setting up the server in a controller called `mycontroller` (on the receiving site), and the client in a controller called `xmlrpc_client` (on the requesting site).

In each case, start off by initializing the CI classes within the constructor. There are two; for a client, you only need to load the first one, for a server you need to load them both:

```
$this->load->library('xmlrpc');
$this->load->library('xmlrpcs');
```

Now, for the server, close your constructor function, and within the `mycontroller` `index()` function define the functions you are offering to the outside world. You do this by building a `functions` subarray (within the main CI `$config` array), which maps the names of the incoming requests to the actual functions you want to use:

```
$config['functions']['call'] = array('function' =>
                                'mycontroller.myfunction');
$config['functions']['call2'] = array('function' =>
                                'mycontroller.myfunction2');
```

In this case, there are two function calls—`call` and `call2`. This is what the request asks for. It doesn't ask for the functions by name, but by the name of the call. Of course, you can use the same name if you wish. For each call, you define a sub-array giving the `function` within the controller, that is, `myfunction` and `myfunction2` respectively.

You then finish off with your server by initializing and instantiating it:

```
$this->xmlrpcs->initialize($config);
$this->xmlrpcs->serve();
```

It is now ready to listen to requests. Now you need to go to the other website—the client—and set up an XML-RPC client to make the requests. This should be a separate controller on your client site. It's quite short:

```
$server_url = 'http://www.mysite.com/index.php/mycontroller';
$this->load->library('xmlrpc');
$this->xmlrpc->set_debug(TRUE);
$this->xmlrpc->server($server_url, 80);
$this->xmlrpc->method('call');
```

You define the URL of the receiving site, specifying the controller that contains the XML-RPC server that you want. You load the XML RPC class, define the server, and the method you want to use—this is the name of the call you want to make, and not the actual function you want to use. If the function you are calling needs parameters, you pass them this way:

```
$request = array('optimisation','sites');
```

As you see, we're passing two parameters. Then, you check if a response has been received, and do something with it:

```
if ( ! $this->xmlrpc->send_request())
{
  echo $this->xmlrpc->display_error();
}
else
{
  print_r($this->xmlrpc->display_response());
}
```

The simplest option is to display it, but in a real application you may want the machine to analyze it too. For example, using the `simplexml.php` class, and then acting on the results. For instance, if the result contains an error message, you might want to record the error in your database, and take action to report it to the human user.

Formatting XML-RPC exchanges

Let's use a real but simplified example. In this section, we will create an XML-RPC call/response that lets you remotely trigger database optimization. The client, we wrote, is asking for a method known as `call` and supplying two parameters—`optimisation` and `sites`.

The server, on the receiving site, maps this request for `call` from a function called `myfunction`. Let's have a look at this function. It's basically an ordinary function within the controller. It attempts to optimize a MySQL database table, and returns `success` or `failure` depending on the result.

```
function myfunction($request)
{
  $parameters = $request->output_parameters();
  $function = $parameters['0'];
  $table = $parameters['1'];
  if ($this->db->query("OPTIMIZE TABLE $table"))
  {
    $content = 'success';
  }
  else
  {
    $content = 'failure';
  }
  $response = array(
                    array(
```

```
                       'function' => array($function, 'string'),
                       'table' => array($table, 'string'),
                       'result' => array($content, 'string'),
                     ),
                'struct');
    return $this->xmlrpc->send_response($response);
}
```

Note the $request, set as the function parameter. This contains the $request array from the client—remember, it had two values, optimisation and sites. CI has transformed the array into an object, $request. So you can't get the individual parameters by treating it as an array, instead you have to use the $request-> output_parameters() method of the $request object. This returns an array, which you interrogate in the normal way.

Using this we have told the function on the receiving site, which table we want to optimize—the sites table. We've also told it to call the function (optimisation). It adds a further parameter called result, gets the value, and returns all three to us. The result it sends back to the client site looks something like this:

```xml
<?xml version="1.0" encoding="UTF-8"?>
<methodResponse>
<params>
  <param>
    <value>
      <struct>
        <member>
          <name>function</name>
          <value>
            <string>optimisation</string>
          </value>
        </member>
        <member>
          <name>table</name>
          <value>
            <string>sites</string>
          </value>
        </member>
        <member>
          <name>result</name>
          <value>
            <string>Success</string>
          </value>
        </member>
      </struct>
```

```
        </value>
      </param>
    </params>
  </methodResponse>
```

As you can see, our simple three word response (optimisation, exercises, success) has been wrapped in verbose layers of tags, in a way sadly typical to XML, to tell a machine what exactly is going on. There are three <member></member> tag pairs. Each has a <name></name> pair (function, table, result respectively). Each of these has a <value></value> pair, which includes (as well as the data type) the actual information we want, that is, optimisation, sites, and success.

Never mind, I don't like it. Computers thrive on this sort of stuff—it is precise, unambiguous, and easy for a machine to read. Now, the XML-RPC client function on your calling site can extract the values it wants and act on them. For example, you can do this with the simplexml class.

 You can find more info about simplexml at php.net/simplexml.

Debugging

As soon as you start testing your client/sever combination, you will probably get this message:

```
The XML data received was either invalid or not in the correct form
for XML-RPC. Turn on debugging to examine the XML data further.
```

To turn on debugging include the following line in your client:

```
$this->xmlrpc->set_debug(TRUE);
```

This allows you to see what your client/server site combination is sending back to you. Beware, this is where debugging gets quite frustrating.

There are several places where the exchange can go wrong:

- If the remote site is not responding properly: You may have to temporarily set it to display errors in order to work out, why it is not responding. This is annoying if it is an active site. The additional Catch 22 is that it will then display error messages (HTML), which aren't part of the XML response your client expects. So, you will get a second set of error messages, caused by the first set. Debugging this may involve quite a lot of FTP transfers back and forth, until you get it right.
- The client code may not be working properly.

- You have got the URL wrong: This needs to follow CI's way of addressing the controller in which the XML-RPC server sits, that is, `http://www.mysite.com/index.php/mycontroller`. If you put all the server code in the constructor instead of the `index` function, it will still work. You need to address the function you want to call by name, for example, `http://www.mysite.com/index.php/mycontroller/myfunction`.

- The XML interchange may not be exactly right—The `set_debug` function allows you to see, what is being sent back. You can spend quite a while staring at this trying to work out where it has gone wrong.

However, once you get all this right, you've done something quite clever—you've built a function in a remote site, and called it remotely! In other words, you've set up an application that can do maintenance or other operations on remote sites. If you have several remote sites to manage, you can easily replicate this across them, allowing you—for instance—to optimize all your database tables once a day by just one action on the site.

Issues with XML-RPC

Security is an issue, of course. You would want to password-protect your function calls, so the client had to send the password as a parameter before the receiving site responded. This can be done by simply sending the password as an additional parameter in the request, and getting it checked by the called function, before responding.

If you were exposing critical functions, you might want the whole thing to take place behind an SSL layer. Our example looks harmless—you might not mind if a hacker repeatedly broke into your site, as all he/she did was tidy up your database each time. On the other hand, it would be a good basis for a "Denial of Service" attack.

Talking to humans for a change—the email class

We've put together a lot of building blocks for our test website. We have a database of tests, and we've built functions to run different type of tests. We can access our site and check if we are seeing the right page. We can check that all the files are where we expect them to be, on the remote server. We can automatically run functions on the site and get it to optimize itself. It's fairly simple to write code that uses these tools to run a suite of tests whenever we want—when we log on or by some automatic reminder, such as setting a Cron job on a Linux server to run our program at suitable intervals.

It's not really enough to run tests and just store the results in a database. If something is wrong, we need to know it as soon as possible. Here CI's email class comes in. It allows us to program our site to send emails whenever certain conditions are met. You might want to send an email for each failed test, or you might want to run a series of tests, collect the results, and then send just one email report.

To use the email class, first (as always) you have to load it.

```
$this->load->library('email');
```

We have to set some configuration variables now. This is where we can run into problems because the class that is able to send email for us depends on the server that is hosting our code. Once again, we may have to check with the ISP and configure our email account in the server.

 It's difficult to test this on a local site, because XAMPP Lite or WAMP server, for instance, may not be able to offer a mail server to you.

However, once you've sorted out your ISP, you can easily configure the email class. There are a lot of options, all listed in the online user guide. The main ones are:

- protocol: This option sets whether your system uses mail, sendmail, or SMTP to send emails
- mailpath: This option sets, where your system's mail program is stored

You set them like this:

```
$config['protocol'] = 'sendmail';
$config['mailpath'] = '/usr/sbin/sendmail';
$this->email->initialize($config);
```

By default the protocol is set to mail, the PHP mail function, so we don't need to specify the mailpath either. Other options, all of which have sensible defaults, include things such as word wrapping, character sets, whether you want to send text or HTML emails, and so on. Setting the options and getting them to work is the only (potentially) difficult part of using this class.

Once you've loaded the class and initialized it, using it is very intuitive.

```
$this->load->library('email');
$this->email->from('david@mysite.com');
$this->email->to('someone@myownsite.com');
$this->email->bcc('fred@somewhere.com');
```

```
$this->email->subject('Test message');
$this->email->message('Hello world');
$this->email->send();
```

This code snippet will send an email to you, copied to your client, reporting whatever message you want. We can also indicate more than one email address in each of the fields, for example:

```
$this->email->to('someone@myownsite.com, another@anothersite.com');
```

If you're sending more than one email, start each one with:

```
$this->email->clear()
```

This is just to make sure that you start with a clean slate each time:

```
foreach ($contact as $user => $email)
{
  $this->email->clear();
  $this->email->to($email);
  $this->email->from('your@example.com');
  $this->email->subject('Info about your site: '.$email);
  $this->email->message('Hi '.$user.' Here is some important
                         information about your site.');
  $this->email->send();
}
```

The `clear` function will help us to clear the state of the variables, so we can have different values each time.

If you are sending email attachments, maybe you want to send the same attachment to all the contacts. If that is not the case you can clear the attachments by passing TRUE to the `clear` function:

```
$this->email->clear(TRUE);
```

You can also use the `email` class to send attachments. Remember, the attachment file must be saved on the server that is sending the email. You have to specify where it is saved, in terms of the server root file (giving the server's address, not the website's address). Get its address and name like this:

```
$path = $this->config->item('server_root');
$file = $path.'/my_subdirectory/myfile.htm';
```

Then just add this line before `$this->email->send();`:

```
$this->email->attach($file);
```

This CI function is much easier to use than trying to write the PHP code to send attachments. It handles all the protocols involved, without you even having to be aware of them. If you include the following line in your code, and print the $result variable, you'll get a string containing information about the result of the email sent:

```
$result = $this->email->print_debugger();
```

If something went wrong, the debug information will return any server error messages as well. For instance, when you set the delivery method to SMTP without setting the correct host or permissions, as shown:

```
$config['protocol'] = 'smtp';
```

Then it can't send the message, and it tells you:

```
You did not specify a SMTP hostname. Unable to send email using PHP
SMTP. Your server might not be configured to send mail using this
method.
```

Bear in mind that sendmail is potentially misleading here—it returns a success message if it has passed the message within the server. This doesn't necessarily mean that the message has actually been sent. So, if you set the wrong mailpath option, sendmail may report that it has sent the email, when it actually hasn't. CI relies on the messages it gets back from the mail sending application, and is fooled. With emails, the only way to be sure they have gone is to check that they've arrived—but that's another story.

CI's email class includes several useful options, all explained in the online user guide. For instance, you can set it to send text or HTML format mails—if you choose HTML there's a function to allow you to send a separate text message to people who don't accept HTML emails. You can also set it to use different character sets, and to handle word wrapping. You can set batch sizes; if you intend to send a lot of emails to a long mailing list, this way your server doesn't get overloaded.

When sending emails with the data received, from a form in your site, always sanitize the received data. Header injection attacks are not a funny thing, so we need to give basic protection to our form:

```
function send_contact()
{
  $this->load->library('email');
  $config['charset'] = 'utf-8';
  $this->email->initialize($config);
  $this->email->from('demo@site.com', 'demosite.com');
  $this->email->to('admin@demosite.com');
  $this->email->subject('Contact form send from website');
  $name = $_POST['name'];
```

```
$email = $_POST['email'];
$phone =  $_POST['phone'];
$message = $_POST['message'];
/**********************************************/
$ data = "Contact form \n";
$data = "------------------------------------------------------
         \n\n";
$data = "Name: ".$name."\n\n";
$data = "Email: ".$email."\n\n";
$data = "Phone: ".$phone."\n\n";
$data = "Message: ".$message."\n\n";
$this->email->message($data);
if ( ! $this->email->send())
{
  // Error handling
}
redirect('contac/index', 'refresh');
}
```

We can see some interesting things in this sample form, let's check them:

```
$config['charset'] = 'utf-8';
$this->email->initialize($config);
```

First we define the `charset` as `utf-8`; it is a nice idea to make the PHP file as a UTF file also, in order to avoid some `charset` problems. After we have created the `config` array, we initialize the `email` class, making it ready for use.

If you continue reading, you can see a basic "header injection removal" code:

```
$name = preg_replace("/\nfrom\:.*?\n/i", "", $_POST['name']);
$name = preg_replace("/\nbcc\:.*?\n/i", "", $name);
$name = preg_replace("/\ncc\:.*?\n/i", "", $name);
```

It's pretty basic, but it will help us remove the headers that could have been added to the message. If you want to know more about header injection you can check:

- `http://en.wikipedia.org/wiki/E-mail_injection`
- `http://www.damonkohler.com/2008/12/email-injection.html`

After all that is done, the message is composed and sent, and if sending fails we can handle the error in some way. We can do things such as inserting a record in a database table.

Remember that you can also use the `email` helper,
by using the `email` class. You can read more about the `email` helper on:
`http://codeigniter.com/user_guide/helpers/`
`email_helper.html`

Twitter

Wouldn't it be great to let your clients receive instant notifications about their site status using twitter? Imagine that a site has gone down, your check tool traces the error and sends that information to twitter. This way your clients will know, at that very moment, what is happening.

Now, thanks to Simon Maddox, this is a very easy thing to do—first copy the code from this site (it is also on the Wiki, see the second link):

- `http://github.com/simonmaddox/codeigniter-twitter/tree/master`
- `http://codeigniter.com/wiki/CodeIgniter-Twitter_Library/`

Copy the code into a file called `twitter` inside the `application/libraries` folder. Now call this library as always:

```
$this->load->library('twitter');
$this->twitter->auth('twitter_account','password');
$this->twitter->update('We have detected an error in your site, we
                        are working to repair it right now.');
```

Sounds pretty good, doesn't it? Thanks to Simon for this great and easy-to-use library. I think it is full of uses.

Summary

We've now used CI to build some very sophisticated tools for our website, which give it some significant functionality.

Firstly, we used CI's `ftp` class to simplify and automate file transfer operations. Initially, we've just used this class to check the files we expect to find on our site, to see that nothing unexpected has been added. This is a valuable check, as many of the problems websites throw at you involve unexpected alterations of files—usually by site admins and sometimes by hackers. This function will regularly check our remote websites and also offers the possibility of remote maintenance and updating the sites.

Then we looked at developing our own private web services using CI's `XML-RPC` classes. These allow us to automatically call functions on a remote site, pass parameters if necessary, and have the results returned to us—the same as if we were logged on to the remote site, instead of our test site. We used this to have the remote site optimize a table in its database and report back to us. Once again, we've gone beyond our original plan to simply monitoring the remote sites. Now we are able to instruct them to check or optimize themselves as well.

Lastly, we looked at CI's `email` class, which allows our testing site to generate emails. The CI code is extremely simple to use, and means that we are notified whenever the site thinks there is a problem. CI makes it simple to build and send emails and attachments too.

If you want to take a look at some other interesting CodeIgniter classes, you should take a look at:

`http://codeigniter.com/user_guide/libraries/trackback.html`

We hope you find it useful and have a nice time trying it! But don't forget the next chapter is awaiting you!

10

How CI Helps to Provide Dynamic Information

We've put a lot of thought into building our test website now, and CI has made it easy to do some very complex things. We've set up databases, used FTP, built tests, and started to email the test results. But it's easy to get caught in techie things and forget that websites are often judged on presentation, on how well they process data, and how appropriately they display it to human users.

Here are a few CI classes that help with some problems that arise regularly when you are building a website, particularly when it comes to delivering dynamic information to your users:

- The `date` helper translates different date formats and helps you to cope with time zones. With the help of the `calendar` class, we will quickly generate a calendar.

- The `text` helper provides useful functions to manipulate and convert strings.

- The `language` class makes it easier to write websites that display the same information in different languages, depending on user preference.

- The `table` class saves a lot of tedious `<tr><td>` tags.

- You can automatically cache high-load dynamic pages for a faster response.

Each of these can save you a lot of coding time, while making your site look more professional (and keeping it easy to update).

The date helper—converting and localizing dates

Sooner or later we will find the need to work with dates, maybe to create a calendar, a list of events, or even a to-do list. In our sample application, we can keep track of the errors and incidents happening in our websites. With that we could generate some nice reports about our websites.

Working with dates is usually a very repetitive task, but CI will help us and ease this task. First we are going to add a new database table, where we can keep track of the errors:

```sql
CREATE TABLE `error_logs` (
`id` INT UNSIGNED NOT NULL AUTO_INCREMENT PRIMARY KEY ,
`site_id` INT NOT NULL ,
`error` TEXT NOT NULL ,
`date` DATETIME NOT NULL
) ENGINE = InnoDB;
```

Now we can start saving our errors to the database. In order to do that we will first create a controller, `application/controllers/errors.php`:

```php
<?php
class Errors extends Controller
{
  function errors()
  {
    parent::Controller();
  }
  function index()
  {
    $this->load->model('errors_model');
    $site_id = "16";
    $error = "Database unavailable";
    $now = date("Y-m-d H:i:s");
    $data = array(
                'site_id' => $site_id ,
                'error' => $error ,
                'date' => $now
              );
    $this->errors_model->insert_error($data);
  }
}
```

This is a simple controller; we've put in static contents so that we can try it. For now, the only thing the controller does is receive the data, prepare an array, and send it to the errors_model function, where the data will be saved (application/models/errors_model.php):

```php
<?php
class Errors_model extends Model
{
    function insert_error($data)
    {
        $query = $this->db->insert('error_logs', $data);
        return $query;
    }
}
```

If you go to http://localhost/codeigniter/errors you will execute the controller. Now we are going to create another function in the controller to retrieve and format the data with the help of CI date helper. But first we need to add this function to the model:

```php
function get_errors($site_id = '')
{
    if(!empty($site_id))
    {
        $this->db->where('site_id', $site_id);
        $query = $this->db->get('error_logs');
        return $query;
    }
}
```

This function receives a site_id, checks if it's not empty and then sends a query to the database to get all errors. We can use this function in our errors controller; let's add the function we were talking about:

```php
function show_errors($site_id = '')
{
    $this->load->model('errors_model');
    $errors = $this->errors_model->get_errors($site_id);
    if ($errors->num_rows() > 0)
    {
        foreach ($errors->result() as $row)
        {
            echo $row->site_id." - ".$row->error." - ".$row->date."<br/>";
        }
    }
}
```

We are loading the model again; call the `get_errors` function and show the errors on screen. Now if we go to `http://localhost/codeigniter/errors/show_errors/16` we will see a list of errors that will depend on the number of times we have loaded the errors index page. For example, we see:

```
16 - Database unavailable - 2009-07-18 17:15:47
16 - Database unavailable - 2009-07-18 17:37:49
16 - Database unavailable - 2009-07-18 17:37:50
16 - Database unavailable - 2009-07-18 17:37:52
```

This info can be very useful to us, but the date with the current format can be a bit difficult to read. Let's start working! Load the `date` helper, using:

```
function show_errors($site_id = '')
{
  $this->load->model('errors_model');
  $this->load->helper('date');
  $errors = $this->errors_model->get_errors($site_id);
```

Then modify the code within the `foreach` loop:

```
foreach ($errors->result() as $row)
{
  $unix = mysql_to_unix($row->date);
  $format = 'DATE_RFC822';
  $time = time();
  $date = standard_date($format, $time);
  echo $row->site_id." - ".$row->error." - ".$date."<br/>";
```

After loading the page we will see something like:

```
16 - Database unavailable - Sat, 18 Jul 09 18:06:02 +0200
16 - Database unavailable - Sat, 18 Jul 09 18:06:02 +0200
16 - Database unavailable - Sat, 18 Jul 09 18:06:02 +0200
16 - Database unavailable - Sat, 18 Jul 09 18:06:02 +0200
```

Now this is something better, and easier to understand. As we can see we have to first convert the date from MySQL format to a Unix timestamp, after that we will be able to change the format with the `standard_date` helper function. Available formats are:

atom:2006-12-31T11:34:44Q

cookie: Sunday, 31-Dec-06 11:34:44 UTC

iso: 2006-12-31T11:34:44+0000

RFC 822: Sun, 31 Dec 06 11:34:44 +0000

RFC 850: Sunday, 31-Dec-06 11:12:34 UTC

RFC 1036: Sun, 31 Dec 06 11:34:44 +0000

RFC 1123: Sun, 31 Dec 2006 11:34:44 +0000

RFC 2822: Sun, 31 Dec 2006 11:34:44 +0000

RSS: Sun, 31 Dec 2006 11:34:44 +0000

W3C: 2006-12-31T11:34:44Q

There are also functions to convert between different types of date/time values. Their names are self-explanatory, and the exact syntax is described in the online user guide. They enable you to do quite clever conversions very simply.

The Calendar class

With the help of the `Calendar` class we can create a calendar. It will help to place the errors by date, so in case we have lot of errors (well we don't want to have them, but in case we have...) we can filter them easily by date. This calendar can be easily created using the `Calendar` class.

As earlier, we will need a function in the model to help us retrieve the data. It will be quite similar to the one we have:

```
function get_errors_by_date($site_id = '', $year = '', $month)
{
  if(!empty($site_id))
  {
    $this->db->where('site_id', $site_id);
    $this->db->select('site_id, DAY(date) as day, MONTH(date) as
                      month, YEAR(date) as year');
    if(!empty($year)) $this->db->where('YEAR(date)', $year);
    if(!empty($month)) $this->db->where('MONTH(date)', $month);
    $query = $this->db->get('error_logs');
    return $query;
  }
}
```

Most functions are the same as we have used before, and the difference has to be with SQL rather than with CI. We can see the DAY, MONTH, YEAR selectors, which help us work with our `date` field.

Another thing to note is how to add conditions to our query if our variables are not empty—easier, than writing difficult `if`/`else` statements. As for the controller function, it will also be something similar:

```
function show_calendar($site_id = '', $year = '', $month = '')
{
  $this->load->model('errors_model');
  $this->load->library('calendar');
  $errors = $this->errors_model->get_errors_by_date($site_id, $year,
                                                    $month);

  if ($errors->num_rows() > 0)
  {
    $data = array();
    foreach ($errors->result() as $row)
    {
      $data[$row->day] = http://localhost/codeigniter/errors/show_day
                       /{$site_id}/{$year}/{$month}/{$row->day}";
    }
    echo $this->calendar->generate($year, $month, $data);
  }
}
```

The first step to generate our calendar is to load the library; once that is done we get the errors from the database. We put all the errors in an array:

```
$data[$row->day] = "http://localhost/codeigniter/errors/show_day
                  /".$site_id."/".$year."/".$month."/".$row->day;
```

The format is day for the array key and a link for the value; in our case we are putting a link that we will use for showing the errors for that day. Once this is done we only have to generate the calendar:

```
echo $this->calendar->generate($year, $month, $data);
```

If we go to `http://localhost/codeigniter/errors/show_calendar/16/`
`2009/7/18` (remember to change the values for your own) we will see something
similar to the following:

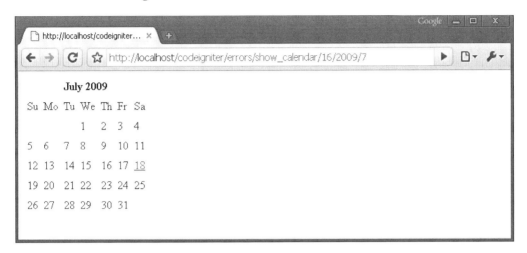

Of course, there is a lot more about the `Calendar` class. You can check all of it at
`http://codeigniter.com/user_guide/libraries/calendar.html`, it will be of
help for sure.

Working with text—the text helper

The `text` helper has a series of functions that help you to manipulate text in various
ways. See the online user guide for details. I'd like to show you a few useful things
you can do. We will see some of the functions while continuing with our example.
Now, if we click on the link we will make a call to the `show_day` function of the `errors`
controller. With little modifications to the `get_errors_by_date` model function:

```
function get_errors_by_date($site_id = '', $year = '', $month = '',
                            $day = '')
{
  if(!empty($site_id))
  {
    $this->db->where('site_id', $site_id);
    $this->db->select('site_id, DAY(date) as day, MONTH(date) as
                       month, YEAR(date) as year, error, date');
    if(!empty($year)) $this->db->where('YEAR(date)', $year);
    if(!empty($month)) $this->db->where('MONTH(date)', $month);
    if(!empty($day)) $this->db->where('DAY(date)', $day);
```

```
        $query = $this->db->get('error_logs');
        return $query;
    }
}
```

We can use the same function to retrieve data for two different functions in our controller, the one we already have, and this new one:

```
function show_day($site_id = '', $year = '', $month = '', $day = '')
{
  $this->load->model('errors_model');
  $errors = $this->errors_model->get_errors_by_date($site_id, $year,
                                                    $month, $day);
  if ($errors->num_rows() > 0)
  {
    $data = array();
    foreach ($errors->result() as $row)
    {
      echo $row->error." ".$row->date."<br/>";
    }
  }
}
```

We will now use the `text` helper to format the data. It would help us to have some headings, so we can identify errors. We can check at a glance most important ones, and then read the rest of the errors. Load the `text` helper, you can place it following the load model line:

```
$this->load->helper('text');
```

Now change the `foreach` loop to this:

```
foreach ($errors->result() as $row)
{
  echo "<h1>".$row->date." : ".word_limiter($row->error, 4)."</h1>";
  echo "<p>".$row->error."</p><br/><br/>";
}
```

This will work as expected. The `word_limiter` function will show the number of words you indicate in the second parameter. In the third parameter, you can indicate what you want to appear as an indicator of more text being available. By default you will see an ellipsis. There is a similar function to this one:

```
character_limiter($row->error, 15)
```

It works the same way, but instead of counting words it counts characters. It's better than the `substr` function of PHP because this one maintains word integrity, so you won't see half cut words. The third parameter works the same way as in the previous function. There are other useful functions in the `text` helper such as:

```
word_wrap($string, length);
```

This one will wrap text at the specified length, passed as the second parameter. We can take a look at the complete documentation and functions at the online user guide `http://codeigniter.com/user_guide/helpers/text_helper.html`; it has some useful functions, so take a look.

Going international—the Language class

Some times it is indispensable for us to be able to communicate in more than one language. For example, take our previous chapter's twitter example. What if, instead of writing the messages to our twitter account, our clients ask us to write the messages to their twitter accounts? Easy isn't it? That way they will be informed about their site's situation only, but then some of them would prefer those notifications in their own language.

For this, we will make use of CI's `language` library. For this library to work correctly, we need some kind of dictionary file with the phrases or words we are going to use. We need to place those files inside our `application/language` folder. We will see that there is already an `english` folder, but there is nothing inside it. Let's build our first file inside this folder; we will call it `info_lang.php`, and it will be like this:

```php
<?php
$lang['error'] = "We have detected an error in your website: ";
$lang['database_unavailable'] = "Database unavailable";
```

You can name the file as you want, but it must end with `_lang.php`. Also avoid placing blank lines after your content as they will be loaded with the file, producing some spaces between content. For example, if you leave a blank line at the end of the file, when loading it, you may get something similar to a `<br/>`. This file is mostly an array with some phrases in it. It is very easy to use, let's build another function in our `application/controllers/errors.php` controller to demonstrate it:

```php
function report_twitter()
{
  $this->lang->load('info', 'english');
  echo $this->lang->line('error');
}
```

English is the default language, so in the previous example, it was not required to specify. For other languages, the language should be specified.

Now, if you go to `http://localhost/codeigniter/errors/report_twitter`, you will see the message—**We have detected an error in your website:**. We have accomplished this in two steps. First, we loaded the language file needed, passing the file name without the `_lang` extension to the load function. The second parameter is for the language, and equates to the folder in which the file resides.

After we have done that we can use the `$this->lang->line` function to retrieve text from the language array. We pass the key we want to this function and the text is returned to us for echo, we save it into a variable if we need to.

But for now, we are much at the same point as we were before we need to write a language file for each language we need. For example, create a `application/language/spanish` folder, create a file called `info_lang.php` in that folder, and paste the following in that file:

```php
<?php
$lang['error'] = "Hemos encontrado un problema en tu sitio web: ";
$lang['database_unavailable'] = "Base de datos no disponible";
```

Calling the file by the same name, we will be able to load the one we need by passing the language to the load function. The array keys inside it are the same, but with the contents translated to the language we need. With all this, we can modify our `error` controller's function to something such as:

```php
function report_twitter($user_lang = 'en')
{
  switch($user_lang)
  {
    case 'en':
      $this->lang->load('info', 'english');
      break;
    case 'es':
      this->lang->load('info', 'spanish');
      break;
  }
  $this->load->library('twitter');
  $this->twitter->auth('account@account.com','password');
  $this->twitter->update($this->lang->line('error'));
}
```

This is a very simple example, let's see how we decide—which language file to load and then use it to send a message to some twitter account, in the desired language. You can try it by loading this `http://localhost/codeigniter/errors/report_twitter` or this page `http://localhost/codeigniter/errors/report_twitter/es`.

You will see that different messages are sent to twitter, as we can see this requires some effort. All we need to do is translations. It is easy to have a multi-lingual site. There is not much about the `Language` class, but you can see it here: `http://codeigniter.com/user_guide/libraries/language.html`

Making HTML tables the easy way—the Table class

Another useful library CI offers is the HTML `Table` class. You can see the details at the online user guide `http://codeigniter.com/user_guide/libraries/table.html`. But we are going to see some of their uses here. For example, if you spend a lot of time writing things such as:

```
echo "<tr><td>$value1</td><td>$value2</td></tr>";
```

CI's `Table` class allows you to auto-generate HTML tables. Let's display details of some of the tests we've run. You start off by loading the class, as always. Then you can specify the table data as an `array`, like this:

```
$this->load->library('table');
$data = array(
                array('name', 'type', 'time'),
                array('test 1', 'ping', '1166627335'),
                array('test 2', 'ping', '1166627335'),
                array('test 3', 'ete', '1166702400')
             );
echo $this->table->generate($data);
```

But the function really comes on its own when you automatically generate the data, using the object returned by a database query. For instance, we can modify our `errors` controller, the `show_errors` function:

```
function show_errors($site_id = '')
{
  $this->load->model('errors_model');
  $this->load->library('table');
  $errors = $this->errors_model->get_errors($site_id);
```

```
if ($errors->num_rows() > 0)
{
  echo $this->table->generate($errors);
}
}
```

If you navigate to `http://localhost/codeigniter/errors/show_errors/16`, remember to change the `site_id` to the one you have used for your site, you will see a table generated from the query result instead of the previous list of errors.

That's an amazing way to save your time—just four lines of code returns a query and wraps it up for you in HTML. In fact, a small tear comes to my eye when I think of the time I used to spend in writing:

```
<table>
<tr><td>$variable1</td><td>$variable2</td></tr> //etc.
```

While, as you can see, CI's basic table layout isn't wonderful, you can set your own template, using CSS styles if you wish, and the function will faithfully follow that. The template is an array inside the `table` class, so you will need to reset it each time you call the class.

```
$tmpl = array (
               'table_open' => '<table border="0" cellpadding="4"
                                                cellspacing="0">',
            'heading_row_start' => '<tr>',
            'heading_row_end' => '</tr>',
            'heading_cell_start' => '<th>',
            'heading_cell_end' => '</th>',
            'row_start' => '<tr>',
            'row_end' => '</tr>',
            'cell_start' => '<td>',
            'cell_end' => '</td>',
            'row_alt_start' => '<tr>',
            'row_alt_end' => '</tr>',
            'cell_alt_start' => '<td>',
            'cell_alt_end' => '</td>',
            'table_close' => '</table>',
            );
$this->table->set_template($tmpl);
```

This is a default template `array`, on which the function's design is based. Note that there are two set of `row` definitions (`row` and `row_alt`), in case you want the colors of the rows to alternate. If you submit revisions to a part or the entire template, the function reacts accordingly, generating different HTML markup.

You'll notice that the template is just an array, and you submit revisions by revising the values for each key. For instance, if you have a CSS file defined somewhere with a class called `mytable`, you can refer to that using:

```
$tmpl = array ( 'table_open' => '<table class="mytable">' );
```

You don't have to alter every value, the ones you don't alter remain at the default setting. Now your table magically jumps into the format you specified.

Caching pages

By now, we're writing some pretty complex code. The server has to sit down and puzzle out each dynamically generated page. While it's simple for you to write a function like the `show_errors`, shown previously, the poor old server has to do more work as a result.

Sometimes, this can lead to your pages taking a longer time to load than you would like. There may be no way out of this. If you're writing a report that will be different each time then you just have to wait. However, you may be generating a page that will remain the same for a while. A blog, for instance, remains the same until you put another entry on it. If your blog gets a thousand views a day, on a day when you didn't add a new posting, each view will be the same. And it's a waste of time, for the system, to regenerate the same page over and over.

The way out of this is to cache the page. You generate the page once, and the HTML produced is saved in a `cache` file with a timestamp, as well as being returned to someone's browser for display on their screen. Then, when the next viewer requests that page, the system checks to see when it was last generated and saved. If this is within a time limit you set, it serves up the cache page. If not, it generates the page from scratch. Sounds like some pretty complex coding is required here. Except if you're using CI. If you are, you need to do two things:

- Find the `/system/cache` folder, which should be empty, except for an `index.html` file. Make sure the folder is writable, that is, has permissions set to 666, if you're on a Linux system.
- Insert the following line somewhere in the controller function that generates an HTML page:

  ```
  $this->output->cache(5);
  ```

  Here 5 is the number of minutes you want your cache to persist, before the page is regenerated.

For example, in our controller:

```
function show_errors($site_id = '')
{
  $this->output->cache(5);
  $this->load->model('errors_model');
  $this->load->library('table');
  $errors = $this->errors_model->get_errors($site_id);
  if ($errors->num_rows() > 0)
  {
    $data['table'] = $this->table->generate($errors);
    $this->load->view('error_table', $data);
  }
}
```

In the `application/views/error_table.php` file we put:

```
<?php
echo $table;
```

It's important to note that only controllers that have views can be cached; if you echo your contents from within the controller, no caching will be done. Also, before caching all your site, think about the pages that really need to be cached. Admin pages usually aren't a good option for caching, for example, when inserting new records we need to see them at the moment.

That's it. If you now load the function, you'll see the page load as usual. If you now look at your /system/cache folder, you'll see a new file in there with a meaningless title.

Open this (in a text editor), and you'll see it contains the HTML code for your page, plus a timestamp. If you request the same page again before the timestamp is five minutes old, you'll get the cached page. If you wait longer and the cache file is out-of-date, your next request will automatically delete it and replace it with a newer version.

If you change your mind about caching the page, delete the this->output->cache(5) line from your controller, and your page will be served afresh each time. The last cached file will stay in your /system/cache folder until you delete it manually. If you want to continue caching, but accidentally delete a cache file at any time don't worry, the system will create a new one when that page is called next.

CI makes this so quick and simple that it is tempting to cache every page! Just remember that you don't always want to do this—it's best for high-load pages that don't change very often, it may not help much on others.

Summary

CI offers a lot of goodies to make coding easier and to make your websites more professional. This chapter looked at just five of them:

- The `text` helper provides useful functions to manipulate and convert strings.
- The `date` helper allows you to convert between different date formats and also to cope with time zones.
- The `Language` class makes it easier to write multi-lingual websites, which respond to user preferences. Alas, you still have to do the translation!
- The `Table` class lets you output properly formed HTML tables, directly from a database query if you need to.
- Automatically caching high-load dynamic pages provides a faster response.

11
Using CI to Handle Files and Images

In this chapter we will see several useful CI functions and helpers. Each of them is a good example of how a few lines of CI code give you seamless access to a range of applications and actions. It would take a lot of specialized knowledge to code them from scratch. In many cases, CI provides an interface to write the code for classes that are already out there—you could download them from PEAR or some other source. CI gives you a standard interface—you just treat it as native CI code, and the framework does all the interfacing work for you.

Let's look at the following activities in this chapter:

- The `file` helper: This makes it easy to write to and read from files
- The `download` helper: This makes it easy for your users to download files directly from the website, rather than displaying them as HTML
- The file uploading class: This works the other way—allowing users to put files on your site, with built-in security precautions to limit what they can do
- The image manipulation class: This allows you to do several useful things with images; we'll look at how to resize and watermark them
- The zip encoding class: This allows you to compress files before your users download them

Each of these examples hides a lot of clever coding and allows you to write practical applications with minimum fuss. In many cases, they add extra code to make the activity more robust.

Let's look at them one by one:

The file helper

PHP syntax for reading and writing files is not easy to grasp at first sight. CI's `file` helper contains a few useful functions, which act as a wrapper for PHP file handling operations. Start by loading the helper:

```
$this->load->helper('file');
```

Life gets much simpler. Now, to write to a file all you need to know is:

- The location of your file.
- The text you want to write to it.
- The mode in which you want to open the file. Modes are defined in the PHP manual (see the page on "fopen"). They include `r` for read, `w` for write (write to the file, overwriting data already there), and `a` for append (write to the file, adding to the existing data). Adding `a+` opens the file for both read and write operations. The parameters `a` and `w`, not `r` and `r+`, create the file if it is not there already.

Then you use these three parameters for the `write_file()` function:

```
write_file('e:/filetest.txt', 'hello world', 'a+');
```

This is simple and more intuitive than PHP's two-step code:

```
if ( $fp = fopen('e:/filetest.txt','r+'))
{
   fwrite($fp, 'hello world');
}
```

The helper returns FALSE if the file operation doesn't take place, so you can use it to report success or failure. You have to specify a title for your file, but if you don't specify a filepath it is placed in the root folder of your site, where your main `index.php` file is.

Of course, any folder that you create or write a file to must have write permissions set. Remember, if you are running on a Windows system you have to use forward slashes (/) to describe your filepath.

In our application, we can combine this helper with the dbutil (database utility) class. For example, we can export our error_logs table to a csv file; this way we can keep the logs, open them with Excel or Calc, check them offline to see the errors that are repeating, and so on.

First, we will use the dbutil class to export the table to a csv file, and then the file helper to write it. Remember our errors controller? It is in application/controllers/errors.php. We are adding a new function to it:

```
function export_csv()
{
  $this->load->dbutil();
  $query = $this->db->get('error_logs');
  echo $this->dbutil->csv_from_result($query);
}
```

Export to CSV format will be done in two steps. First, we load the dbutil class and then we use the db->get method to retrieve data from our error_logs table. The next step produces the CSV format as a result. We can see it at http://localhost/codeigniter/errors/export_csv. We are now using the file helper to write this result to a file:

```
function export_csv()
{
  $this->load->dbutil();
  $this->load->helper('file');
  $query = $this->db->get('error_logs');
  $result = $this->dbutil->csv_from_result($query);
  if( ! write_file('backups/file.csv', $result))
  {
    ccho "Unable to write file";
  }
}
```

After loading the `file` helper, we save the results to a variable, instead of sending data to the screen. The `write_file` function is used to save this variable to a file. It returns FALSE if it's not able to generate the file. This way we can check if everything is fine and if so, we will have a file that will look something like this:

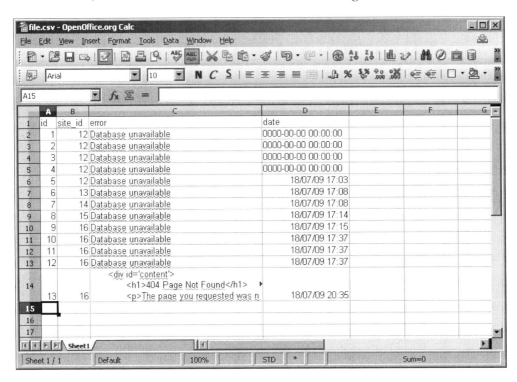

We can use the `database` class for more functions than just generating `csv` files. It allows us to create, back up, repair, and optimize databases and tables—only on MySQL and MySQLi databases. Combine it with the `file` helper, and you create a neat backup routine. For this purpose we are writing a new function inside our controller:

```
function database_backup()
{
  $this->load->dbutil();
  $this->load->helper('file');
  $backup = $this->dbutil->backup();
  if( ! write_file('backups/backup.gz', $backup))
  {
    echo "Unable to write file";
  }
}
```

It's pretty much the same as we had before, but instead of the csv_from_result function we are calling backup, and writing its contents to a .gz file. If we go to http://localhost/codeigniter/errors/database_backup, the file will be created inside our backups directory. Decompress and open it, you will see an SQL export file with the database structure, even with the data inserted.

The backup function can be fed with an array of options, to help us customize the result. You can check them in the online user guide http://codeigniter.com/user_guide/database/utilities.html, but we are going to use only one of them for now:

```
function database_backup()
{
  $this->load->dbutil();
  $this->load->helper('file');
  $prefs = array(
                 'tables' => array('error_logs'),
               );
  $backup = $this->dbutil->backup($prefs);
  if( ! write_file('backups/backup.gz', $backup))
  {
    echo "Unable to write file";
  }
}
```

We have used the $prefs array to indicate the tables we want to back up; if we don't pass any more values to the array, default values will be used. The rest of the values are well documented in the online user guide.

Inside the file helper there's also a function that returns an array of all files and/or folders in a given directory:

```
$filenames = get_filenames('c:/')
```

You can use this in a simple piece of code to check that the files and folders are actually what you expect. Start by using the CI function to find the files present, and a reference array of files you expect to find, and use array_diff() to compare them. Given two arrays, array_diff() tells you which values are in the first and not in the second. So, you have to use it twice, putting each array first.

```
//list files actually found
$files_there = get_filenames('C:/wamp/www/codeigniter/application/
                             controllers');
// list files we expected
$files_expected = array('start.php', 'index.php');
```

```
// any found that we didn't expect?

$difference = array_diff($files_there, $files_expected);
echo "<br />Missing files are:";
print_r($difference);

// any expected that we didn't find?

$difference = array_diff($files_expected, $files_there);
echo "<br />Extra files are:";
print_r($difference);
```

There are more useful functions inside the `file` helper, just check them at
http://codeigniter.com/user_guide/helpers/file_helper.html.

The download helper

The `download` helper only has one function, but it complements the `file` helper very
nicely. You might create a file on a website and then want to serve it up to the reader
as a text file, rather than converting it to a web page. A good example would be a
database backup file, like the one we just created for our application.

In order to code this over an internet connection, you must specify the type of
page you want in the HTTP headers. CI's `download` helper does this for you in the
background. Load the helper with:

```
$this->load->helper('download');
```

Its single method is used like this:

```
force_download($name, $data);
```

Where $name is the name you give to the downloaded file, and $data represents
the file contents. If you want to download an existing file, you have to read it into a
string first:

```
function backup_download($file = '', $ext = '')
{
  $this->load->helper('file');
  $this->load->helper('download');
  $data = read_file("backups/".$file.".".$ext);
  force_download($file.".".$ext, $data);
}
```

This time we have created a new function inside the `errors` controller, which receives two parameters to create a file name (you can't pass dots in the URL, hence the need for two parameters). The file is then read and the `download` helper is called in order to download the file. We can check it at `http://localhost/codeigniter/errors/backup_download/backup/gz`; if all goes well our download should start in some seconds.

Behind the scenes, the helper takes care of identifying the MIME type and setting HTTP headers. It relies on the `mimes` file, located at `system/application/config/mimes`, which is also used by the `upload` class, which we'll look at next. This file stores an array of MIME types and the appropriate HTTP extensions. For example:

```
'rtf' => 'text/rtf',
'text' => 'text/plain',
```

It saves you from remembering them!

If you regularly use file types that aren't included on CI's list, you can easily add them to the `application/config/mimes.php` file.

The file upload class and CI's image class

Now we are using those two libraries to add some cool functionalities to our website monitoring tool. Among all the data we have collected for our sites, it would be very helpful to have an image of the site itself. This will allow us to have a list of sites with a thumbnail helping us recognize the site very easily.

Our first step will be to create a folder, where we can keep the uploaded files. These may be text, images, or more exotic file types such as MP3 audio or MPEG video. Uploading is a more complex process than the file downloads we just discussed, but CI's `upload` class takes care of most of the work for you. It also looks after some of the security issues. The folder must be set with the correct permissions, allowing users to write to it (that is, 777 on a Unix/Linux system). Let's assume you call this folder `uploads`, and put it in your website's root folder.

If we want to upload files we will need an upload form. Let's build a controller and a view. First, build the controller at `application/controllers/uploader.php`:

```php
<?php
class Uploader extends Controller
{
  function uploader()
  {
```

```
      parent::Controller();
    }
    function index()
    {
      $this->load->helper('form');
      $this->load->view('upload_form');
    }
  }
```

Apart from loading the `form` helper, we are loading the view from, `application/ views/upload_form.php`.

```
<?php
echo form_open_multipart('uploader/upload');
echo form_upload('file')."<br/><br/>";
echo form_submit('submit', 'Send');
echo form_close();
?>
```

This time we are using the `form_open_multipart` function so that the form is created with `enctype="multipart/form-data"`, and we are able to upload files. The `form_upload` function will generate the input of field type. With that done we can navigate to `http://localhost/codeigniter/uploader` and we will see our form. The next step is to create a function in the controller that actually uploads the file.

```
function upload()
{
  $config['upload_path'] = 'uploads';
  $config['allowed_types'] = 'gif|jpg|png';
  $config['max_size'] = '8000';
  $this->load->library('upload', $config);
  if ( ! $this->upload->do_upload('file'))
  {
    echo $this->upload->display_errors();
  }
  else
  {
    print_r($this->upload->data());
  }
}
```

Our controller is divided into three parts. The first one prepares a `config` array with the data needed to upload the file. The `upload_path` will indicate the folder where want the file to be placed. The `allowed_types` will define which file types will be allowed for upload; don't leave it blank—it will prevent all file uploads. The `max_size` allows us to define the maximum size for file uploads; if we set it to zero, there will be no limits.

Next we will load the library. By default, it expects the form field to be named `userfile`:

```
echo form_upload('userfile')
```

But if you look at our code we have called it:

```
echo form_upload('file')
```

As we have changed the form field name, we need to pass it to the `do_upload` function:

```
$this->upload->do_upload('file')
```

The last part of our function is used to perform some checks, to ensure the file has been uploaded. If there are any errors, the function will show them so that we can correct. If all goes fine, the array with information about the file will be output to the screen.

The `config` array can either be in the controller, or we can create a `config/upload` folder to contain it (this would be in `system/application/config/upload/upload.php`).

```php
<?php
if (!defined('BASEPATH')) exit('No direct script access allowed');
$config['upload_path'] = 'uploads';
$config['allowed_types'] = 'gif|jpg|png';
$config['max_size'] = '8000';
?>
```

It's important to grasp the difference between these two ways of setting your defaults. If you set the defaults from the upload file, you don't need to specifically initialize the file upload class. Just load it and it will find the defaults for itself. However, if you leave the defaults in the controller, you need to specify where they are when you load the class, using the second parameter in the `load` function, like this:

```
$this->load->library('upload', $config);
```

Where `$config` is the name of your array for defaults.

If you need to set different values or change them, you can initialize the library again:

`$this->upload->initialize($config);`

To know more about the parameters you can configure, look in the online user guide at `http://codeigniter.com/user_guide/libraries/file_uploading.html`.

Now we are able to upload a file, let's try it. Select one image file and upload it using the form. After completion, if all goes well, you will see the file info array in the upload folder, the file will be there.

You may be wondering what happens if we try to upload the same file twice. No problem, by default if a file already exist, the one we are trying to upload is renamed. For example, if we have already uploaded `forest.jpg`, the second time we upload it, it will be called `forest1.jpg`.

Of course, this behavior can be changed in the `config` file, setting the overwrite parameter to TRUE:

```
$config['overwrite'] = TRUE;
```

CI's image class

Now that we have our file uploaded we can use CI's image class to manipulate it. This library works with the three most popular image libraries for PHP—GD/GD2, NetPBM, and ImageMagick. Use `phpinfo()` to find which of these is supported by your server. Image watermarking only works with GD/GD2, though:

The image manipulation class allows you to perform four basic functions with images:

- Resize: You may want to fit them into a standard size on your screen or you may want to cut them right down to thumbnail images

- Crop

- Rotate

- Watermark (only available with GD/GD2): This is often used to put a copyright notice on an image so that people can't download it from your site and pass it as their own work

The GD library is always needed in order to calculate image properties. You can use the library you want to manipulate the image.

First we will take a look at image resizing.

 Remember, for us to be able to manipulate the images, we will need to have write permissions for them.

First, load the library. We will do this inside our upload function, so we can work with the image after uploading it:

```
else
{
  $this->load->library('image_lib');
  print_r($this->upload->data());
}
```

Then, you need to set a few configuration details. As with the file upload class, you can either do this in your code, or in a separate system/application/config/image_lib.php file.

There are several preferences you can set and they are listed in the online user guide. Perhaps the most important ones are:

- Which image library you are using. The default is GD2.

- The image you want to manipulate. This should be the path (relative to your site's root folder) and filename.

- The size you want the image to be after processing — where x is a number of pixels, the width is set by $config['width'] = x;, and the height by $config['height'] = x;.

These are enough to resize our image, let's change the code inside the else loop:

```
else
{
  $file_data = $this->upload->data();
  $droot = $_SERVER["DOCUMENT_ROOT"];
  $config['image_library'] = 'GD2';
  $config['source_image'] = $droot.'codeigniter/uploads/'
                            .$file_data['file_name'];
  $config['new_image'] = $droot.'codeigniter/uploads/t_'
                         .$file_data['file_name'];
```

```
$config['maintain_ratio'] = TRUE;
$config['width'] = 75;
$config['height'] = 75;
$this->load->library('image_lib', $config);
if ( ! $this->image_lib->resize())
{
  echo $this->image_lib->display_errors();
}
else
{
  $this->load->helper('url');
  $data['file'] = $file_data['file_name'];
  $this->load->view('image', $data);
}
}
```

What exactly are we doing here? First, we save the uploaded file's data to an array and we also save our server's document root in a variable. Then, we start writing our `config` array, with the library to be used—GD2 in this example—and the source image, which would be the file we just uploaded. We also specify the new file that will be created from the image. We then indicate that we want to maintain the ratio of the width and height of the image.

Then we load the library and call the `resize()` function to try to resize the image. If all goes well, we call the view at `application/views/image.php`:

```
<img src="<?php echo base_url()."uploads/".$file; ?>"/>
<br/><br/>
<img src="<?php echo base_url()."uploads/t_".$file; ?>" />
```

If we go to `http://localhost/codeigniter/uploader` and upload an image we will end up with a screen similar to:

With the uploaded image and the resized one. That was fun, isn't it?

 Remember, if you want to resize another image just after finishing with the first, you need to create/modify the `config` array and initialize the library again:

```
$this->image_lib->initialize($config);
```

You can go to `codeigniter.com/user_guide/libraries/image_lib.html` for more details.

Easy file compression with CI's zip class

If you're moving around large files like images, you might need to compress them. CI contains a handy library for doing this. For example, if we want to download our `uploads` folder, we can easily achieve it with the help of this library. To see this in action create a download function inside `application/controllers/uploader.php` controller:

```
function download()
{
  $this->load->library('zip');
  $this->zip->read_dir('uploads/');
  $this->zip->download('uploads.zip');
}
```

That's all we need to download the `uploads` folder. Don't forget to put the `/`, or it won't work. The `read_dir` function reads all the contents of the folder you pass to it, and then the download function sends the file to your browser for download.

What if we want to keep the file in our server, so we can download it more times without the need to generate it again? Easy again, instead of:

```
$this->zip->download('uploads.zip');
```

We write:

```
$this->zip->archive('uploads/uploads.zip');
```

And the `.zip` file will be created inside our `uploads` folder for us to download as many times as we want. The `read_dir` function can be changed to `read_file` so that we can read a single file instead of a folder, you only need to pass the complete path to the function.

The CI zip encoding class is more complex than this and gives you several options. As usual, they're all set out in the online user guide. But this should give you an idea of how easy CI makes it to zip downloads from your site—minimizing the bandwidth they consume and saving your user's time.

Summary

This chapter brings together a few CI helpers and classes with similar themes. They help you to:

- Write and read files on your system with minimal coding, while CI locks and unlocks the files in the background
- Download files, rather than show them as HTML on the screen—with CI providing the HTTP headers and worrying about MIME types for you
- Upload files to your site, allowing you to specify security constraints such as the size and type of files you allow
- Easily manipulate images, to resize them
- Compress your files before you download them to your users

This is what frameworks are all about. Instead of a lot of tedious coding, they let you get on with building an application that works. They give you a standard and easy interface, and worry about the details for you.

12
Moving Your Site to the WWW

The great day has come. Your development site is running well enough on your local server to transfer it to a production site hosted on a remote web server. It should be easy to do this. Copy all the files, including the entire `system` folder, update the configuration settings, copy over and link to the database, and away you go. Sometimes, it is really that easy.

We will do this step by step; we will try to identify potentially problematic points so that this guide helps you in future. In this chapter we are going to see:

- Uploading our site and modifying it to work on a shared server
- Errors and error pages
- The site updating screen
- Updating CI to a new version
- Uploading and configuring our site

This is the easiest part—don't worry the rest is going to be easy too. For uploading our site we can use one of the hundred FTP programs out there. We will use FileZilla (`http://filezilla-project.org/`), but any other will also work fine for us.

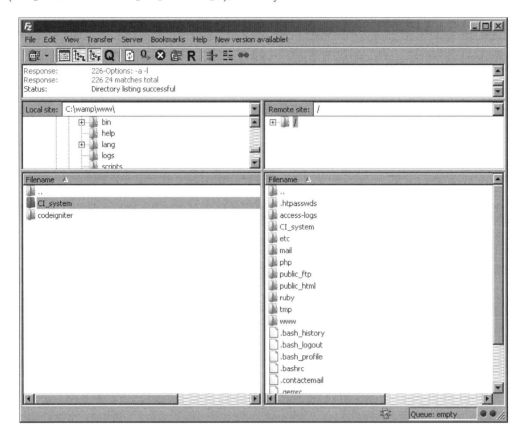

First, we are going to upload our `CI_system` folder to the root folder of our shared server. The `system` folder is the core of the CodeIgniter framework, which we don't need to be reachable for our site visitors, so placing it outside www will be safer. Also we can use a single `system` folder for as many websites we want, and upgrade it easily.

 In fact we could have placed everything outside www, except the `index.php` file and any assets we would need to be publicly accessible, such as images, `.js` files, `.swf` files, and so on.

Next, open the CodeIgniter folder inside `c:\wampp\www` and upload all its contents to the www folder of our server, and then we can see a structure like this:

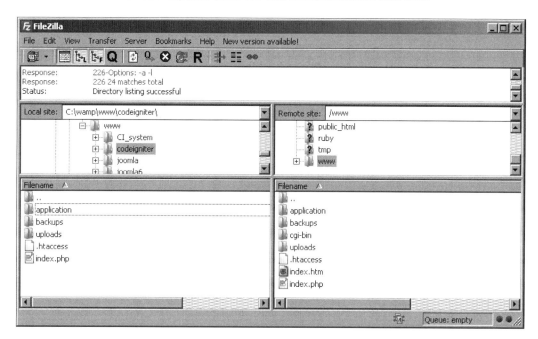

 Don't forget to edit the `index.php` file, and modify the `$system_` folder and `$application_` folder according to your server paths.

You think it is done? Let's take a dose of reality. Take a look at your site:

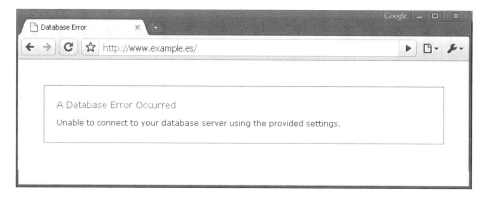

Ah, the old database error. We need to create the database in our server and modify the CI database configuration file. We can export our database using the phpMyAdmin application that comes with WAMP. In the server we can find some tool such as `cpanel` with phpMyAdmin installed, so we can easily create and import the database.

 If you need help for using phpMyAdmin you should read:
`http://www.packtpub.com/`
`mastering-phpmyadmin-3-1-fourth-edition/book`

Before importing the data, we need to create a database, a user, and give privileges to this user for the created database. When giving privileges to the user do it with care; maybe this user doesn't need drop table permissions, or create privileges. Assigning only the needed privileges will make your website safer.

After that is done, we can import the data to our newly created database. Last and very important, edit `application/config/database.php` to:

```
$active_group = "default";
$active_record = TRUE;
$db['default']['hostname'] = "localhost";
$db['default']['username'] = "example_demo";
$db['default']['password'] = "demo";
$db['default']['database'] = "example_database";
$db['default']['dbdriver'] = "mysql";
$db['default']['dbprefix'] = "";
$db['default']['pconnect'] = TRUE;
$db['default']['db_debug'] = TRUE;
$db['default']['cache_on'] = FALSE;
$db['default']['cachedir'] = "";
$db['default']['char_set'] = "utf8";
$db['default']['dbcollat'] = "utf8_general_ci";
```

Most of the values can remain the same, but take care of the following ones:

- `hostname`: When we were working with WAMP this parameter was `localhost`; maybe for our shared server it may remain as `localhost`, as some shared hosts have it this way. You may need to check with your hosting provider for the value you need to put here.

- `password`: Here we need to change the value to that of our new user password.

- `username` and `database`: These may be a little problematic, as sometimes the hosting provider places the site name or abbreviation before the user and database name.

It would be better to have two configuration arrays, one for our local configuration, and the other one for the online site. For example:

```
$active_group = "online";
$active_record = TRUE;
$db['default']['hostname'] = "localhost";
$db['default']['username'] = "root";
$db['default']['password'] = "root";
$db['default']['database'] = "websites";
$db['default']['dbdriver'] = "mysql";
$db['default']['dbprefix'] = "";
$db['default']['pconnect'] = TRUE;
$db['default']['db_debug'] = TRUE;
$db['default']['cache_on'] = FALSE;
$db['default']['cachedir'] = "";
$db['default']['char_set'] = "utf8";
$db['default']['dbcollat'] = "utf8_general_ci";
$db['online']['hostname'] = "online_host_name";
$db['online']['username'] = "online_username";
$db['online']['password'] = "online_password";
$db['online']['database'] = "online_database";
$db['online']['dbdriver'] = "mysql";
$db['online']['dbprefix'] = "";
$db['online']['pconnect'] = TRUE;
$db['online']['db_debug'] = TRUE;
$db['online']['cache_on'] = FALSE;
$db['online']['cachedir'] = "";
$db['online']['char_set'] = "utf8";
$db['online']['dbcollat'] = "utf8_general_ci";
```

Now if we need to use the online database configuration, we only need to change the $active_group variable, and upload the file. This way we only need to change one value and we can maintain both configurations.

With all these settings in place don't forget to upload the modified file to our site. This time, if we reload the page we will see:

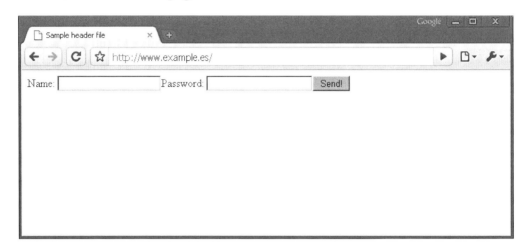

Much better now, but though it may seem to be working we still need to make some changes to our code. For example, in our `application/config/config.php` file, we will need to change our `base_url`:

```
$config['base_url'] = "http://www.example.es/";
```

Configuration is almost done, though if we try to load another controller or page, for example, our `charts` controller, we would get this error:

This kind of error is very different than the usual CI "Controller not found" error. This time it has to be with our .htaccess file, remember? We were using it to rewrite our URLs and remove the index.php from them. Let's look inside it:

```
<IfModule mod_rewrite.c>
  RewriteEngine On
  RewriteBase /

  #Removes access to the system folder by users.
  #Additionally this will allow you to create a System.php
  #controller, previously this would not have been possible.
  #'system' can be replaced if you have renamed your system folder.
  RewriteCond %{REQUEST_URI} ^system.*
  RewriteRule ^(.*)$ /codeigniter/index.php?/$1 [L]

  #Checks to see if the user is attempting to access a valid file,
  #such as an image or css document, if this isn't true it sends
  #the request to index.php

  RewriteCond %{REQUEST_FILENAME} !-f
  RewriteCond %{REQUEST_FILENAME} !-d
  RewriteRule ^(.*)$ /codeigniter/index.php?/$1 [L]
</IfModule>

<IfModule !mod_rewrite.c>

  # If we don't have mod_rewrite installed, all 404's
  # can be sent to index.php, and everything works as normal.
  # Submitted by: ElliotHaughin

  ErrorDocument 404 /index.php
</IfModule>
```

We need to change those lines, removing the /codeigniter/ part, thus they will look like:

```
/index.php
```

Note, if you have moved your system folder out of the www folder, you won't need these two lines:

```
RewriteCond %{REQUEST_URI} ^system.*
RewriteRule ^(.*)$ /codeigniter/index.php?/$1 [L]
```

But if, for some reason, you can't move the system folder out of www, leave these lines in the .htaccess file, as they will prevent your users from accessing your system folder.

If we now try to reload the page, or any other controller, this time it will work fine. So we are done with modifying files now, but there is one last thing we need to check, permissions given to some folders, like our uploads folder or the CI_system/cache folder. These folders need to be writable so we need to change their permissions to 766 or 777. With that done our image uploads and cache should work as expected.

If you upload to a Windows server you may encounter some differences, most of which are related to using \ rather than / in your paths and some permission definition differences.

A very annoying one—remember that a Windows system doesn't make a difference between uppercase and lowercase names. So Image.jpg is the same as image.jpg, but on a Unix system it wouldn't be so.

Errors and error pages

While developing, it is a good idea to see programming errors that really help us. But it may not be a good idea letting our visitors to see those errors, for example, a missing semicolon would end up showing the following screen to our visitor:

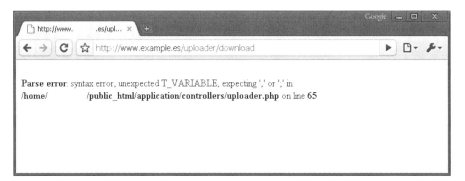

While this helps you, you need to refrain from showing this to your visitors. Open your index.php file and find this line in it:

```
error_reporting(E_ALL);
```

Change it, or better comment it and add:

```
error_reporting(0);
```

Now, after uploading the file, no errors will be shown any more. But other errors such as "404 Page Not Found", will require some tweaking. We will try to make them more useful for our visitors, for example, if they try to load a non-existent controller they will see this screen:

This is of no help to our visitors. If we want to help them in case they reach that error page, we need to modify the `application/errors/error_404.php` file. When we open it we will see something like this:

```php
<?php header("HTTP/1.1 404 Not Found"); ?>
<html>
<head>
<title>404 Page Not Found</title>
<style type="text/css">
  body
  {
    background-color: #fff;
    margin: 40px;
    font-family: Lucida Grande, Verdana, Sans-serif;
    font-size: 12px;
    color: #000;
  }
  #content
  {
    border: #999 1px solid;
    background-color: #fff;
    padding: 20px 20px 12px 20px;
  }
  h1
  {
    font-weight: normal;
    font-size: 14px;
```

```
      color: #990000;
      margin: 0 0 4px 0;
    }
  </style>
  </head>
  <body>
    <div id="content">
      <h1><?php echo $heading; ?></h1>
      <?php echo $message; ?>
    </div>
  </body>
  </html>
```

We are going to modify the last part like this:

```
<div id="content">
  <h1>Oooops, it seems the page you are searching is no longer here.
      You can navigate to one of these others:</h1>
  <a href="/start">Home</a> -> This is our home page <br/>
  <a href="/charts">Charts</a> -> This is our charts page <br/>
  <a href="/uploader">Uploader</a> -> This is our uploader <br/>
</div>
```

This way we are helping our visitors to find their way to a page that already exists. There are some other error files in the `application/errors` folder that we can tweak to give better error pages to our users. This is an important part of site development and will give a nice experience to your visitors.

So, should we update if a new version of CI comes out?

New versions of CI come up from time to time. They come with comprehensive instructions for updating. Usually, this involves copying a new set of files to your `CI_system` folder. Sometimes, you need to change `config` files, or your `index.php` file as well. Because the folder structure keeps your application files in their place, it's usually easy to update the system without touching the applications.

But, say you've written your killer application in version 1.7.1. It's uploaded to your production system and is working fine. Then CI version 1.7.2 comes out (or 2.8 or whatever…). It has interesting new features and some bug fixes. Do you upgrade to it?

We would say, "Yes", if it's a minor upgrade. But if it's a major version change, and your existing system is working fine, it may take some more time to update it, so you will need to decide if the changes are going to help you or not. You can tell the difference partly from the numbering, but also from the "change log" published with each upgrade when it is released. The sort of changes that have been made in CI over the last year fall into three categories:

- Bug fixes: There are surprisingly few of these—CI has excellent code, and most of the base classes have been well tested by hundreds if not thousands of users.

- New features: These appear regularly, but if you managed to build your application without them, will they be really helpful now?

- Subtle changes: As described, CI has gone through a process of internal evolution, and it may well continue to do so. Some of these might be backwardly compatible, or they might require fairly major rewrites of your code.

We can check the changes in the change log at:
`http://codeigniter.com/user_guide/changelog.html`

It's a good idea to take a look into the change log, when a new version comes out. This way we can see how those changes affect our existing code.

Steps/advice to follow when updating our CI version

Updating a site, especially when it is a production one, producing a working site, maybe an online shop or anything else needs care. We don't want our visitors to see any errors.

- Try to have a cloned version of your online site, be it in your localhost or any other place, but in an environment similar to the online one, that is the same PHP version, and so on. In this "clone" version you can make all the modifications and check if everything works without compromising the online version. This is a good idea not only when updating, but for adding new functionalities to the site, or changing some code, and so on.

- Back up your database, always. Before doing anything else, make a copy of the database, in case you need to restore it.

- It would be a good idea to make a copy of the files too—before updating, or even better, rename your `system` folder and upload the new one—this way if something goes wrong you can rename it again. You can name your `system` folder for CI version.

- If you have renamed your `system` folder you will need to edit your `index.php` file and change it too.

With these simple steps, you can update your sites with safety, and if something goes wrong, go back to your previous version quickly.

Summary

In this chapter, we've seen some of things that we need to do when moving our site from our development environment to a shared server, or production environment. We have also seen how to give our visitors better error screens and, what to do in case of CI updates.

This has been a light chapter, but a very important one, as you will need to upload your site to a different server, or update the CI version you are using.

13

CRUD—or Putting It All Together

The most essential and repetitive part of designing any dynamic site is the CRUD. You have one or more database tables; you need to be able to Create, Read, Update, and Delete entries on each of these. Later, you'll do clever things with the data, but until there is some user-friendly way to put it there and maintain it, your site isn't viable.

This involves writing CRUD functions and though conceptually quite easy, they are fairly complex and time-consuming. But CI will help us make them faster and more reusable. For this example we are going to take our `sites` table and make some functions to read, insert, edit, and delete. This is a good way of summing up and using many of the lessons that we've learned in the previous chapters.

So we are writing code for:

- A controller for our `sites` table, with some functions to read, insert, edit, delete
- Some views to present the data
- A model to work with the data

We will also take a look at pagination and ordering. Let's start; this is going to be a very useful chapter!

Building our CRUD controller, model, and views

We will start with the controller, so we can load the views from it and see exactly what are we doing. We are going to create the `sites` controller; if you remember, we have a table like the following one:

```
CREATE TABLE `sites` (
  `id` int(10) NOT NULL auto_increment,
  `name` varchar(100) NOT NULL,
  `url` varchar(100) NOT NULL,
  `un` varchar(50) NOT NULL,
  `pw` varchar(50) NOT NULL,
  `client1` int(10) NOT NULL default '0',
  `client2` int(10) NOT NULL default '0',
  `admin1` int(10) NOT NULL default '0',
  `admin2` int(10) NOT NULL default '0',
  `domainid` int(10) NOT NULL default '0',
  `hostid` int(10) NOT NULL default '0',
  `webroot` varchar(50) NOT NULL,
  `files` text NOT NULL,
  `filesdate` int(11) NOT NULL default '0',
  `lastupdate` int(11) NOT NULL default '0',
  `submit` varchar(25) NOT NULL,
  PRIMARY KEY  (`id`)
) ENGINE=MyISAM  DEFAULT CHARSET=latin1 AUTO_INCREMENT=15 ;
```

The first function we will build inside our controller will be the `index` function. This function will show a list of the records existing in the table, let us insert new ones and read, edit, or delete existing ones. Quite a lot of things, so let's get started! Create a `application/controller/sites.php` file:

```php
<?php
class Sites extends Controller
{
  function Sites()
  {
    parent::Controller();
  }
  function index()
  {
    echo "This is working!";
  }
}
```

Well, for now we have only created the basic structure, but we can navigate to `http://localhost/codeigniter/sites` and check if it is working. Now we will create a simple view to put that message into it. Go to `application/views` and create a `sites` folder. Create a view inside it, for example, `application/views/sites/index.php`:

```
This also works
```

With this in the view, we are going to modify our controller, so it shows this view; instead of doing an echo inside it, change the echo line to:

```
$this->load->view('sites/index');
```

You can appreciate how the folder is passed as well as the filename, this way we can organize our files in a convenient structure. As now we have a controller and a view, we are going to create a model; this model will help us retrieve data from the table.

```php
<?php
class Sites_model extends Model
{
  function get_sites()
  {
    $query = $this->db->get('sites');
    return $query;
  }
}
```

For now, our model has only one function, the `get_sites()` function. Maybe, we can write this query in our controller. But then what? We will then place more complex queries in the model? That way, we will have some queries in our model, and some in our controller. It's better to keep things organized—even the simplest query should be placed in a model. If for one unavoidable case you have to put a query in a controller, you can, but it's always better to keep things in place.

Now, it's time to put our controller to work. This time, we will call our model, retrieve the data, and prepare it, before loading the view. Remember the `table` class? Well, we are going to use that one too; this is going to help us get things done faster, let's see:

```php
function index()
{
  //First we load the library and the model
  $this->load->library('table');
  $this->load->model('sites_model');
  //Then we call our model's get_sites function
```

```
$sites = $this->sites_model->get_sites();

//If it returns some results we continue

if ($sites->num_rows() > 0)
{
  //Prepare the array that will contain the data

  $table = array();

  //Prepare the table headers, one column for each table field

  $table[] = array('id','name','url','un','pw',
                   'client1','client2','admin1',
                   'admin2','domainid','hostid',
                   'webroot','files','filesdate',
                   'lastupdate','submit');

  //Then we loop through our query results

  foreach ($sites->result() as $row)
  {
    //For each one of the results we create an array of values, one
    //for each field, that will be under our table headers
    $table[] = array($row->id,$row->name,$row->url,
                     $row->un,$row->pw,$row->client1,
                     $row->client2,$row->admin1,$row->admin2,
                     $row->domainid,$row->hostid,$row->webroot,
                     $row->files,$row->filesdate,
                     $row->lastupdate,$row->submit);
  }

  //Next step is to place our created array into a new array
  //variable, one that we are sending to the view.

  $data['sites'] = $table;
}

//Also we put into that array another variable, "heading" that we
//will use to echo the heading title

$data['heading'] = "Sites admin";

//Now we are prepared to call the view, passing all the necessary
//variables inside the $data array

$this->load->view('sites/index', $data);

}
```

Now that's a bit of change—from a simple phrase, to a fully working function. But don't worry; we will check every change step by step. First, we load the `class` table, and our `sites` model. The order in which we do it doesn't really matter, you can place them the way you like. Next we call our model function:

```
$sites = $this->sites_model->get_sites();
```

The query data is then saved to the `$sites` variable, then we check if that variable contains any record and prepare an array that will contain the data, if any. This will be a multidimensional array, being the first subarray in our table headers. The `foreach` loop will create the other subarrays. The data is placed into another array, `$data`, which will also contain a header variable. We then load our view and send all this data to it.

We have done a lot of things there, but with the help of CI we have done them in a very elegant and easy way. Our view will only have one function, to show our data on the screen, not much, for now:

```
<?php
//First we echo the $heading variable
echo "<h1>".$heading."</h1>";
//And if the $site variable is not empty we echo it's content by
//using the generate method of the table class / library
if(!empty($sites)) echo $this->table->generate($sites);
```

See, how we are doing it—using the `table` class `generate` function, passing all the data as a parameter. We can check what we have already done, but as there is no data in our database we are not going to see anything but the heading. Anyway go to `http://localhost/codeigniter/sites` to see that, at least, there are no errors. After checking it, we can continue.

We are now going to prepare a form, to help us insert data into the database. We need a link in our `index` view for us to click on and call the `form` view; just add this line to the view:

```
<?php
echo "<h1>".$heading."</h1>";
//Using the url helper's anchor function we create a link to our
//controller's new_site function
echo anchor('/sites/new_site', 'Add new element')."<br/><br/>";
```

This will render a new link; when clicked it will call the new function inside our `sites` controller. This is done with the help of the `url` helper. We have it autoloaded for this application, but in other cases you will need to load it manually:

```
$this->load->helper('url');
```

Remember, if you don't autoload the `url` helper in your `config` file at `application/config/autoload.php`, you will need to do it in every function that needs it using `$this->load->helper('url');`

Our new controller is going to be really simple. We will create it inside our `sites` controller, under the `index` function:

```
function new_site()
{
  //We are going to need the form helper
  $this->load->helper('form');
  //And then we load the view, "new" in this case
  $this->load->view('sites/new');
}
```

We load the `form` helper, and just after that load the `new.php` view. We are going to create that file in the same folder as our previous `index.php` view, in `application/views/sites/new.php`.

```
<h1>Add new site</h1>
<?php
//First open the form using the form helper
echo form_open('sites/add');
?>
<ul>
<!-- And then we use the form helper's input function to create the
form fields -->
<li>Site name: <?php echo form_input('name'); ?></li>
<li>Site url: <?php echo form_input('url'); ?> </li>
<li>Site username: <?php echo form_input('un'); ?></li>
<li>Username password: <?php echo form_input('pw'); ?></li>
<li>Client name 1: <?php echo form_input('client1'); ?></li>
<li>Client name 2: <?php echo form_input('client2'); ?></li>
<li>Admin name 1: <?php echo form_input('admin1'); ?></li>
```

```
<li>Admin name 2: <?php echo form_input('admin2'); ?></li>
<li>Domain id: <?php echo form_input('domainid'); ?></li>
<li>Host id: <?php echo form_input('hostid'); ?></li>
<li>Webroot: <?php echo form_input('webroot'); ?></li>
<li>Files count: <?php echo form_input('files'); ?></li>
<li>Files upload date: <?php echo form_input('filesdate'); ?></li>
<li>Last update: <?php echo form_input('lastupdate'); ?></li>
<li>Submit date: <?php echo form_input('submit'); ?></li>
</ul>
<!-- Create the submit button -->
<?php echo form_submit('add', 'Add site'); ?>
```

This is a very basic form, but it will help us send some data to another function in our controller—the add function. For the moment we are only using the form_input function of the form helper, along with form_submit and form_open. If we go to http://localhost/codeigniter/sites/new_site, we will see something like:

Though it's not the best looking form in the world, it will do the work for now. When we, or a user, fill the form and click the **Add site** button it will send all the data to the add function in our controller. In that function we will receive all the data and prepare an array to save it into the database. It's just that easy; later we can do some validation and other things, but for the moment we are going to keep it simple:

```
function add()
{
  //we are going to use the session library to create some flash data
  $this->load->library('session');
  //Also we are going to need the sites model
  $this->load->model('sites_model');
  //Put the received data into an array.
  $data = array(
              'name' => $_POST['name'],
              'url' => $_POST['url'],
              'un' => $_POST['un'],
              'pw' => $_POST['pw'],
              'client1' => $_POST['client1'],
              'client2' => $_POST['client2'],
              'admin1' => $_POST['admin1'],
              'admin2' => $_POST['admin2'],
              'domainid' => $_POST['domainidr'],
              'hostid' => $_POST['hostid'],
              'webroot' => $_POST['webroot'],
              'files' => $_POST['files'],
              'filesdate' => $_POST['filesdate'],
              'lastupdate' => $_POST['lastupdate'],
              'submit' => $_POST['submit'],
            );
  //We call the model add_site function, passing the created array as
  //a parameter, we save returned data into the $sites variable.
  $sites = $this->sites_model->add_site($data);
  //If data was inserted ok we create a new flashdata with an ok
  //message
  if($sites)
  {
    $this->session->set_flashdata('status', 'Data added
                                  ok<br/><br/>');
  }
  else
```

```
{

   //But if something has gone wrong, we also need to tell that to
   //our users

   $this->session->set_flashdata('status', 'Data was not added,
                                  please try again<br/><br/>');
}

//Then we redirect to the index page again

redirect('sites/index', 'refresh');
}
```

The data sent by our form is received and put into an array. You can see that there is a new model function being called; we are going to build it in a moment. That model function will insert our data, and if all goes well, it will return true; if not it will return false.

We are using that to prepare a `flash` variable so that we can inform the users. The last line redirects us to the `index` view again.

Remember that `set_flashdata` creates a `session` variable that will be available only in the next server request.

The redirect is used to do a "header redirect" to the URI specified. The second parameter can have two values `refresh` and `location`; `location` is faster but may give some problems on Windows servers. You can read more about `redirect()` on:

http://codeigniter.com/user_guide/helpers/
url_helper.html

With all this in place, inserting data is going to be much easier; open your file in `application/models/sites_model.php` and copy the following code:

```
function add_site($data)
{
  //We create $result variable with a default value of 0, so if no
  //insert is done, $result will be returned with 0 value, and we
  //will be able, in the controller, to create the flash data
  //accordingly.

  $result = 0;

  //Check if $data is not empty

  if(!empty($data))
  {

    //insert $data with the insert method
```

```
    $result = $this->db->insert('sites', $data);
}
//return the value
return $result;
}
```

After adding data to the database, our function loads the view, and if we modify the view and add the following line, after inserting some data in our form, we will see a screen similar to this one:

```
echo $this->session->flashdata('status');
```

Now that we are able to insert data, and show it in a list, what can we do next? Maybe add a view link, so that we can load the contents of some record to check it. After that, in a similar way, we can create an edit link and lastly a delete link. But we are going to add the view link first.

Doing this involves several steps; one of them is to modify our `index` controller and we will change the following lines of the `index` function:

```
$table[] = array('id','name','url','un','pw','client1',
                 'client2','admin1','admin2','domainid',
                 'hostid','webroot','files','filesdate',
                 'lastupdate','submit');
foreach ($sites->result() as $row)
```

```
{
  $table[] = array($row->id,$row->name,$row->url,
                   $row->un,$row->pw,$row->client1,
                   $row->client2,$row->admin1,$row->admin2,
                   $row->domainid,$row->hostid,$row->webroot,
                   $row->files,$row->filesdate,$row->lastupdate,
                   $row->submit);
}
```

With these new ones:

```
//We are reducing the number of fields to show
$table[] = array('id','name','url','un','pw','client1','view');
//keep looping through results as before
foreach ($sites->result() as $row)
{
  //but now for each result returned, we show the needed fields, but
  //also create a link to the view_site function, attaching the id of
  //the current result row, the second parameter will be the text
  //that will appear in the link
  $table[] = array($row->id,$row->name,$row->url,$row->un,
                   $row->pw,$row->client1,
                   anchor('sites/view_site/',
                   $row->id, 'View'));
}
```

This will reduce the amount of data shown in our index view, also we are using the anchor function to create links in our view to our new controller function — view_site. Each link will have a record id that will make possible to retrieve the exact record from the database. The second parameter indicates what text we want to appear in the link.

So, now we have a link that calls a controller function, let's build it:

```
function view_site($id = '')
{
  $this->load->model('sites_model');
  //we call our model's get site function, we will create that
  //function in a moment
  $site = $this->sites_model->get_site($id);
  $data['title'] = "Record view: ";
```

```
//Returned data will be put into the $row variable that will be
//send to the view.

$data['row'] = $site;
$this->load->view('sites/view', $data);
}
```

As for the previous ones, this controller makes use of our `sites` model, and calls a function inside it, calling a view with the data obtained. This time, our model function will be:

```
//We don't give a default value to the $id variable, but will make
//the necessary checks inside the function

function get_site($id)
{
  if(!empty($id))
  {

    //use the where function to add a filter to our query, this time
    //the id, with the $id value

    $this->db->where('id', $id);

    //and then execute the query

    $query = $this->db->get('sites');
  }

  //If data is returned, the $row variable will be loaded with it

  if ($query->num_rows() > 0)
  {
    $row = $query->row();
  }
  else
  {

    //if no data, then we put FALSE into the variable

    $row = FALSE;
  }

  //and then return one value or the other one.

  return $row;
}
```

Though this function would need some more validation, it will do the work for this sample. We have seen these functions in previous chapters; with them we read from the database and return a record to the controller, which will feed the view with it. Our view will only need to output the data to the screen. We will create a `application/views/view.php` file:

```php
<h1><?php echo $title ?></h1>
<?php

//If our query returned no data, we created the $row variable with
//the FALSE value, we now use this to pick out the correct info to
//show

  if($row == FALSE)
  {
    echo "The record does not exist";
  }
  else
  {
    ?>
    <ul>
    <!-- If all was ok, then we show the values of each field -->
    <li>Site name: <?php echo $row->name; ?></li>
    <li>Site url: <?php echo $row->url; ?> </li>
    <li>Site username: <?php echo $row->un; ?></li>
    <li>Username password: <?php echo $row->pw; ?></li>
    <li>Client name 1: <?php echo $row->client1; ?></li>
    <li>Client name 2: <?php echo $row->client2; ?></li>
    <li>Admin name 1: <?php echo $row->admin1; ?></li>
    <li>Admin name 2: <?php echo $row->admin2; ?></li>
    <li>Domain id: <?php echo $row->domainid; ?></li>
    <li>Host id: <?php echo $row->hostid; ?></li>
    <li>Webroot: <?php echo $row->webroot; ?></li>
    <li>Files count: <?php echo $row->files; ?></li>
    <li>Files upload date: <?php $row->filesdate; ?></li>
    <li>Last update: <?php echo $row->lastupdate; ?></li>
    <li>Submit date: <?php echo $row->submit; ?></li>
    </ul>
    <?php
  }
  ?>
  <a href="javascript:history.back()">Back</a>
```

Now we are able to go to `http://localhost/codeigniter/sites/index` and click on the view link from the list of the record we want. A page with the contents of that record will be shown to us.

Now we are merging our view and add functions to have an edit form. We are going to retrieve some record from the database and use its data to fill the form fields. This way we will be able to change the data in the form. We will call this function inside our controller `edit_site`:

```
function edit_site($id = '')
{                 .
  $this->load->helper('form');
  $this->load->model('sites_model');
  $site = $this->sites_model->get_site($id);
  $data['title'] = "Record edit: ";
  $data['row'] = $site;
  $this->load->view('sites/edit', $data);
}
```

As you see, it's same as the view function, it only changes the view it is loading. Again, we need to modify our `index` function first:

```
//add a new header column, this time it will be "edit"
$table[] = array('id','name','url','un','pw',
                 'client1','view','edit');
foreach ($sites->result() as $row)
{
  //this is mostly the same, but with a new link and edit link which
  //calls our new edit_site function
  $table[] = array($row->id,$row->name,$row->url,
                 $row->un,$row->pw,$row->client1,
                 anchor('sites/view_site/'.$row->id, 'View'),
                 anchor('sites/edit_site/'.$row->id, 'Edit'));
}
```

We are adding a link, that when clicked on will call the `controller` function. Our model function, the one we used for the view, can be reused for the `edit` function. This way, and for now, we only need to create the view. Let our file be `application/views/edit.php`:

```
<h1><?php echo $title; ?></h1>
<?php
//Again if there are no records, a message will be shown, if there is
//a record, we will see the form.
if($row == FALSE)
{
  echo "The record does not exist";
  ?>
```

```
   <a href="javascript:history.back()">Back</a>
   <?php
}
else
{
   ?>
   <?php
   //Again we make use of the form helper, this time we pass the
   //current record id into the third parameter, as an array. We will
   //use it to know which record to edit later. We could have also
   //appended the id to the first parameter as 'sites/edit/'.$row->id
   echo form_open('sites/edit','',array('id' => $row->id));
   ?>
   <ul>
   <!-- Now create each form field, adding the current value, got from
   the database, in the second parameter -->
   <li>Site name: <?php echo form_input('name', $row->name); ?></li>
   <li>Site url: <?php echo form_input('url', $row->url); ?> </li>
   <li>Site username: <?php echo form_input('un', $row->un); ?></li>
   <li>Username password: <?php echo form_input('pw', $row->pw);
   ?></li>
   <li>Client name 1: <?php echo form_input('client1', $row->client1);
                   ?></li>
   <li>Client name 2: <?php echo form_input('client2', $row->client2);
                   ?></li>
   <li>Admin name 1: <?php echo form_input('admin1', $row->admin1);
                   ?></li>
   <li>Admin name 2: <?php echo form_input('admin2', $row->admin2);
                   ?></li>
   <li>Domain id: <?php echo form_input('domainid', $row->domainid);
                 ?></li>
   <li>Host id: <?php echo form_input('hostid', $row->hostid); ?></li>
   <li>Webroot: <?php echo form_input('webroot', $row->webroot);
               ?></li>
   <li>Files count: <?php echo form_input('files', $row->files);
                   ?></li>
   <li>Files upload date: <?php echo form_input('filesdate', $row-
                       >filesdate); ?></li>
   <li>Last update: <?php echo form_input('lastupdate', $row-
                   >lastupdate); ?></li>
   <li>Submit date: <?php echo form_input('submit', $row->submit);
                   ?></li>
   </ul>
   <?php echo form_submit('edit', 'Edit site'); ?>
   <?php
}
?>
```

This is pretty much the same form, but we are using the second parameter of each input function—we want to be able to edit—to pass the data,. Also if we look at the following line, we will see some changes:

```
<?php echo form_open('sites/edit','',array('id' => $row->id)); ?>
```

We have three parameters there; the second one is empty. The first continues to be the parameter that indicates where to send the data from our form. The second one will allow us to add an array containing CSS styles, an `id`, and so on. The third one allows us to create hidden fields. This line will generate the following code:

```
<form action="http://localhost/codeigniter/sites/edit" method="post">
<input type="hidden" name="id" value="17" />
```

Note that hidden fields, `name=" id"`, and `value="id"` for row `id` have been created. We will use them to indicate, to our update model function, the record to be updated. Now if we try to edit one of the records we will be presented with a screen like the following one:

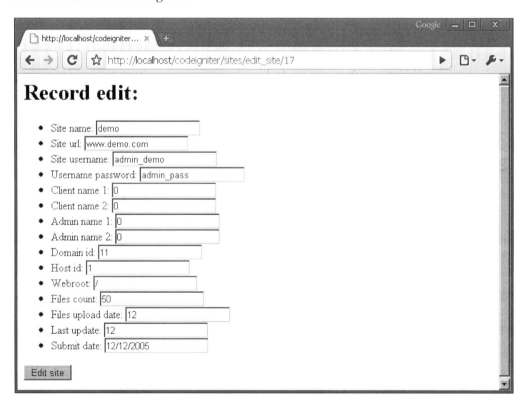

Now, we can change or modify this data, but we need one new function to take care of the data. As you may have noticed, when reading the previous code, we are calling this new function `edit`. This function will receive the data, and prepare it to send to another model function:

```
function edit()
{
  $this->load->library('session');
  $this->load->model('sites_model');
  $data = array(
                'name' => $_POST['name'],
                'url' => $_POST['url'],
                'un' => $_POST['un'],
                'pw' => $_POST['pw'],
                'client1' => $_POST['client1'],
                'client2' => $_POST['client2'],
                'admin1' => $_POST['admin1'],
                'admin2' => $_POST['admin2'],
                'domainid' => $_POST['domainid'],
                'hostid' => $_POST['hostid'],
                'webroot' => $_POST['webroot'],
                'files' => $_POST['files'],
                'filesdate' => $_POST['filesdate'],
                'lastupdate' => $_POST['lastupdate'],
                'submit' => $_POST['submit'],
               );

  //Here we call a new model function, the edit_site one
  $sites = $this->sites_model->edit_site($data, $_POST['id']);
  if($sites)
  {
    $this->session->set_flashdata('status', 'Data updated
    ok<br/><br/>');
  }
  else
  {
    $this->session->set_flashdata('status', 'Data was not updated,
    please try again<br/><br/>');
  }
  redirect('sites/index', 'refresh');
}
```

As in the add function, we are creating an array that will help us send data to a model function, which will update the data. Write the following function into the model:

```
function edit_site($data, $id)
{
  $result = 0;
  if(!empty($data))
  {
    $this->db->where('id', $id);
    $result = $this->db->update('sites', $data);
  }
  return $result;
}
```

With all this in place, we can update our records. You can try, and it will work as we want it to. Only one task needs to be done now – delete records. Don't worry, that will be easy. Modify your index controller function, to add a new link to it:

```
$table[] = array('id','name','url','un','pw','client1',
                 'view','edit','delete');
foreach ($sites->result() as $row)
{
  //This time we are not only adding a new link, but, in the third
  //parameter of the anchor function we are adding an onclick
  //behavior to ask the user if he/she really wants to delete the
  //record.
  $table[] = array($row->id,$row->name,$row->url,$row->un,
               $row->pw,$row->client1,
               anchor('sites/view_site/'.$row->id,
               'View'),anchor('sites/edit_site/'.$row->id,
               'Edit'),
               anchor('sites/delete_site/'.$row->id,
               'Delete',array('onclick' => 'return
               confirm(\'Are you sure you want to delete
               the record?\');')));
```

This time we are using the third parameter of the anchor function to pass the parameter that specifies how we want our link to be created. For example, adding a simple JavaScript, to ask if we really want to delete the record. If we cancel the message nothing will happen, but if we accept it the delete_site function will be called. Let's prepare it:

```
function delete_site($id = '')
{
  $this->load->library('session');
  $this->load->model('sites_model');
  $sites = $this->sites_model->delete_site($id);
  if($sites)
  {
    $this->session->set_flashdata('status', 'Record deleted
                                   ok<br/><br/>');
  }
  else
  {
    $this->session->set_flashdata('status', 'Data was not deleted,
                                   please try again<br/><br/>');
  }
  redirect('sites/index', 'refresh');
}
```

Again the same pattern, we are only changing the model function, and the messages that will be shown in the index view. This time our function will be:

```
function delete_site($id)
{
  $return = 0;
  if(!empty($id))
  {
    $this->db->where('id', $id);
    //this time we will use the delete function
    $result = $this->db->delete('sites');
  }
  return $result;
}
```

Now when a record is deleted, we are informed about it.

Upgrading our CRUD

Of course, you may be thinking about lot of things that we can do to upgrade our application's CRUD. We will see some that are quite useful, for example, pagination—something that is needed in almost every project. Also, we are going to see how to order our records.

Pagination class

Paginating our results is a good way of making life easier for our visitors, as they won't need to search through thousands of records. For us, developers, paginating will be very easy; with this CI class, it will be implemented in a matter of seconds. Want to see how? Let's start. Open your `application/controllers/sites.php` file, take a look at the `index` function, that's the one we will modify.

For our pagination to work we need to make some changes. First, change the following line:

```
function index()
```

To:

```
function index($page = "0")
```

This will help us determine the page and the function call we are in, the default being the first one. Also, we need to change our model function call:

```
$sites = $this->sites_model->get_sites($page);
```

We will pass the page we are on, at the moment, to that function. Some other changes to our controller include:

```
//as we are going to change our model, we need to change this line,
//this is needed because this time we are returning two arrays into
//the $sites one. One with the results and another one with the total
//row number, without the pagination.
if ($sites['query']->num_rows() > 0)
{
  $table = array();
  //table headers
  $table[] = array('id','name','url','un','pw','client1',
                   'view','edit','delete');
  foreach ($sites['query']->result() as $row)
  {
```

This needs to change, because we are also modifying the way in which our model function returns the data. Take a look at your model file, before continuing, in `application/models/sites_model.php`. The `get_sites` function will now look this way:

```
function get_sites($page)
{
  //we limit the number of results we want to have returned, also
  //passing the current page as the second parameter.
  $this->db->limit(5, $page);
```

```
$query = $this->db->get('sites');
//also we need the total number of records.
$query2 = $this->db->get('sites');
$total_rows = $query2->num_rows();
//as only one value can be returned, and as we have two values, we
//need an array for that.
$data['query'] = $query;
$data['total_rows'] = $total_rows;
return $data;
}
```

We have introduced a lot of changes there, the first one in the function definition, where we catch the page variable sent by the controller. We use that later to limit the number of results returned by the query. For one part we take the records we want to show, but in the other part we make a query to know the total number of records that we have. Both data results are put in a query, for us to be able to return it to the controller.

Back to the controller; we need to add this code before the view loading line:

```
//Pagination code
//load the pagination library
$this->load->library('pagination');
//the base url that will be used in the links
$config['base_url'] = 'http://localhost/codeigniter/sites/index/';
//the total number of records
$config['total_rows'] = $sites['total_rows'];
//how many records we want in each page
$config['per_page'] = '5';
//we indicate in which segment the current page will be indicated,
//this time /sites/index/page, third position
$config['uri_segment'] = 3;
//and then we initialize the library
$this->pagination->initialize($config);
//***************
//***************
```

This is the part that in fact prepares the navigation. Let's check some of the parameters we are using. First, as always, we need to load the library, and after that is done, we can create the $config array with its configuration. The most important part is the base_url, which is where we indicate the base path of our pagination.

Then we have `total_rows` that, as you may expect, indicates the number of records in all. This works with the next parameter, `per_page`, to calculate the number of links to be produced, as the `per_page` parameter indicates the number of records to be shown on each page.

Lastly you can find the `uri_segment` part, which is also very important, as it indicates the position in which the current page parameter is expected to be found. Now, you only need to add one line to your view, at the bottom or wherever you want your pagination to be shown:

```
echo "<br/><br/>".$this->pagination->create_links();
```

With that, your pagination will be in place when you load your page `http://localhost/codeigniter/sites/index/`.

> The pagination class has many other configuration possibilities; you can find them all in the online user guide:
> `http://codeigniter.com/user_guide/libraries/pagination.html`

Your pagination, without styling, will look this way:

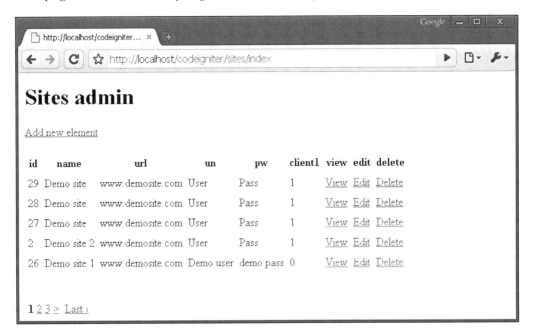

Now, we will continue with ordering our records.

Putting some order into our records

To continue with development we are going to add the possibility to order our records. As we already have data in our table we will need to make some preparations. For example, to add a new column, which we will call "order":

```
ALTER TABLE `sites` ADD `site_order` INT NOT NULL
```

Here we will save the order of our records, but as it is a new column there won't be any initial data. That can be solved easily with one small query:

```
UPDATE sites SET site_order = id
```

For example, we can execute this query in phpMyAdmin, and then we will have the foundation necessary to work. So, we may have some records such as:

id	site_order
1	1
2	2
3	3

So, now imagine we want our record with id number 1 to appear under the record with id number 2. The easiest thing to do is swap their site_order number, giving the record with id number 1 the site_order number 2, and the record id 2 the site_order number 1. Let's see it:

id	site_order
1	2
2	1
3	3

So if we order our queries we will get:

id	site_order
2	1
1	2
3	3

For ordering we only need to swap the `site_order` value of the two records involved. Now, we will write the code for that.

Our next step will be to make some modifications to the `index` function of the `sites` controller:

```
$table[] = array('order','id','name','url','un','pw','client1',
                 'view','edit','delete');

//initialize the order variable
$order = 0;
foreach ($sites['query']->result() as $row)
{
  //with the row() function, we can indicate which row we want to
  //get, this time we add 1 to the current one, thus obtaining the
  //next record
  $next = $sites['query']->row(($order)+1);

  // And now the previous one
  $previous = $sites['query']->row(($order)-1);

  //add 1 to the order variable for the next iteration
  $order++;

  //If we are in the first record, only the down link will be created
  if($order == 1)
  {
    //we create links to our order function, passing the needed
    //parameters
    $order_line = anchor('sites/order/'.$row->site_order.'/'.
                         $next->site_order.'/'.$row->id.'/'.$next-
                         >id, '>>');
  }
  else if($order == $sites['total_rows'])
  {
    //if we are at the last record only the up link will be created
    $order_line = anchor('sites/order/'.$row->site_order.'/'
                         .$previous->site_order.'/'.$row->id.'/'
                         .$previous->id, '<<');
  }
  else
  {
    //for every other record, we will need up and down links
    $order_line = anchor('sites/order/'.$row->site_order.'/'
                         .$previous->site_order.'/'.$row->id.'/'
```

```
                        .$previous->id, '<<');
    $order_line = "  ".anchor('sites/order/'.$row-
                                    >site_order.'/'.$next-
                                    >site_order.'/'.$row-
                                    >id.'/'.$next->id, '>>');
    }
    //we add our $order_line variable contents to each one of our
    //records.
    $table[] = array($order_line,$row->id,$row->name,$row->url,$row-
                     >un,$row->pw,$row->client1,
                     anchor('sites/view_site/'.$row->id, 'View'),
                     anchor('sites/edit_site/'.$row->id, 'Edit'),
                     anchor('sites/delete_site/'.$row->id, 'Delete',
                     array('onclick' => 'return confirm(\'Are you sure
                           you want to delete the record?\');')));

}
```

These changes include adding a new column to the table, in which we will put the arrows that control the changes in record order. With this line:

```
$sites['query']->row(($order)+1)
```

We can see how to pass a number to the row function to retrieve the record we want; in this case we are reading the next and previous records that will help us to prepare the arrows accordingly. Each arrow will have a call to our order function. We will add that to the controller too:

```
function order($current = '', $destiny = '', $current_id = '',
              $destiny_id = '')
{
    $this->load->model('sites_model');

    //we call our model function
    $sites = $this->sites_model->change_order($current,
                                              $destiny,$current_id,
                                              $destiny_id);

    redirect('sites/index', 'refresh');
}
```

There's not much to see in that function, as it is only a call to a similar function in the model:

```
function change_order($current,$destiny,$current_id,$destiny_id)
{
  //the current record, $current_id, will get the $destiny order
  //number
  $data = array('site_order' => $destiny);
  $this->db->where('id', $current_id);
  $this->db->update('sites', $data);

  //the other, $destiny id, record will get the current record order
  //number, thus swapping order numbers
  $data = array('site_order' => $current);
  $this->db->where('id', $destiny_id);
  $this->db->update('sites', $data);
}
```

This function, in the model, is the one that makes changes in the order. Finished, now we can check the site using `http://localhost/codeigniter/sites/index` and see the result of our work:

Only one last thing needs to be done, when a new record is inserted we need to apply the order to it, this can be easily achieved by modifying our `add_site` model function:

```
function add_site($data)
{
  if(!empty($data))
  {
    $result = $this->db->insert('sites', $data);

    //the insert_id() function gets the id of the last inserted
    //record
    $last_id = $this->db->insert_id();
    $data = array('site_order' => $last_id);
    $this->db->where('id', $last_id);

    //so the created record will have the same order number as its id
    $this->db->update('sites', $data);
  }
  return $result;
}
```

We are using the `insert_id` function to retrieve the last inserted ID, then we use that number to get the last record. That's all, we are done with ordering our links.

Summary

This has been a long chapter, but it has drawn a lot together. We've seen:

- CRUD operations
- Pagination
- Ordering

Now, we could extend this simple CRUD to do many other things, but it has helped us to summarize many things learned in previous chapters.

Using CI has allowed us to write all of this in around hundred lines of (relatively) simple code, which we can reuse on almost any site we build.

14
The Verdict on CI

This book started with some specific examples on how CodeIgniter can save your time and effort when you are designing websites using PHP. We've gone through some of the many things CI can do—using as a basis some parts of a website that will conduct regular tests on other websites. I hope that these examples have shown how CI makes coding much easier at the macro level.

In this chapter, I'd like to step back a little and look at the overall impact of using the CodeIgniter framework. Does it make writing a complete application easier? Can it produce professional results? I'm sure at this point we would say "yes", but let's see where CI is of help to us.

When you write a book like this, it's important to divide it into sections and focus on one new trick at a time. It's sometimes difficult to see how all the bits fit together. I hope the CRUD code in the previous chapter went some way in putting different bits of code together, mixing up Active Record, unit testing, and forms. Looking at our site from top to bottom, we can see that CI has helped with:

- Organizing the files of our site
- Organizing the logic of our site
- Centralized configuration
- Code conventions
- Database tools
- Simpler and more powerful code
- Adding security to our site
- Making our site more scalable and our code more reusable
- Documentation and community

Organizing the files of our site

From the start CI gives you something very useful. Just after downloading it and decompressing the ZIP file you download, you have a structure to work with, We can also separate the framework part from our application. Inside our `application` folder, where we will be working for most part, we can find:

At first sight we can think it is a tight structure that will make working more difficult, but we have learned that it will help us organize our project. Also it is a well thought out structure, very similar to that found in other frameworks. Having a good structure is a key point in every project as it will help us know where our files are, and hence where our code is placed. Benefits of this structure are:

- Organized structure, that helps us find our files easily and in writing code

- Helps with team work, as all the members know where to find and place the project files

- Easy to update from one CI version to another, as our files and code are separated from the framework's

Organizing the logic of our site

This is possible, thanks to the structure of CI, as for this to be possible we need to separate our code in more than one file. CI follows the MVC design pattern, which means that we have our code divided into:

- A controller — as a central point of our code, where data manipulation and other data operations are carried

- A model — to retrieve data from a database or databases

- A view — or more if necessary, to present the code to our visitors

Again, at first this may seem tight to work with. But it is very convenient and will make our code more maintainable. For example, if we want to read the records from our users2 table, we will need three files, one for each—controller, model, view.

A model

To retrieve the data we will create a model:

```php
<?php
class Users2_model extends Model
{
  function get_users()
  {
    return $this->db->get('users2');
  }
}
```

With the help of the Active Record we are able to retrieve our data in an easy way using the get function. We will place all our database queries in our model. This way those queries can be reused by more than one controller, as we can load as many models as needed from our controllers. The next thing we need is a controller.

A controller

Controllers are the central point of our site, where we call models to retrieve data from the database, organize, and prepare it. We can call models and views only from a controller. From here, views are loaded and data is passed to them, which in turn create our site's pages. Controllers are called from our site URLs.

```php
<?php
class Users2 extends Controller
{
  function Users()
  {
    parent::Controller();
  }
  function index()
  {
    $this->load->model('users2_model');
    $users = $this->users2_model->get_users();
    $data['heading'] = "Sites users";
    $data['users'] = $users;
    $this->load->view('users2', $data);
  }
}
```

A view

Views are tools to show data to the visitors and create the site's contents. It's best not to place code or queries in the views; just the necessary code to show our data should be there.

```php
<h1><?php echo $heading; ?></h1>
<br/><br/>
<?php
if ($users->num_rows() > 0)
{
  foreach ($users->result() as $row)
  {
    echo $row->id."<br/>";
    echo $row->username."<br/>";
    echo $row->password."<br/>";
    echo $row->f_name."<br/>";
    echo $row->l_name."<br/>";
    echo "<br/><br/>";
  }
}
?>
```

Benefits are:

Structured ways of working, which will help us organize our site and code. This will in turn make our site easier to modify and code more maintainable.

Preventing our code from being a mix of HTML, SQL, and PHP—keeping everything in place.

Centralized configuration

All the configuration needed by our application is kept in one folder, that is the config folder; this is very convenient and will make our application easy to configure. CodeIgniter doesn't need a lot of configuration, all we need to change can be found inside this folder. Among other files we can find:

- autoload.php: Here we place the libraries, helpers, plugins, and so on. They will be loaded for every controller function throughout our application. Useful for autoloading database configuration or the libraries, helpers, and so on, you find that you are using a lot.

- `config.php`: Our main configuration file, with important parameters such as `base_url`, `charset`, `log`, `cache`, and more.

- `database.php`: Here our database configurations are kept, for as many databases as we need.

- `routes.php`: URLs and other application routes are defined here. Our default controller is also defined here. This is a very important thing to add, as this is the default controller when no other controller is specified.

> Benefits are:
>
> Organized configuration files. This is an important part, as it not only helps us, but if another developer has to take our project it will be an easy task for him/her to change or check project configuration.
>
> We can define global variables in the `config.php` file so we will not be spreading them all over our application files.

Code conventions

Most code conventions in CI aren't mandatory, they are just recommendations that will keep code organized. This is very useful, as we are able to decide whether we want to use them or continue to use our own. These include class names, spaces, closing tags, and so on. Though I recommend you to adhere to these conventions, as they will make your code more consistent and easier to read, you can keep your own code conventions or even mix them.

> Benefits are:
>
> Though we are able to use these conventions, CI doesn't force us to do so, unlike other frameworks. This way you can use CI out of the box without the need to learn the conventions. It makes your code more consistent, better organized, and cleaner, even between projects.

Database tools

CodeIgniter also offers a good pack of database utilities, ranging from ease of database configuration, to using configuration files, to Active Record features such as query structures and transactions.

It lacks some of the powerful Active Record utilities and table relationships that exist on other frameworks by default, but you can also have those with some coding. At first you may find it more difficult to use the Active Record functions than plain queries, but with the help of the profiler and some time, you can learn to write Active Record queries that are easy to read.

Benefits are:

Wide range of possibilities and tools that make our coding experience more productive, when working with databases, with a gradual learning curve. Enhanced security when using Active Record, as data is escaped automatically. Some powerful tools such as query caching and transactions. Active Record, gives us the possibility to switch databases as and when needed, from MySQL to Postgres, or even MSSQL.

Much much more.

Simpler and more powerful code

One of the key points of CI is the number of libraries and helpers that help us in our site development. You can find HTML helpers, pagination libraries, image libraries, and a lot more easy-to-use and very powerful code. As always, we as developers decide whether we want to use them or not; CI isn't going to force us, though it is always a good idea to use them. For example, you can write this line of code:

```
<!DOCTYPE html PUBLIC "-//W3C//DTD XHTML 1.0 Strict//EN" "http://www.
w3.org/TR/xhtml1/DTD/xhtml1-strict.dtd">
```

Or use the HTML helper and write:

```
echo docytype();
```

You obtain the same result. CI has lot of helpers and libraries that will help us write less code, write it faster, and hence, be more productive.

Benefits are:

Many libraries that will help us with most common tasks such pagination, resizing photographs, and so on. Write less code and save time.

Adding security to our site

Security is an important concern for every website or online application. CI helps us keep our site safe, starting from URI security to global variables turned off, XSS filtering, data validation, and so on.

Some of these tools are run by default by CI, like the URI security, and we can even define the XSS filtering to run globally; this is done in our `config` file:

```
$config['global_xss_filtering'] = FALSE;
```

Other of these tools are run manually such as the form validation class and query escaping. Together these functions help us with securing the application.

Benefits are:

Ease of use when adding security to our application and forms. And very important—thanks to some of those functions—our sites are more secure by default.

Making our site more scalable and our code more reusable

CI makes extensive use of libraries, helpers, and plugins. This makes coding very easy and modular. Moreover, we can create our own libraries or place third-party code in a library. This way we can make use of code from our previous projects or, as we have said, third-party code. This way we can reuse code from one site on another very easily. Libraries can be very modular, and to use them in another project we simply copy them.

Benefits are:

We can reuse code easily from one project for another, creating our own CI libraries, helpers, and so on.

Documentation and community

When you start working with a new framework there are three things that can help you get started very easily:

- A good book that you can learn from—like this one, for example.

- Good documentation to help us when in doubt. CI has one of the best documentations out there. We've been using PHP frameworks for quite some time now, and we know what we are talking about. Some people don't think this is a must, but it is.

- A good community. There will be times when you won't find a solution in the online documentation or in this book. In those cases you may post your question in the forums, so other users can help you.

Benefits are:

A very important benefit! You can download CI and start working; when in doubt you can check this book, the online documentation, or the forums. This will help you to develop your site without having much problem.

Summarizing all that CI offers

We find that CI is a great framework to work with. It helps us organize our files and code. From the start we have seen that CI only offers ease of use. There will be very few to no occasions when you will be lost using CodeIgniter and for those, help is easy to find.

After we download CI we only have to make some changes in our `config` and `database` files to start working. Very few code conventions or ways of working are needed, so we can start at once. You can use CodeIgniter the way you want, for example, you may not use models, and so on.

Once you try CI you will never want to work without it. It's easy to use, with lot of libraries that help you in coding, it provides security, has an active community, and so on. All this makes CI a great framework.

Summary

This chapter covers everything CI has to help us in our site development. Though we have not seen any code here, this chapter is useful to remember all the possibilities CI offers. We have seen how to organize the files and logic of our site. We have seen the centralized configuration, code conventions, and database tools. Later we saw how to write simple and powerful code, add security, and make our site scalable and reusable. And last, but not least, we talked about the great documentation CI has, and its community. All of these make CI one great framework, and our favorite out there.

15
Resources and Extensions

Well, we've looked at CI pretty thoroughly, and we hope all we have been through helps you in your day-to-day programming. We've also developed some of our code in the process. When you must have gone through some of the code in this book, you must have thought "I could write that better…". Everyone has their own style, and CI gives you a lot of freedom.

The CI community is full of people who write good code and luckily many of them make it available free of cost to the rest of us. So there's a lot of code out there that may save you a lot of work. For example, if you want to create dynamic graphs of data drawn from your database—you can sit down and write the code yourself or search for a ready-made solution.

Using third-party code in our applications and websites is something quite usual, because we can't develop everything, it wouldn't be productive. Luckily for us CI's Wiki is very extensive and has a lot of libraries that we can use.

In this chapter we will see some of the resources from which you can draw help, to make coding quick and easy. CI has a thriving and active community of users and the available resources are changing all the time, so we don't have an exhaustive list, but will just give you an idea of what's there and where to look for help.

There's a caution note too. There is so much code out there that it can be very confusing. People write their pet projects—some brilliant, some just quite good. Many of us are better at writing code than writing explanations or comments. As a result, it can be quite difficult to work out just what each library or plugin does, and if it's the best one for you. We can always open the files, take a look at the code, and if the license permits us to, adapt it to our needs.

So, let's take a look at the available help.

- First, let's look at the sources from which you can get code
- Then, let's look at a few subjects and compare the code that's available
- Lastly, let's look at more general sources of help on PHP, MySQL, and Apache

CI's user forums

CI has two main resources:

- The user forums at `http://www.codeigniter.com/forums/`, offer a lively discussion of most CI issues on a regular basis. Comments and suggestions made are not always helpful (or accurate), but there are a number of "senior members", who usually make sense. It's a kind forum where people ask very obvious "newbie" questions, and get patient and helpful replies. But there's much more in the CI forums than just questions and answers—news, job boards, a place to request features, bug reports, and so on. Going through the forum from time to time can make us stay inline with the CI community and let us know what is being cooked.
- The Wiki, at `http://www.codeigniter.com/wiki/`, is a repository for tips, tricks, hacks, plugins, and enhancements. It contains a lot of useful code, though coverage is not systematic.

If you are very curious to know what is going on, you can take a look at the SVN on `http://dev.ellislab.com/svn/CodeIgniter/trunk/`; you can download the latest version from there, but remember it's not a stable version.

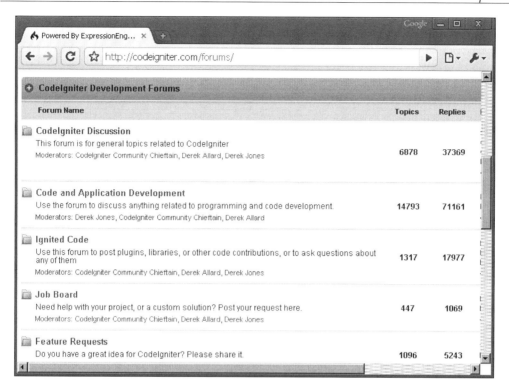

The previous screenshot shows how active the CI forums are with lot of topics and posts. With this great community the forums are a big and important source of help. It is one of the first places where you should look for help, when in need.

Using the forum or the Wiki is easy—you just create a membership for yourself (free) and then log on and search for what you want. If you are seriously using CI, it's worth setting your RSS reader to subscribe to the **Recent Changes** feed on the Wiki. You can find the RSS Feed here: `http://codeigniter.com/feeds/rss/news/`.

Remember:

- Though plugins and libraries can really save us time, they may have bugs or security problems. So it's a good idea to check them if time permits you to do so.

- Some of the older plugins written before CI version 1.5 came out may need alteration, because the way in which those libraries were initialized is different (see Chapter 12). This should not be very difficult to do, but it does mean that these libraries won't work straight out of the box.

Video tutorials

If you want to be literally talked through your first CI application, there are some excellent **Video Tutorials** out there, which you can find on the CI site.

- An introduction to CI.

- Create a blog in 20 minutes: Derek Jones builds basic blog pages, showing how to set up the site, make database queries, and present the results in views.

And others are out there on the net, for example:

- A link to an external video by Derek Allard (see `http://video.derekallard.com/`), which describes, among other things, how to use the `scriptaculous` library to integrate AJAX and JavaScript effects. Using the following view it shows how to build an autocomplete text entry drop-down, using AJAX to update it.

- CodeIgniter from scratch series:
    - `http://net.tutsplus.com/videos/screencasts/codeigniter-from-scratch-day-1/`
    - `http://net.tutsplus.com/videos/screencasts/codeigniter-from-scratch-day-2/`
    - `http://net.tutsplus.com/videos/screencasts/codeigniter-from-scratch-day-3/`

Of course, there may be others, but this is just an interesting sample of what can be found.

Available plugins and libraries

Due to CI's huge community, it's quite usual for users to contribute to plugins or libraries to help other CI users. The number of plugins and libraries is growing steadily, and those already there are undergoing change. So, the next section is not a systematic account of what's there—just a few notes on some of the things you might find useful. Sorry, as we had to miss out on a lot of good stuff—please take a look at the Wiki.

AJAX or JavaScript

The Wiki contains some AJAX packages—one using xajax and the others using `prototype.js/scriptaculous.js` libraries.

Name	YUI Ajax **helper**
URL	`http://codeigniter.com/wiki/YUI_Ajax_Helper/`
Author	Anonymous

Name	Xajax
URL	`http://www.codeigniter.com/wiki/XAJAX/`
	CI frontend for the xajax library. Includes its own JavaScript `include` file—`xajax.js`.
Author	Greg McLellan—based on the `xajax` PHP library (see `http://www.xajaxproject.org/`).

Authentication

Wiki users have also wrestled with security, the following three packages help in authenticating your users and avoiding the possible pitfalls of storing session data in cookies.

Name	DX Auth
URL	`http://codeigniter.com/wiki/DX_Auth/`
Author	Erick Hartanto

Name	SimpleLoginSecure
URL	`http://codeigniter.com/wiki/SimpleLoginSecure/`
	This library offers an easy way of having login functionality in our application, using the **Secure Password Hashes (phpass)** framework for secure passwords instead of straight **MD5 (Message-Digest algorithm 5)** without salt. Very easy and simple to use.
	Tested in CI 1.6.3
Author	Alex Dunae

Name	DB Session
URL	http://www.codeigniter.com/wiki/DB_Session/
Author	Dready

PDF generation

Sometimes, we will need to generate PDF documents for our site—it may be a print version of a page, a bill, or any other type of document. CI has some libraries available for this task. One that I like—for its ease of use—is not really a library but a step-by-step guide. You can find this guide here:

Name	**PDF generation using** dompdf
URL	http://codeigniter.com/wiki/PDF_generation_using_dompdf/

The dompdf library is very easy to use, though it has no support for CSS styles. Its ease of use resides in the fact that dompdf generates PDF files from your HTML code. So, we don't have to learn a specific way of building our PDFs. Sure you have other libraries where you have to create the PDF line-by-line, just like creating HTML tables.

This library does the job, at least for PDF creation needs. It's very easy to use, so take a look at it and decide if it does the job for you. If you like to compare between different options, you can take a look at fpdf CIed that makes use of the fpdf library:

Name	fpdf CIed
URL	http://codeigniter.com/wiki/fpdf_CIed/

This one has a different approach to PDF creation, a bit more difficult but as always, it's better to check different options for deciding what is best for us.

Comparisons: Which charting library to use?

Here you have quite a range of options. Sometimes, there can be almost too much choice. To demonstrate this, let's look at three options for doing the same thing and see how they differ.

Making dynamic charts of data is not an easy thing to code on your own. But it does make your site look good. In Chapter 8, we saw how to make charts with the help of the `googlecharts` API, and a library we built from third-party code. There will be times when we don't want or are unable to use the `googlecharts` API. Then, we will need a library on our own server to generate those charts. Let's look at some add-ons available for CI that do just this, and try to compare their strengths and weaknesses, as well as look at the results they produce.

Name	`3d-pie-chart`
URL	`http://codeigniter.com/wiki/3d-pie-chart/`

Generates a pie chart from two arrays of data (labels and values) and saves it on your site. Looks great, but this is all it does.

It is simple to set up' just put the `piechart.zip` file in your `application/libraries` folder, and write a controller based on the example. It requires a font; and that is all you need to modify a view to display the results. It works with CI version 1.5.

Author	Craig

Name	`Panaci`
URL	`http://bleakview.orgfree.com/` or `http://codeigniter.com/wiki/Charting/`

Dynamically generates charts and graphs, including bar, line, area, step, and impulse charts (but not pie charts). The Wiki entry states: "Please note, this is NOT a commercial grade library such as `jpgraph` or `chartdirector`, but it is quite adequate for basic plots". The code example and specimen plot that follow show what it looks like and how to use it.

Works with CI version 1.5. As with `3d-pie-chart`, you copy the file into your `application/libraries` folder, and call it from your controller, supplying basic parameters and an array of data.

Short discussion in CI Forums, no major bugs found at the time of writing.

Author	Oscar Bajner

Name	`JP Graph`
URL	`http://codeigniter.com/wiki/JP_Graph/`
Author	`Anonymous`

Three options—the first two are relatively simple, the third is more complex; it depends on what you need (and if you are prepared to pay).

HTML purifier

HTML purifier is a library that helps you to filter your HTML code to make it standard compliant and helps you remove malicious code. You can find HTML purifier here: `http://htmlpurifier.org/`. For working with this library and CI, look for information at:

Name	`htmlpurifier`
URL	`http://codeigniter.com/wiki/htmlpurifier/`
Author	Thorpe Obazee

At the Wiki you will find the code, necessary to create the plugin and after that using it is very easy. Remember that you'll also need to download the original HTML purifier library.

CRUD—the final frontier

You need to write CRUD pages for almost every application. It seems simple and logical to automate the process of creating those pages. They are tantalizingly standard—and yet they have a deceptively large number of possible variations. It's impossible to write one without imposing your own rules and assumptions on the user. There is always a trade-off between covering more and more possible options on one hand, and simplicity of use on the other. The more exceptions and possibilities you try to cover, the more complex your code becomes, and the larger the download is.

So, quite a few people have had a go at simplifying the basic CRUD operation. For example, try `iScaffold`; it gives great results. You can learn more about this on `http://codeigniter.com/forums/viewthread/113223/`, and download it from `http://code.google.com/p/ci-crud-generator/`.

Though it is great to use this kind of tools—as they really save us time—you have to be very careful when using them. Checking the generated code and adapting it to suit our needs would be necessary most of the time. Remember that these are generic tools, which don't go down to the details, they just help with the most repetitive tasks.

However, for very big projects with a lot of relationships between tables, it will be more difficult to use those tools. For small projects, it is easier to use them, as they are less complicated. They should be used in projects where they would be more useful, as they will save us from having to write the same code again and again.

Invoicing

This is not a CodeIgniter library, but a complete CodeIgniter application built by Derek Allard. Why have we added it here? Well there are two reasons. First, it's a great example of what can be built with CI—powerful sites and applications. Second, it's a useful application that you can use to take care of your invoices. As Derek says, you have your data on your own server, be it a shared one or local, so you are not sharing your data with a third-party company.

Take a look at what it looks like:

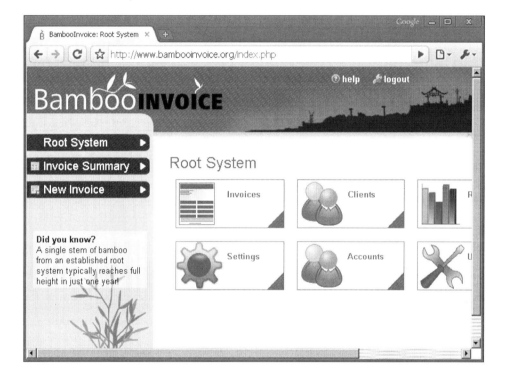

Doesn't it look great? A good example of what can be done with CodeIgniter. Take a look at it here `http://bambooinvoice.org/`.

Additional resources

For a developer, staying up-to-date is a very important thing. New technologies are continuously emerging and though it is not considered necessary to use the last one, it's a good thing to know what is happening.

We would like to make some recommendations, in the hope that they will help you:

- Dzone

  Dzone is a great place to check for programming news, tutorials, and a lot of resources. It is good to take a look at it almost everyday. Check out this link: `http://www.dzone.com/links/index.html`.

- Firebug

  You must have heard about Firebug—a Firefox extension that helps us debug the code—especially useful when working with AJAX. If you haven't heard about it, now is the perfect time to download it from `https://addons.mozilla.org/en-US/firefox/addon/1843`.

- CSSViewer

  This is another Firefox extension I couldn't live without. This one helps you hover with your mouse pointer through any document, telling you the CSS classes of the elements hovered upon. As always, it's better to have an image than a thousand words, so take a look at what it looks like, downloading it from `https://addons.mozilla.org/en-US/firefox/addon/2104`.

Some books that could help

Books are my favorite source of knowledge. I like reading them so I can compare my way of doing things, learn, and have some entertainment. Packt has some great books related to PHP and Web programming. I would recommend the following:

- *Mastering phpMyAdmin 3.1 for Effective MySQL Management*, by Marc Delisle, Packt Publishing: Most of the time you will use phpMyAdmin to configure a database, create tables, run some SQL queries, and so on. This book will teach you all you need to know about phpMyAdmin.

- *Object-Oriented Programming with PHP5*, by Hasin Hayder, Packt Publishing: Though it's not necessary to know about OO to work with CodeIgniter, you should learn about it, as it would be very useful for your site development.

- *cPanel User Guide and Tutorial*, by Aric Pedersen, Packt Publishing: This one can be useful when uploading your site to a shared server; as this part is always a bit problematic, a little help is always useful.

- *Building Websites with ExpressionEngine 1.6*, by Leonard Murphy, Packt Publishing: ExpressionEngine is a CMS, built using components found in CodeIgniter. With good knowledge of CodeIgniter and the help of this book, it will be of great advantage for your site development.

Of course, there are many more, but these books are very useful for the topic at hand.

Resources for other programs: XAMPP Lite, MySQL, and PHP

There are a lot of useful resources for PHP. Let's take a brief look at some of them:

- PHP can be downloaded from `www.php.net`, which also includes a detailed manual. It is free of cost.
- Notepad++ is a free programming editor with a lot of powerful characteristics. If you don't want to use an IDE, this editor will do a great job.

To run a local web server on your machine, try looking at `http://www.apachefriends.org/en/index.html` — a site that offers free downloads of the XAMPP package. This installs an Apache web server with MySQL, PHP, and Perl. If the XAMPP package is too comprehensive for you, try MiniXAMPP, which is available on the same site — the code used in this book is written on MiniXAMPP.

Another application that I like for running on a local server is WAMP, which is available at `http://www.wampserver.com`. WAMP also provides an easy way to have Apache, MySQL, and PHP installed on your PC without the need to configure them. It also provides a very easy-to-use menu to activate or deactivate PHP and Apache extensions and libraries such as `mod_rewrite`, PHP `Zip` library, and so on.

MySQL has its own web page — `http://www.mysql.com/` — if you want to download the latest versions for free, go to `http://dev.mysql.com/`. Bear in mind — many ISPs don't use the latest version. See, *Creating your MySQL Database: Practical Design Tips and Techniques*, by Marc Delisle, Packt Publishing.

Although MySQL comes with its own tools, the most popular (and most common) tool is phpMyAdmin. You can download all these tools separately (PHP, MySQL, and so on), but it's easier to install WAMP or XAMPP. Take into account that most of the times the configuration that these tools provide is not the same as you will find on a shared host. For example, there are many shared host providers that don't allow you to use a `.htaccess` file.

It's always good to check what the provider offers before starting to develop and adapt your local server to that configuration.

Summary

In this chapter, we've looked at some of the resources available when you start writing code with CI. There's a lot of ready-made code available. You have to check the code before you use it—don't just take the first plugin or library that seems to do what you want and start using it. You need to study each to see what it really does; it also helps you to go through the code and make sure you understand it. However, if you are prepared to do this, you can find libraries with different levels of scope and complexity that will take up many of the tasks that would otherwise involve a lot of hand coding.

Lastly, we looked at some of the resources available for PHP and MySQL, and for running a local web server. We hope you have enjoyed reading this book, and that it helps you in your site development. We've tried our best to make it as useful as possible and we really hope it has been a nice experience for you, reading through this book.

Appendix

Now we will see a last-minute addition to the book—the `cart` library. This library was added in CI 1.7.2 and is a very interesting addition to an already great framework. In this appendix we will see a very small example, just to explain the key points of this library.

We will see:

- What we need to use the library
- Adding products to the cart
- Showing the cart
- Updating the cart

What we need to use the library

In order to use this library, we will need CI version 1.7.2, so if you have been following this book with a previous version, download version 1.7.2 and unzip it. We have unzipped it in a folder called `codeigniterc`. If you do the same, you will be able to check your CI installation in `http://localhost/codeigniterc/`. Once this is done, we will create a new database; call it `cart` or whatever you want. For our example we will call it `cart`.

 Don't forget to change the `base_url` value in your `application/config/config.php`. For example:
`$config['base_url'] = "http://localhost/codeigniterc/";`

We need to configure our CI installation to be able to use this database. Remember that the database configuration file was placed in `application/config/database.php`:

```
$db['default']['hostname'] = "localhost";
$db['default']['username'] = "root";
$db['default']['password'] = "root";
$db['default']['database'] = "cart";
$db['default']['dbdriver'] = "mysql";
$db['default']['dbprefix'] = "";
$db['default']['pconnect'] = TRUE;
$db['default']['db_debug'] = TRUE;
$db['default']['cache_on'] = FALSE;
$db['default']['cachedir'] = "";
$db['default']['char_set'] = "utf8";
$db['default']['dbcollat'] = "utf8_general_ci";
```

Again, the most important values are:

- `hostname` is the database server where our database is located, in this example, `localhost`
- `username` is that of a user who has permissions to use the database
- `password` is the password for that user
- `database` is the database we will use

The easiest way to see if this configuration is working, is to `autoload` the `database` library. Remember this was done in the `application/config/autoload.php` file; we can see the `libraries`, just add `database` in the array name as shown:

```
$autoload['libraries'] = array('database');
```

After this is done, when we refresh `http://localhost/codeigniterc/`, we can check if the configuration is working. If something goes wrong we will see a message like:

```
A Database Error Occurred
```

We are almost done with the preparations. Now we need to create a new table in our database using the following code:

```
CREATE TABLE IF NOT EXISTS  `ci_sessions` (
session_id varchar(40) DEFAULT '0' NOT NULL,
ip_address varchar(16) DEFAULT '0' NOT NULL,
user_agent varchar(50) NOT NULL,
last_activity int(10) unsigned DEFAULT 0 NOT NULL,
user_data text NOT NULL,
PRIMARY KEY (session_id)
);
```

The cart library also uses the Session class. To save cart data into the database, we need to create the mentioned table. Once this is done, we can start using the cart library.

 For using the database in the Session class, we need to change another parameter in application/config/config.php file. This time it will be sess_use_database; we need to set it to TRUE:

```
$config['sess_use_database'] = TRUE;
```

Note: This class seems to work without the database, but as the user guide tells us to do so, we are keeping to that in this example.

Adding products to the cart

To keep with the example, we will build a list of products, with their prices and an **Add** button. Now create a controller in application/controllers, call it shop.php, and for the moment, only add the following code:

```php
<?php
class Shop extends Controller
{
  function Shop()
  {
    parent::Controller();
  }
  function index()
  {
    $this->load->view('home');
  }
}
```

We are only defining the class, the constructor, and creating an index method, which calls the view. This view will be the place where we build our list of products, but for now create the file in application/views/home.php, and place some simple content in it:

```
<h1>This is our shop home page</h1>
```

If we want to check that everything is working fine, we only need to go to http://localhost/codeigniterc/index.php/shop.

As you can see, this time we have the `index.php` part in the URL. This is so that we can see another way of working, not that we like having it, but just to see how fast it is to start working with CI. We have just downloaded it and configured the database connection, we don't need anything else.

Let's continue; we will now create our shop's list of products. For this to be easier, we will make use of the `form` helper, so load it in the controller, `application/controllers/shop.php`, in the `index` function:

```
function index()
{
  $this->load->helper('form');
  $this->load->view('home');
}
```

As we have loaded the `form` helper, we are able to use it in our view; let's add some code to it. Remember it was in `application/views/home.php`:

```
<h1>This is our shop home page</h1>
<table border="2">
<tr>
  <td>
    <?php
    //Here we are opening the form

    echo form_open('shop/add');

    //Adding some hidden values

    echo form_hidden('id', '1');
    echo form_hidden('price', 12);
    echo form_hidden('name', 'Vegetable 1');

    //Echoing our product name

    echo "Vegetable 1";
    ?>
  </td>
  <td>
    <?php
    //Creating an input box so our users can write how many of our
    //products do they want

    echo "Quantity ".form_input('qty', 1);
    ?>
  </td>
  <td>
    12 $ / u
```

```
      </td>
      <td>
        <?php

        //And then we create the buy button and close the form

        echo form_submit('buy', 'Buy!!!');
        echo form_close();
        ?>
      </td>
  </tr>
  <tr>
      <td>
        <?php

        //And start another form for the next product

        echo form_open('shop/add');
        echo form_hidden('id', '2');
        echo form_hidden('price', 5);
        echo form_hidden('name', 'Vegetable 2');
        echo "Vegetable 2";
        ?>
      </td>
      <td>
        <?php
        echo "Quantity ".form_input('qty', 1);
        ?>
      </td>
      <td>
        <?php
        echo form_submit('buy', 'Buy!!!');
        echo form_close();
        ?>
      </td>
  </tr>
  </table>
```

Now, if we go to the URL `http://localhost/codeigniterc/index.php/shop`, we will see a table showing our products. It is a very simple table, but see the idea behind it. We have created two forms, one for each product, so when our visitors click on the **Buy** button, the information contained in the form is sent to the controller.

The field names we have used are not arbitrary, the cart library expects to receive this data. In order to insert product data in the session, we need:

- id is a unique identifier for the product
- qty is the quantity of products of this type added to the shopping cart
- price is the price of the product
- name is, of course, the name of the product

> However, we can add our own keys to the array if we want to, but remember two things:
>
> There is an options array, in which we can place additional data in the form of an array. For example:
>
> 'options' => array('class' => 'A', 'type' => 'some type')
>
> Also there are two reserved words, rowid and subtotal, which are used internally by the library, so it's better not to use them.

The cart library expects to receive all this data. We can name the form fields in any way and create variables in the controller with the required name, but that would be a bit confusing.

Now back to the controller; let's see what we can do with this data. Create a new function in application/controllers/shop.php and call it add:

```
function add()
{
  $data = array(
                'id'      => $_POST['id'],
                'qty'     => $_POST['qty'],
                'price'   => $_POST['price'],
                'name'    => $_POST['name']
              );
  $this->cart->insert($data);
  redirect('shop/index/', 'refresh');
}
```

In this function we create an array with the received data. Remember that the cart library expects these variables, hence, they are all required, so changing them may cause failure in adding this data to the session.

After the array is prepared, we call the cart->insert method, passing the array as a parameter, and we are done with inserting the data. Now we can redirect to a view of the cart, but as we don't have it yet, we will return to the index page.

Don't worry if you have not seen the `load->library` method or the `load->helper` one; we have put them in the class constructor, as we will need them throughout all the methods of our class:

```
function Shop()
{
  parent::Controller();
  $this->load->library('cart');
  $this->load->helper('url');
}
```

We are loading the necessary libraries and helpers, and as we load them in the class constructor, they will be available for each function in our class.

 The `cart` library loads the `Session` class automatically, so we don't need to load the `Session` class too.

Now you can go to `http://localhost/codeigniterc/index.php/shop/index` and give it a try. It should look something similar to:

When you click on the **Buy** button, you will be returned to this page again. Don't worry, if no errors are shown, all has gone well. In the next section we will see how to show the cart.

Showing the cart to our clients

This task is also very easy to accomplish with the new `cart` library. We will need a controller and a view. Just go to `application/controllers/shop.php`, and add a new function to it; `show_cart` would be a good name:

```
function show_cart()
{
  $this->load->helper('form');
  $this->load->view('cart');
}
```

Nothing much happening there, we only load the `form` helper and the `cart` view. We will do most of the work in `application/views/cart.php`:

```
<h1>This is our cart</h1>
<?php

//Open the form and point it to the update function

echo form_open('shop/update');
?>
<table border="2">
<tr>
  <th>Product</th>
 <th>Quantity</th>
  <th style="text-align:right">Price</th>
  <th style="text-align:right">Total</th>
</tr>
<?php $i = 1; ?>
<?php

//Then loop through the cart contents

foreach($this->cart->contents() as $items):
?>
<?php

//Create a hidden input field for each element, adding the rowid
//value to it

echo form_hidden($i.'rowid', $items['rowid']);
?>
<tr>
  <td>
    <?php
    //Also create an input field for the quantity value, this will
    //allow us to modify this value
```

```
        echo form_input(array('name' => $i.'qty', 'value' =>
                              items['qty'], 'maxlength' => '3',
                              'size' => '5'));
      ?>
  </td>
  <td>
    <?php

    //show the product name
    echo $items['name'];
    ?>
  </td>
  <td>
    <?php

    //show the product price
    echo $this->cart->format_number($items['price']);
    ?>
  </td>
  <td>
    $<?php

  //show the total price
    echo $this->cart->format_number($items['subtotal']);
    ?>
  </td>
</tr>
<?php $i++; ?>
<?php endforeach; ?>
<tr>
  <td colspan="2">
  </td>
  <td><strong>Total</strong></td>
  <td>$<?php echo $this->cart->format_number($this->cart->total());
  ?></td>
</tr>
</table>
<p>
  <?php

  //Send the form
  echo form_submit('submit', 'Update cart');
  ?>
</p>
<p>
  <?php
```

```
    //Or go back to the index
    echo anchor('shop/index', 'Continue shopping');
    ?>
</p>
```

Let's see what we are doing in this piece of code. This works pretty much the same way as other edit forms we have seen in the previous chapters. We start by opening the form, and pointing it to the `edit` function.

The next step is to loop through the contents in our cart. In order to retrieve our cart contents we need to call the following function:

```
foreach($this->cart->contents() as $items):
```

The `cart->contents()` function returns all that is in our cart, and using the `foreach` loop we put each result into an `$items` array. In each loop we create the fields necessary to modify the elements in our cart. For example, first we create a hidden field:

```
echo form_hidden($i.'rowid', $items['rowid']);
```

This hidden field contains the `rowid` of the element. To understand what the `rowid` is, we can take a look at the source code this field generates:

```
<input type="hidden" name="1rowid" value="c4ca4238a0b923820dcc509a6f7
5849b" />
```

The name is not important, we can name it the way we want; the `$i` variable helps us to name it and give a different name for each field. The `rowid` is the value for this product.

 Why not use the product ID to identify it? Sometimes, for products that have options, we can have cart products with the same ID, but with different options. Thus we need a way of distinguishing different products; the `rowid` is used to identify them.

Next we create an input field to show and let us change the quantities, using the following line:

```
<?php echo form_input(array('name' => $i.'qty', 'value' =>
                    $items['qty'], 'maxlength' => '3', 'size'
                    => '5')); ?>
```

This works in much the same way as the previous field. Again, the name is formed with the `$i` variable and a string, `qty` in this case—using the `$items['qty']` array—which contains the quantity of items for this product. The name of the product is also inside the `$items` array:

```
<?php echo $items['name']; ?>
```

Other values that we can find inside the `$items` array are:

- `$items['price']` is the singular price for this element
- `$items['subtotal']` is the subtotal price, meaning the price of the product multiplied by the number of products of this type

Once we have run across all the elements we have in the cart, we can show the total price for the cart, which is contained in:

```
$this->cart->total()
```

Then we create two things:

- `echo form_submit('submit', 'Update cart');`

  This creates the button that will submit the form, with all the changes we have made to the quantities
- `echo anchor('shop/index', 'Continue shopping');`

  This creates a link to go back to the index page

Let's check what we have done; go to `http://localhost/codeigniterc/index.php/shop/index` and "Buy" something. Now if you go to `http://localhost/codeigniterc/index.php/shop/show_cart`, you will see a screen that more or less resembles the following:

Don't click on the **Update Cart** button for now, remember that we need to prepare our controller; we need an `update` function:

```
function update()
{
  //create the array variable

  $data = array();

  //create a loop that runs as many times as items we have in the
  //cart

  for($i=1;$i<=$this->cart->total_items();$i++)
  {
    //add an array for each item, with the posted rowid and the new
    //quantity

    $data[] = array('rowid' => $_POST[$i.'rowid'], 'qty' =>
                 $_POST[$i.'qty']);
  }
  //execute the cart update method

  $this->cart->update($data);

  //return to the show_cart function to show the user the changes we
  //have made

  redirect('shop/show_cart/', 'refresh');
}
```

To update the items in our cart, we use one of the library's `update` methods. This method receives values that we want to change, in the form of an array.

We use a loop, which goes to all the items we have in the cart. This is not a problem, because even if we change only one element in the cart, the others are sent too, maintaining their quantity value. For each of the loops we put an array into the main array:

```
$data[] = array('rowid' => $_POST[$i.'rowid'], 'qty' =>
             $_POST[$i.'qty']);
```

Here we find the `rowid`, with the value sent by the form in the $_POST global variable, which will be used to determine which product to update, and the quantity value, which will update the product's quantity. Then we execute the update method:

```
$this->cart->update($data);
```

That's all; you can check it at `http://localhost/codeigniterc/index.php/shop/` `show_cart`. So go ahead and give it a try.

 To delete a product give it a value of 0; doing this will delete it from the cart.

We can also add, in the `application/views/home.php`, a link to the `show_cart` screen:

```
<p><?php echo anchor('shop/show_cart', 'See cart'); ?></p>
```

So we can access the `show_cart` screen every time we want. One more thing I would like to share with you is one detail of the `cart` library; maybe you have noticed it before. When you go to `http://localhost/codeigniterc/index.php/` `shop/index`, and add a product to the cart and then go to `http://localhost/` `codeigniterc/index.php/shop/show_cart`, you will see that the product is added. Now, if you return to the shop index and add two products what will happen? You will see that there are two products on the `show_cart` page.

By default the `cart` library places the last quantity added to it. So, if we have one product added to the cart, and after that if we try to add two of the same product, then there will be two items of that product. But sometimes it would be desirable to sum products as we add them, so we would have three products of the same type in the cart.

If we want to have this functionality, we can achieve it in a very easy way. Let's modify the `add` function in our `shop` controller:

```
function add()
{
  //First we get all the contents in the cart
  $data = $this->cart->contents();
  //then we loop through the contents
  foreach($data as $row)
  {
    //If we are in the array of the element we want to modify
    if($row['id'] == $_POST['id'] && $_POST['qty'] != 0)
    {
      //we get the current quantity and sum the quantity we have just
      //added
      $qty = ($row['qty']) + ($_POST['qty']);
    }
```

```
    }
    $data = array(
                    'id'      => $_POST['id'],
                    'qty' => (empty($qty)  ? $_POST['qty'] : $qty),
                    'price' => $_POST['price'],
                    'name' => $_POST['name']
                );
    //we use a short hand if to check if the $qty variable is empty,
    //and if it is we get the value of the $_POST array
    //And then we insert the data
    $this->cart->insert($data);
    redirect('shop/index/', 'refresh');
}
```

With these little modifications we are able to make the `cart` library behave as we want. Another thing that won't work as expected is the `cart->total_items()` method, as this one will not return the total of all elements in the cart; instead it will return the total of distinct product types. As before, this is very easy to solve. We can create a new method in our `shop` controller:

```
function total_items()
{
  $data = $this->cart->contents();
  $qty = 0;
  foreach($data as $row)
  {
    $qty += $row['qty'];
  }
  return $qty;
}
```

Pretty much the same as before, we can now call this method in any of our controller's methods:

```
$data['qty'] = $this->total_items();
```

So, if we send this variable to the view, we will be able to output the correct quantity of elements in the cart:

```
Total elements in cart <?php echo $qty; ?>
```

These two problems have been commented on in the forums, and some solutions have been given for them on:

`http://codeigniter.com/forums/viewthread/129037/`

But it is preferable not to modify the `cart` library directly, as it could be changed in the next CI update, causing us to lose all of our changes.

At this time we may have a basic cart, but one that works. However, there's much more in the `cart` library. We have only seen the basics; if you want to learn more, you can check this page:

`http://codeigniter.com/user_guide/helpers/cart.html`

Don't forget to check the options in products; that can be very useful in some projects, also this basic example can be easily modified to support that feature.

Summary

In this appendix we have seen how to create a basic shopping cart with the `cart` library in four steps. Of course, this is by no means a working shopping cart; it's only a working example of the basics.

As always CI helps us to make it an easy task by giving us the basics, so we can extend it with our own coding skills.

Index

Symbols

3d-pie-chart 255

A

Active Record
  about 62
  advantages 63
  complex queries, dealing with 73-75
  mixing, with classic styles 72
advantages, Active Record
  about 63
  automatic functionality 64
  queries, creating 69-71
  queries, deleting 72
  queries, updating 69-71
  query reading 66-68
  query results, displaying 69
  time saving 63
advantages, CI form helper
  automation 95, 96
  clarity in code 92- 94
Ajax packages
  Xajax 253
  YUI Ajax helper 253
assessme method 106
authentication package
  DB Session 254
  DX Auth 253
  SimpleLoginSecure 253

B

backup function 191

C

CakePHP
  selecting 18
calendar class
  about 175-177
call method 159, 160
cart
  products, adding 263-267
  showing, to clients 268-275
cart library
  about 261
  requisites 261, 262
centralized configuration, CI
  about 244
  autoload.php 244
  config.php 245
  database.php 245
  routes.php 245
charting library
  3d-pie-chart 255
  about 254
  JP Graph 255
  Panaci 255
CI. *See* **CodeIgniter**
  URL, handling 50
CI classes
  control and data, passing between themselves 52
CI file structure
  about 36
  default controller 40, 42
  views, working with 39, 40
  welcome controller 38
  working 36, 37

CI form helper
  about 91
  advantages 92- 95
  features 91
CI form validation class
  about 98
  controller, setting up 99
  forms, setting up 100
  validation class, setting up 98, 99
CI guidelines
  file format 84
  PHP closing tag 86
CI session class
  about 111-115
CIs image class
  about 196-198
CI site
  base url 106
  class 106
  database, designing 61
  error pages 208-210
  example 107-110
  file types 44, 45
  index file 106
  issues, site architecture 89, 91
  method 106
  plus any parameters 106
  programming errors 208-210
  start controller 107
  uploading 202-208
CI super-object
  code, adding to 130
  issues 132-134
  working 126-128
CI user forums
  about 250
  libraries 252
  plugins 252
  video tutorials 252
  wiki 250
CI version
  updating 210
  updating steps 211
code conventions, CI
  benefits 245
  routes.php 245

CodeIgniter
  about 7
  Active Record 59, 62
  centralized configuration 244
  code conventions 245
  code, making reusable 247
  community 247
  community libraries 118-121
  comparing, with CakePHP 16
  comparing, with Joomla! 16
  configuration settings 60
  database tools 245
  data helper 172
  documentation 247
  email class 163
  features 7, 248
  file, compressing 199
  installing 22
  invoicing 257
  language class 179
  limitations 14
  license 19
  pages, caching 183
  powerful code 246
  resources 258
  security 122
  security, adding to site 246
  selecting 18
  session mechanism 111
  site files, organizing 242
  site logic, organizing 242
  site, making scalable 247
  site, setting up 21
  table class 181
  text helper 177
  updates 210
  XML-RPC 157
  zip encoding class 200
CodeIgniter helper
  creating 137-139
CodeIgniter installation
  about 22, 23
  apache .htaccess 29
  application directory, moving 31
  configuration file 26, 27
  file structure, exploring 23
  helpers, autoloading 28, 29

libraries, autoloading 28, 29
mod rewrite 29
system directory, moving 31
testing 26
CodeIgniter library
creating 139, 140
excel.php 140
Google charts plugin 145-150
My_Parser.php 144, 145
php-excel library 139
sitemap 141, 143
CodeIgniter site
setting up 21
CodeIgniter site, setting up
CodeIgniter, installing 22
prerequisites 21, 22
CodeIgniter syntax rules
about 42
controller 43
view 43
community 247
community libraries 118-121
component singularity 36
configuration settings, CodeIgniter
about 60
options 60
configuration file 26-28
**control and data, passing between them-
selves**
about 52
CI helper example 53
controllers, interacting with 52, 53
functions, calling directly 52
simple library example 55
views, calling 52
controllers 34
CRUD
about 256
controller, building 223
controller, working 215, 216
data, inserting in database 221
form helper, loading 218-221
form, preparing 217
model, creating 215
model function, calling 217
pagination class 232
site controller, creating 214

starting with 213
upgrading 231
view, creating 215
view function, merging with add function
226
view link, adding 222
CSSviewer 258

D

database, CI site
designing 61, 62
database tools, CI
about 245
benefits 246
data helper
about 172
calendar class 174-177
dates, working with 172-174
DB Session 254
default controller, CI file structure 40-42
display model 96, 97
documentation 247
dompdf library 254
do_upload function 195
download helper 192
DX Auth 253
Dzone 258

E

email class
about 163, 164
clear function 165
features 166
using 164
errors controller 177
escape function 68

F

features, CodeIgniter
about 7
conditions 8
save time 8, 9
site performance, improving 9
sophisticated codes, achieving 13

file helper
  about 188
  loading 190
files, CI site
  organizing 242
file structure, CodeIgniter installation
  application folder 24
  exploring 23
  index.php 25
  license.txt 25
  system folder 23
  user_guide 25
File Transfer Protocol. *See* FTP
file types, CI site
  about 44
  helper 45
  library 44
  model 44
  plugin 45
file upload class
  about 193-196
Firebug 258
foreach loop 178
form helper 264
fpdf CIed 254
fpdf library 254
frameworks 15
FTP 153
FTP class
  using, for testing remote files 153-156

G

Google charts types
  about 150
  bar-horizontal 150
  bar-vertical 150
  bhs 150
  bvs 150
  lc 150
  line 150
  lxy 150
  pc 150
  pie 150
  pie3d 150
  parkline 150

H

HTML purifier 256

I

index() function 159
index method 263
installing
CodeIgniter 22

J

Joomla!
  selecting 18
JP Graph 255

L

language class 179-181
last_query method 75
limitations, CodeIgniter 14
local web server
  running 259
logic, CI site
  controller 243
  model 243
  organizing 242, 243
  view 244
loose coupling 36

M

model, CRUD
  get_sites() function 215
models 34
MVC 34
MySQL 259

N

nested header view
  $base 87
  $css 87
  $myrobots 87
  $mywebtitle 87
  about 86
Notepad++ 259

O

object-oriented programming. *See* OOP
oop
  code, adding to CI super-object 130, 131
  copying by reference 129
  issues, CI super-object 132
OOP
  about 125
  super-object, working 126-128

P

pages
  caching 183, 184
pagination
  about 232-234
Panaci 255
PDF generation using dompdf 254
PHP
  resources 259
php-excel library 139
PHP syntax
  long form 84
  short form 83
products
  adding, to cart 263-267

R

read_dir function 199
records
  ordering 235-239
resize() function 198
resources
  CSSviewer 258
  Dzone 258
  Firebug 258

S

scope 125
security
  about 122, 123
  settings 122
security, CI site 246
session mechanism
  about 111

session, destroying 117
sessions, turning into security 115-117
show_day function 177
simple library example 55, 56
SimpleLoginSecure 253
site performance, improving
  database SQL injection attacks, preventing 10-12
  form prepping, preventing 10-12
  links, keeping up-to-date automatically 10
  site, protecting from XSS attacks 12
sophisticated codes, achieving
  email attachments, sending without hassles 13
  ZIP files, with four lines of code 14
start controller
  data, passing to view 50, 51
  designing 48
  function, defining 49
substr function 179
system folder, file structure
  application folder 24
  cache folder 25
  codeigniter folder 25
  database folder 25
  fonts folder 25
  helpers folder 25
  language folder 25
  libraries folder 25
  logs folder 25
  plugins folder 25
  scaffolding folder 25

T

table class 181-183
test view, CI site
  designing 46
text helper
  about 177
  data, formatting 178
twitter 168

U

update method 272
URL helper 53
user_agent class 122

V

video tutorials 252
view
  nesting 86- 89
  writing 81-83
views 34
views, CI file structure
  working with 39, 40

W

WAMP 259
welcome controller, CI file structure 38
word_limiter function 178
write_file() function 188

X

Xajax 253
XML-RPC
  about 157
  client, setting up on requesting site 158-160
  debugging 162, 163
  exchanges, formatting 160-162
  issues 163
  server, setting up on remote site 158-160
XML-RPC class 159
XML-RPC process
  issues 158
XSS 12
xss_clean() function 68

Y

YUI Ajax helper 253

Thank you for buying
CodeIgniter 1.7

Packt Open Source Project Royalties

When we sell a book written on an Open Source project, we pay a royalty directly to that project. Therefore by purchasing CodeIgniter 1.7, Packt will have given some of the money received to the CodeIgniter project.

In the long term, we see ourselves and you—customers and readers of our books—as part of the Open Source ecosystem, providing sustainable revenue for the projects we publish on. Our aim at Packt is to establish publishing royalties as an essential part of the service and support a business model that sustains Open Source.

If you're working with an Open Source project that you would like us to publish on, and subsequently pay royalties to, please get in touch with us.

Writing for Packt

We welcome all inquiries from people who are interested in authoring. Book proposals should be sent to author@packtpub.com. If your book idea is still at an early stage and you would like to discuss it first before writing a formal book proposal, contact us; one of our commissioning editors will get in touch with you.

We're not just looking for published authors; if you have strong technical skills but no writing experience, our experienced editors can help you develop a writing career, or simply get some additional reward for your expertise.

About Packt Publishing

Packt, pronounced 'packed', published its first book "Mastering phpMyAdmin for Effective MySQL Management" in April 2004 and subsequently continued to specialize in publishing highly focused books on specific technologies and solutions.

Our books and publications share the experiences of your fellow IT professionals in adapting and customizing today's systems, applications, and frameworks. Our solution-based books give you the knowledge and power to customize the software and technologies you're using to get the job done. Packt books are more specific and less general than the IT books you have seen in the past. Our unique business model allows us to bring you more focused information, giving you more of what you need to know, and less of what you don't.

Packt is a modern, yet unique publishing company, which focuses on producing quality, cutting-edge books for communities of developers, administrators, and newbies alike. For more information, please visit our website: www.PacktPub.com.

Mastering phpMyAdmin 3.1 for Effective MySQL Management

ISBN: 978-1-847197-86-3   Paperback: 352 pages

Increase your MySQL productivity and control by discovering the real power of phpMyAdmin 3.1

1. Covers version 3.1, the latest version of phpMyAdmin

2. Administer your MySQL databases with phpMyAdmin

3. Manage users and privileges with MySQL Server Administration tools

cPanel User Guide and Tutorial

ISBN: 978-1-904811-92-3   Paperback: 208 pages

Get the most from cPanel with this easy to follow guide

1. Everything you need to manage files, email, and databases using cPanel

2. Organise your web siteâ€¦ create subdomains, custom error messages, and password protected areas

3. Analyse site logs, ensure your site and data remain secure, and learn how to create and restore data back ups

Please check **www.PacktPub.com** for information on our titles

Printed in Great Britain by
Amazon.co.uk, Ltd.,
Marston Gate.